Hard and Unreal Advice

Hard and Unreal Advice

Mothers, Social Science and the Victorian Poverty Experts

Kathleen Callanan Martin

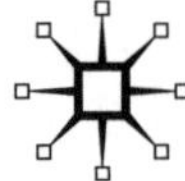

First published 2008 by
PALGRAVE MACMILLAN
Houndmills, Basingstoke, Hampshire RG21 6XS and
175 Fifth Avenue, New York, N.Y. 10010
Companies and representatives throughout the world

PALGRAVE MACMILLAN is the global academic imprint of the Palgrave Macmillan division of St. Martin's Press, LLC and of Palgrave Macmillan Ltd. Macmillan® is a registered trademark in the United States, United Kingdom and other countries. Palgrave is a registered trademark in the European Union and other countries.

ISBN 13: 978–0–230–20189–7   hardback
ISBN 10: 0–230–20189–X   hardback

This book is printed on paper suitable for recycling and made from fully managed and sustained forest sources. Logging, pulping and manufacturing processes are expected to conform to the environmental regulations of the country of origin.

A catalogue record for this book is available from the British Library.

A catalogue record for this book is available from the Library of Congress.

10   9   8   7   6   5   4   3   2   1
17   16   15   14   13   12   11   10   09   08

Printed and bound in Great Britain by
CPI Antony Rowe, Chippenham and Eastbourne

Contents

Prologue: Victorian Social Science in a Twentieth-Century World

Long after the Victorian Poor Law had ceased to function, long after the last workhouse in Britain had shut its doors, the U.S. Congress began to debate how to "end welfare as we know it." A widespread belief that public assistance does the poor more harm than good prompted legislators to a drastic overhaul of the U.S. welfare system, setting limits to the period of eligibility and imposing "workfare" requirements on recipients. Among the sparks that ignited this movement for reform was, by all accounts, a study of the effects of public welfare by political scientist Charles Murray, in a 1984 book called *Losing Ground*.

That *Losing Ground* had a significant influence on politicians and public alike no one disputes, although the extent of that influence can be debated. Murray himself points out that the Reagan administration had in mind drastic reform, while the logic of Murray's argument points toward actual abolition of the system. "And yet," he acknowledges, "observers from left and right agree that it has had an enormous impact on the social policy debate."[1] Lest Murray's assessment be written off to self-promotion, we should note the comment of sociologist William Julius Wilson, no friend of Murray's perspective, on *Losing Ground*: "Probably no work has done more to promote the view that federal programs are harmful to the poor."[2] This influence has not, of course, met with uniform approval. Michael Katz, prominent historian of American welfare policy, has characterized it as "the most notable right-wing attack on the social programs of the 1960s and early 1970s" – which of course it was.[3] Murray's affiliation with the Manhattan Institute and later with the American Enterprise Institute made aspersions on his political motives inevitable. But, politics aside, was he correct in his analysis?

Murray presents a dazzling array of statistical graphs and charts purporting to show that the social programs of the "War on Poverty" and its successors actually worsened the lot of the poor and hastened the deterioration of family life in the inner cities, promoting the proliferation of illegitimacy and female-headed households. These statistics he supplements with a series of "thought-experiments" about how the incentives provided by public welfare assistance have affected decision-making among the poor. The most famous of these, the hypothetical couple called "Harold and Phyllis," is intended to demonstrate that more generous AFDC payments, coupled with the removal of "man in the house" restrictions, changed the incentives governing decisions to marry (or not to marry) made by low-income people confronted with an unplanned pregnancy – with disastrous effects on the lives of ghetto children. As Murray sees it, "Interconnections among the changes in incentives I have described and the behaviors that have grown among the poor and disadvantaged are endless. So also are their consequences for the people who have been seduced into long-term disaster by that most human of impulses, the pursuit of one's short-term best interest."[4]

Impressive as Murray's graphs and tables seem at first glance, they have not held up well under close examination. Katz's comment that Murray's use of statistics "has been attacked with devastating effectiveness" is nothing short of the truth, although Murray insists in the tenth-anniversary edition of *Losing Ground* that, "surprising though it may seem for such a controversial book, there are not any errors of numbers or facts in *Losing Ground* that need to be corrected."[5] William Julius Wilson, whose analysis of changes over time in the structure of the unskilled labor market and in patterns of residential segregation points to "the extraordinary rise in black male joblessness" as "the most important factor in the rise of black female-headed families," sees Murray's approach as ignoring the economy in favor of a return to an old-fashioned focus "exclusively on individual characteristics."[6] Ironically, Murray predicted in the introduction to the tenth-anniversary (1994) edition of *Losing Ground*, that, following upon his successful wake-up call to the poverty experts, "Sooner or later, social science will catch up."[7]

In reality, the approach taken by Charles Murray in *Losing Ground* is not something new to which social science must "catch up." What Murray is doing, in a very real sense, is Victorian social science. Anyone familiar with the Victorian social science of poverty recognizes immediately in Murray's analysis of public welfare its typical concerns, techniques, assumptions, blind spots, and behavioral models. Far from thinking outside the box, Murray is marching confidently down a path laid out long ago, a path now so comfortable to people raised in the culture of the English-speaking world that they scarcely notice the other possible paths they might have taken instead. Anyone truly wishing to understand poverty, rather than to parrot what is usually said about poverty, must therefore take a closer look at how the customary path was established and the reasons for its comfortable continuing use. To do this, it is necessary to begin with the world of Murray's predecessors, the Victorian poverty experts.

Acknowledgments

This book has been many years in the making. Along the way I have amassed quite a few debts that in justice should be acknowledged here.

I owe profound thanks to two of my undergraduate instructors at Dickinson College. One of them is Professor Marvin Israel, who taught me why I should be skeptical of all numbers in social science. He ruined me for an academic career in sociology but prepared me admirably to write this book. The other is Professor Vytautas Kavolis, whose many kindnesses sustained me and who taught me what social theory is really for, as well as how best to use it. For what he gave me, no thanks could ever be enough.

Thanks are also due to the graduate program in Comparative History at Brandeis University. The archival research for this project was done on a research travel grant from Brandeis. I am very grateful to Professor Eugene Black for giving me the chance to return after a long absence to complete my work, to Professor John Schrecker, Professor Silvia Arrom, and Dean Milton Kornfeld for generous moral support. Thanks to Professor Mark Hulliung for encouraging my faith in this project when I most needed a boost.

I am grateful as well to colleagues at the College of General Studies, Boston University, who read part of the manuscript and offered useful suggestions: Professors Shelley Hawks, Susan Lee, and Polly Rizova. I am particularly grateful to Susan Lee for reassurance on my analysis of the religious foundations of Victorian poverty theory.

My thanks to Cambridge University Press for permission to reprint the passages used as epigraphs in Chapters 1 and 10. They are taken from Owen Chadwick, *The Secularization of the European Mind in the Nineteenth Century* (Cambridge: Cambridge University Press, 1975), pages 14 and 202 respectively.

The passage used as an epigraph to Chapter 2 is reprinted with the permission of The Free Press, a Division of Simon & Schuster Adult Publishing Group, from *How We Know What Isn't So: The Fallibility of Human Reason in Everyday Life* by Thomas Gilovich. Copyright 1991 by Thomas Gilovich. All rights reserved.

The passage used as an epigraph to Chapter 5 is reprinted with the permission of Simon & Schuster Adult Publishing Group, from *Stigma: Notes on Management of Spoiled Identity* by Erving Goffman. Copyright

1963 by Prentice Hall, Inc. Copyright renewed 1991 by Simon & Schuster, Inc. All rights reserved.

The passages used as epigraphs to Chapters 6 and 7 are taken from *The Mismeasure of Man* by Stephen Jay Gould. Copyright 1981 by Stephen Jay Gould. Used by permission of W.W. Norton & Company, Inc.

Finally, I am grateful to my husband, Joseph Martin, for endless moral support, patient computer consulting, and superb, uncomplaining proofreading. Words alone cannot convey how much his participation in this project has meant to me.

1
Introduction to Victorian Poverty Studies

On first inspection, the literature of Victorian poverty studies seems undeniably quaint. In its denunciations of the routine use of pawn-shops, its paeans to oatmeal, its obsession with dirt, and its blithe assumptions about intemperance, it sounds like the voice of a long dead world. Closer acquaintance, however, reveals very modern concerns: the emergence of an unemployable urban underclass, the effect of inadequate parenting on slum children, the presence among the poor of an alien subculture difficult to assimilate into the value system of the majority. (In the mid-Victorian era, of course, that alien Other was the Irish, later to be joined by a wave of Eastern European immigrants, many of them Jews.) Above all we recognize the fear that public assistance undermines its recipient's sense of personal responsibility and is, therefore, self-perpetuating. Whether the problem bedeviling slum neighborhoods is called "welfare dependency" or "fecklessness," the world of welfare reform is not so far removed as we might imagine from the world of the Victorian poor law. Our most prominent living scholar of Victorian views on poverty, in fact, feels that the two worlds should be closer still. Gertrude Himmelfarb has based her influential argument that generous welfare payments undermine the morality of the poor on what she sees as the strengths of the Victorian system. In this she joins a long tradition of social science research on the relief of poverty. While Himmelfarb is quite familiar with the Victorian poor law, most of the readers who follow the debate over welfare reform in their daily newspapers know relatively little about the New Poor Law or the social science tradition behind it, let alone what was "new" about the Victorian system.

From the perspective of the early 1970s, the Victorian approach to poverty appeared to many a matter of purely antiquarian interest. The dominant narrative had become a sort of Whig history of social policy, in which the benighted notions of our moralizing ancestors had yielded to the progressive policies of the welfare state. From the perspective of the era of Welfare Reform, however, the story looks very different. To anyone who does not unquestioningly accept them, the obvious survival of many of those "benighted notions" requires explanation, which must begin with the origin of the notions themselves.

This is the story of a set of ideas that, in Britain and the United States, have dominated public opinion and public policy on the subject of poverty for nearly two centuries. From the beginnings of social science in Britain, these ideas have shaped the motivations and methods of poverty researchers. In their role as experts, these poverty researchers have in turn shaped public opinion and public policy on social welfare.

Much of this volume will be concerned with the role of the emerging social sciences in the construction, maintenance, and evaluation of the Victorian Poor Law. The system of relief customarily known as the New Poor Law or the Victorian poor law began and, in effect, ended in two great Royal Commissions. Each consisted of experts selected to consider the efficacy of relief efforts in England, Wales and (to some extent) in Ireland.[1] Since 1601 relief had been governed by "the Statute of Elizabeth," which attempted to keep the "able-bodied poor" from becoming vagrants by tying them to their home parishes. Responsibility for the "impotent poor" was assigned to their parish vestries. The statute authorized a levy on local landowners to pay for the support to which the poor of the parish were entitled by settlement. The powers and practices of overseers were reinforced and codified by law in 1662 in the Act of Settlement. In different locations at any given time, and under changing circumstances in any given location, provision for the poor might be relatively generous or parsimonious, and monetary relief supplementing low wages might or might not be granted to laborers and their families.

For about a half-century before 1832 the subject of poor relief had come under increasing discussion and criticism, leading to the appointment of a Royal Commission to study the existing system and to recommend changes. Most students of the Victorian poor law have attributed this controversy to the "great structural changes in the economy and in society" that accompanied early industrialization.[2] Whatever the reasons for its appointment, the Royal Commission did recommend, and Parliament did authorize, significant changes in the administration of relief. The system, reexamined by another Royal

Commission in 1905–1909, endured into the twentieth century, when it was largely replaced by the social insurance reforms of a Liberal Government.

Almost from the first, discussion of the New Poor Law has been narrowly focused on issues of personal responsibility, of individualism versus socialism, of *laissez-faire* versus state intervention. These themes, developed by contemporary observers, have directed nearly all analysis of the rise and fall of the Victorian system ever since.[3] Late Victorian commentators, as we shall see, generally approved. By the time the Edwardian Royal Commission filed its reports, however, some dissenting voices had begun to be heard. Socialist economic historian Richard Tawney, for one, pointed out some of the deficiencies of the inquiry of 1832, calling its report "a wildly unhistorical document" and noting that the Edwardian commissioners believed, almost as strongly as their predecessors, that everyone who wants a job can somehow find one regardless of the circumstances.[4]

Sidney and Beatrice Webb, whose views on poverty and on public relief policy will be examined in some detail in this study, were not only participants in the framing of poor law policy but historians of the poor law. Undertaken as part of their enormous history of English local government, their account of the adoption and operation of the Victorian poor law, as well as their account of the Edwardian Royal Commission that failed to reach a consensus on how to improve it, had a significant impact on all future discussions of the subject. Because Beatrice Webb was a member of the Royal Commission, and because she and Sidney were the principal authors of its Minority Report, all parties have interpreted their account as partisan. And so it was. Nonetheless their approach has helped to shape the views of friends and foes alike. The focus of their narrative, powerfully reinforced by their public identities as Fabian socialists, strongly encouraged the tendency to see the struggle over the Victorian poor law as the struggle of "collectivism" or socialism against individualism, of activist government versus *laissez-faire*.

Their history of the Statute of Elizabeth or "Old Poor Law," in operation until 1834, paints a picture of maladministration by local authorities, insufficiency of relief, and inconsistency in enforcement that cried out for central control. The Webbs note with indignation that a Parliamentary inquiry of 1760 found a mortality rate of about 80 per cent among infants born in the poorhouses of London, leading to inadequate attempts to regulate the practice of "baby-farming."[5] In their treatment of bastardy they accept at face value all of the claims of the report of the 1832 Royal Commission, reporting uncritically that paternity was often falsely sworn against innocent parties and that many women in the Speenhamland counties deliberately bore several bastards for the purpose of collecting the allowance – "a direct premium" on "female unchastity."[6]

With respect to the Royal Commission of 1905, the Webbs characterized it as "a body of experts, either in Poor Law administration or social investigation," appointed because of an uneasy perception that the administration of relief had drifted too far away from "the Principles of 1834."[7] In their view, virtually all of the Commissioners and expert witnesses agreed on several key issues. Levels of relief were generally inadequate. Some classes of the poor, such as the sick and children, deserved more specialized treatment than the workhouse could afford. Unsupervised relief was to be avoided at all costs.[8] For whatever reason, most subsequent students of the poor law have paid less attention to this assertion of agreement than to the differences the Webbs and others saw between the two reports issued by the Royal Commission. The Majority wanted to maintain the apparatus of the poor law for most members of "the pauper class" and to keep its services deterrent, while the Minority wanted to abolish the apparatus of the poor law and hand its functions over to more specialized agencies dealing with health, education, and employment.[9] As the Webbs saw it, this difference was the result of the Minority's ability to discard the outdated concern with "pauperism" that had motivated the men of 1834 and move on to an attempt to eliminate "destitution" instead. Destitution, according to the Webbs, is a "social disease" best treated systemically by the state.[10] This framing of the issue has been honored by most subsequent historians. Whether they prefer the "social disease" view of the Webbs or the "moral" view of the Majority, most have agreed that this was the essential issue between the two reports and have emphasized the differences, rather than the commonalities, of their viewpoints.[11]

Curiously, the attitude of the Webbs toward social insurance has been either ignored or misunderstood by many commentators. In the conclusion of their poor law history, as well as in other writings, the Webbs expressed strong reservations about the appropriateness of social insurance, even of unemployment compensation, because of its lack of supervision and "treatment."[12] Yet many historians of the poor law have assumed that the Webbs favored the move to social insurance, thus missing one of the commonalities of the Majority and Minority perspectives. This may be because the Webbs were later members of the inner circles of the British Labour Party, or because they are assumed to have been more "modern" in their views than the upholders of the "principles of 1834," environmentalists rather than moralists.

Subsequent studies of the New Poor Law, many of which are detailed in the Bibliography, have tended to accept the conventional framing of the issues while examining particular details of administration. A provocative contribution has been Ian Anstruther's examination of one of the great scandals of the early administration of the New Poor Law. Emphasizing the desire of rural ratepayers to save money by cheaper administration, Anstruther saw the New Poor Law as framed with good intentions but ending badly in some local instances. His narrative of the horrors of the Andover workhouse and others like it indicates that the law could be very cruel, indeed.[13] His tale of routine semi-starvation and draconian – occasionally fatal – punishments for minor infringements of workhouse discipline is somewhat at odds with his assumption of good intentions, especially since, by his account, the Guardians of the Andover workhouse were reluctant to dismiss its master in spite of actions that might have been indictable at Nuremberg as crimes against humanity. The desire to save money does not seem to provide an adequate explanation.

The dominant chord has continued to be the role of the New Poor Law in the growth of the welfare state. The typical narrative details the development of a central bureaucracy in response to growing evidence that existing relief efforts were inadequate in dealing with industrial dislocations.[14] Social caseworkers, accordingly, represent the modern approach to providing both public support and individualized help. Historians in the Marxist tradition, especially Gareth Stedman Jones, have contested this viewpoint. Jones argues that after the early 1880s, prompted by "fear of the casual residuum," the professional elite began to reclassify immorality as a symptom, rather than as the cause, of poverty.[15] Subsequent historians of the "social control" school have continued to develop some of these themes, arguing that welfare provisions both before and after 1909 have been aimed at least as much at controlling the poor as at relieving their poverty.

Like the Webbs, most historians have been inclined to see the Majority Report of the Edwardian Royal Commission as reflecting "the older view" of poor relief, while the Minority Report called for "radical change."[16] Vincent, in contrast, argues that "the two reports represent mere differences of emphasis on the same point about the causes of poverty," both demonstrating the widespread ambivalence of their era as to the respective roles of environmental and moral causes of poverty.[17] While

Vincent disapproves of the moralizing approach, his point about the shared ambivalence of the two reports is quite compatible with the view of Gertrude Himmelfarb, the dominant figure in the debate over the Victorian Poor Law since the early 1980s. Her two-volume history of Victorian and Edwardian poverty policy is primarily the story of the emergence of a moral consensus on how social policy should be approached: a consensus that, first and foremost, social policy should enhance individual moral responsibility. In Himmelfarb's view it was Mayhew and his imitators who transformed poverty into a "social pathology" – a development she clearly deplores.[18] From her perspective this idea is "not entirely in the interests or to the credit of the poor," unlike the viewpoint of the Victorians, who were more truly egalitarian in expecting moral behavior from both rich and poor alike.[19]

Himmelfarb argues that there was "a strong consensus that the primary objective of any enterprise or reform was that it contribute to the moral improvement of the poor – at the very least, that it not have a deleterious effect."[20] She makes a compelling case that such a consensus did in fact exist without, however, addressing the issue of how the Victorians could know whether or not this policy was succeeding. By what criteria could it be assumed that various aspects of slum life reflected immorality rather than other – perhaps unrecognized or misunderstood – phenomena? No careful reader of her work, much less of her more popular writings on the subject, can fail to apprehend that Himmelfarb feels twentieth-century social policy has erred in no longer caring about the morality of the poor, whether or not the reader accepts as proven that these judgments were well-founded in the Victorian era or that they are absent in the modern era.[21] In her defense of "Victorian values" Himmelfarb notes that Beatrice Webb, as much as any member of the Edwardian Majority, cared about the morality of the poor; she was "a moralist as well as a collectivist."[22] In this she implicitly agrees with Vincent on the commonalities of the Majority and Minority viewpoints, although her opinion of the appropriateness of these moral concerns could not be more different from his. "It was the welfare state that finally brought about the divorce of morality from social policy. The divorce was finalized when the services and benefits provided by the state were made available to everyone regardless of merit or even need."[23] Himmelfarb thus provides a dark echo of the standard narrative of the development of the welfare state, tracing the same history not as a story of progress toward more enlightened social policy but as the story of moral decline based on a terrible mistake in judgment whose effects are with us still. Our encounter with Charles Murray in the Prologue suggests just how influential this view has been in the last half of the twentieth century.

Lynn Hollen Lees, the most recent major historian of the Victorian Poor Law, has adhered for the most part to the paradigm of progress toward the welfare state although, as might well be expected after two decades of Thatcherism, without the sense of inevitability that characterized a number of her predecessors. With respect to the Edwardian Royal Commission, Lees was more struck by the commonalities of the two reports than by their differences. Both acknowledged the impact of environmental causes and considered the workhouse inappropriate for at least some of the poor. Both showed a continued interest in moral causes of poverty. Both were willing to move away from the concept of a deterrent poor law toward providing "treatment" for the specific problems of the poor. In her view "the most striking point about the two documents is not their differences, but the distance between both of them and the Royal Commission report of 1834."[24]

This book argues precisely the opposite: although the two reports did have a great deal in common, the most striking thing about them is their *closeness* to the report of 1834. Both of them assume that the poor need some kind of improvement, that there is something fundamentally wrong with poor people aside from their lack of money. The key to understanding this continuity is to ask a very different question from the ones historians of the Victorian poor law have always asked. Leaving aside the issues of Malthus versus Bentham, of economic interests, and of the progress (or regress) toward the welfare state, we shall ask this question: what did the poverty experts of the period know about the poor, and how did they know it? The answer to this question lies in the realm of Victorian and Edwardian social science.

Mothers, social science, and the Victorian poverty experts

I think – and believe this judgment to be derived from inspection of history and not from desire in my soul – that without the intellectual enquiry the social enquiry is fated to crash; as fated as was the intellectual enquiry when historians asked no questions about the nature of the society in which ideas were propagated and repudiated.

Owen Chadwick, *The Secularization of the European Mind*

A review of the literature on the Victorian Poor Law leaves many questions unanswered, indeed unasked. If the inquiry of the 1832 Royal Comission was as biased and flawed as virtually all observers since the Webbs have believed it to be, then why was it plausible to so many Victorians? If levels of relief under the Old Poor Law were as inadequate as the Webbs believed, then why did the Webbs also believe that many rural men had married in order to obtain it, or that many rural women had produced multiple bastards toward the same goal? If levels of outdoor relief under the New Poor Law were as inadequate as both the Majority and the Minority believed them to be, then why did they also believe that applicants must be rigorously screened and supervised? If, as Lynn Lees argues, the members of both factions had learned that "Destitution had roots in the human life cycle and in the industrial economy," then why were they so concerned with "treatment" of the destitute by professional social workers? [25] And why were they so opposed to social insurance?

This seeming illogic, of course, could easily give rise to an argument that the avowed concerns and intentions of social policy makers were in fact a mask for the exercise of power. This is, in fact, essentially the argument that the "social control" school of poverty theorists makes with respect to both nineteenth-century and twentieth-century social policy. Their perspective seems particularly compelling when one examines phenomena like the scandal of the Andover workhouse, in which propertied people were willing to tolerate atrocious administration in order to keep their taxes low. Brutal workhouse masters, like brutal Gestapo agents, arguably represent cases of individual psychopathology. Just as many historians have asked why millions of Germans tolerated the crimes of the Nazis, however, it is appropriate to ask why it was so difficult to get the Andover Board of Guardians to part with their cost-cutting administrator. The attitudes embodied in the Victorian poor law were demonstrably shared by more people than could ever have profited directly from harsh dealings with the poor. Rather than assume bad faith on the part of so many people, it would seem more fruitful to attempt to understand their attitudes.

As the Webbs indicated in their examination of the Royal Commission on the Poor Laws appointed in 1905, its members were selected for their expertise either in poor law administration or in "social investigation." The expertise of this latter group, which included the authors of both the Majority and the Minority Reports, had been acquired in the context of Victorian social science, which from its earliest days displayed a marked concern for problems of poverty. They drew on a long tradition of analysis, first by political economists and then by pioneers in the fields of public health and sociology, of the reasons for poverty and the best methods of alleviating it. This tradition cannot have failed to shape their thinking about the issues they addressed as members of the Royal Commission. The aim of this study is to examine the nature of this influence and thus to search out the logic behind the apparent illogic that characterized Victorian and Edwardian poverty policy. Our own contemporary public policies, based on a social science of poverty born in the Victorian era, should come into clearer focus in the process.

In order to do this, it will be necessary to examine how well the professional knowledge of the poverty experts fits what we know about the lives of the destitute people they studied. Inconsistencies between the two would seem to be the most promising territory in which to search for the influence of ideas on their observations – the intersection, as it were, of intellectual and social history.

To trace the influence of social science on all aspects of poverty policy would be far too vast an enterprise for the scope of this study. From among the common subdivisions of welfare policy – unemployment, old age, mental and physical infirmity, and support for impoverished women with dependent children – the last has been chosen because it both was and is the "hot-button" topic drawing out the most impassioned discussion. The emotional intensity of this discussion has led many participants to reveal, often inadvertently, their innermost and least examined assumptions about the behavior of the poor. From Malthus to Daniel Patrick Moynihan to Charles Murray, this topic has always generated the most heat; it would seem particularly appropriate, therefore, to see how much light it can be made to generate as well.

2
Two Royal Commissions

People's preferences influence not only the *kind* of information they consider, but also the *amount* they examine. When the initial evidence supports our preferences, we are generally satisfied and terminate our search; when the initial evidence is hostile, however, we often dig deeper, hoping to find more comforting information.

Thomas Gilovich, *How We Know What Isn't So*

The Royal Commission on the Poor Laws, 1832

Nine members signed the Royal Commission's formal report, issued in 1834: Charles James Blomfield, Bishop of London; John Bird Sumner, Bishop of Chester; William Sturges Bourne; Nassau William Senior; Henry Bishop; Henry Gawler; Walter Coulson; James Traill; and – last but certainly not least – Edwin Chadwick.[1] Analyzing the work of this Royal Commission, Cowherd designates some of its personalities "dignified" members and others "effective" members – a distinction that is generally useful in approaching the Royal Commissions of the nineteenth century.[2] The "dignified" members, who "lent their prestige and credibility to the Commission" but were not closely involved in its detailed work, were the two bishops and William Sturges Bourne, a Tory Member of the House of Commons considered an expert on poor law administration. All three had long been critical of the existing system.[3] The "effective members" were Senior, Chadwick, and Walter Coulson. The last two had served as private secretaries to Jeremy Bentham.[4] Not much is known about the roles played by Coulson or by the other three members – a fact that probably speaks for itself, given the attention the work of the Royal Commission has received.

Most commentators agree that all three of the "dignified" members favored abolition of the poor law on Malthusian grounds.[5] We shall consider this viewpoint in detail in our examination of the influence of political economy. Sumner, "a prominent Evangelical," had written a defense of Malthus as consistent with divine providence, while Blomfield had testified before a committee on emigration in 1826 that it was desirable to reduce "surplus population."[6] Even the representatives of the Established Church were amenable to change.

Chadwick and Senior dominated the Royal Commission.[7] Chadwick, a former private secretary of Jeremy Bentham, was a member of the "Benthamite team" at the *Westminster Review*.[8] In keeping with his Benthamite perspective, Chadwick was most concerned about administration – both the administration of the New Poor Law, which he later oversaw, and the management of the Royal Commission itself.[9] Chadwick dispatched questionnaires to the parish authorities and sent out the 26 Assistant Commissioners who visited about 3,000 (one fifth) of the local parishes. Chadwick himself, in fact, served as an Assistant Commissioner in addition to his duties as a Commissioner.[10] Over the course of the inquiry Chadwick received – and ignored – numerous complaints about his selection of biased witnesses.[11] For this and for many other reasons, critics like the Webbs and R.H. Tawney have regarded the Commission's inquiry as fundamentally unfair.[12] All recent students of the Commission conclude that criticisms of this type did not shake Chadwick's certainty that his procedures were appropriate. Chadwick has been described as "hasty and doctrinaire," defined by his "arrogance, abrasiveness, and intolerance."[13] Not surprisingly, the milder-mannered Nassau Senior was the more effective lobbyist for adoption of the Commission's recommendations.[14]

Nassau William Senior, Drummond Professor of Political Economy at Oxford, was a member of the Whig Party and a senior Whig advisor on economic policy.[15] Senior's special concerns were surplus labor and labor mobility, so he took a particular interest in the settlement laws.[16] In the final Report of the Royal Commission Senior was the principal author of the sections on settlement, vagrancy, and bastardy, while Chadwick collated the collected evidence and wrote the section on remedial measures.[17]

Findings of the 1832 Royal Commission

The Report of the Royal Commission was presented to the government in full and was abstracted into a single volume intended for wide distribution to arouse public support for the remedies proposed. Finer recounts the process by which the product of "a manipulated inquiry" was used in "a manipulated publicity," arguing that Chadwick and his lieutenants achieved "an orchestrated fanfare of comment" and a "carefully timed press campaign" to accompany release of the Report.[18] Harriet Martineau was given an advance look at the Report for use in her "poor law tales," intended to popularize (and dramatize) the Commissioners' view of the sad state of poor relief in Britain.[19] Martineau's widely read tales were not, as her biographer notes, "an accurate reflection of the general operation of the poor laws ... nor, for that matter, are the Commissioners' reports."[20]

Although most nineteenth-century English experts took the validity of the Royal Commission's findings for granted, few, if any, students of the subject do so today. As early as 1909 Tawney referred to the Report as "a wildly unhistorical document" – a description with which Sydney Checkland would certainly agree. In his view "the thinking that drove it was rural rather than urban based" and resulted in a law "entirely unsuited to and unworkable in the industrial urban setting."[21] Both, of course, had the benefit of hindsight. Gertrude Himmelfarb, generally more sympathetic to the aims of Victorian social policy than most twentieth-century commentators, acknowledges that the Report was "grossly biased" and that the Victorian poor law was "obsolete almost from the time of its enactment."[22] The focus of the inquiry was on rural labor at a time when the English workforce was becoming increasingly urban.[23] Another problem was the Report's narrow focus on the able-bodied poor to the near exclusion of the elderly, incapacitated, and children, whose numbers were far greater.[24] As we examine the assumptions of the Royal Commission in detail in subsequent chapters, we shall gain additional understanding of why the inquiry proceeded as it did and why the Report seemed, at the time of publication, plausible.

The Report marshaled testimony to support its contention that the existing system of poor relief inhibited labor mobility, encouraged laziness and excessive procreation among the poor, and reduced personal responsibility for the care of family members. The Commissioners recommended, therefore, that relief be granted only in a well-run parish workhouse, not as "outdoor relief" in aid of wages and especially not as family allowances for additional children. In order to discourage the work-shy from applying for relief and to encourage families to take care of their own, while ensuring that the truly needy received aid, workhouses were to be established in each parish (or union of parishes) and all cash allowances were to be abolished. The Commissioners further recommended that the Act of Settlement be abolished, in order to facilitate the mobility of labor, and that the responsibility for bastard children fall entirely on their mothers. Finally, the Commissioners recommended the creation of a central authority to oversee local administration of the poor law. This proved to be highly contentious, arousing vehement and long-lasting opposition on grounds of the traditional liberties of Englishmen, but creating in the end what Checkland calls "the first effective element of centralised British bureaucracy."[25]

Some of the recommendations proved more politically attractive than others. When legislation based on the Report was introduced in Parliament, the Government chose to word the provisions on the workhouse test rather vaguely, sensing that the concept might be controversial. They also chose not to set a firm date for the abolition of outdoor relief, as had originally been intended, but to leave the matter to the discretion of the local authorities under the supervision of the central poor law authority – which would presumably discourage outrelief. The Poor Law Amendment Act of 1834 did spell out the replacement of the parish overseers of the poor with an elected board of guardians and the procedures for incorporating several small parishes into one poor law union.[26] And it did contain, in its original version, the recommended language placing the responsibility for bastard children entirely on their mothers rather than on their putative fathers or – failing that – on the parish. This provision had to be withdrawn after meeting resistance from members of both Houses so intense that it endangered passage of the entire bill.

The legislation of 1834 set up the basic outlines of the New Poor Law, which despite occasional tinkering survived into the twentieth century. Over its course, poverty became the subject of the growing body of social science that forms the principle concern of this study, and this social science, in turn, produced many of the experts who were called to serve on the 1905 Royal Commission to reexamine the poor laws. Beatrice Webb, one of those chosen, began her service with high hopes because, as she noted in her diary, "the unique characteristic of this Commission was the inclusion in it of members who had proved their capacity for the work of social investigation."[27] Many disagreements later, in 1908, she was to record the hope that "If I ever sit again on a Royal Commission, I hope my colleagues will be of a superior caliber..."[28]

The Royal Commission on the Poor Laws, 1905

Beatrice Webb accurately characterized her fellow commissioners as "predominantly a body of experts, either in poor law administration or social investigation."[29] The chairman was Lord George Hamilton, a Conservative and former Secretary of State for India. He had long been a supporter, if not an active member, of the Charity Organisation Society (hereafter known as the COS), but his strongest credential was his experience in organizing famine relief in India.[30] Hamilton would seem, at first glance, to have been merely a "dignified" member. He appears, however, to have been an effective arbiter of some of the many disputes among Commissioners, and he undertook with George Lansbury a personal tour of the poor law facilities of East London.[31]

Two differences in the composition of the two Royal Commissions on the Poor Laws are apparent at a glance. The Edwardian Commission included three women and no official representative of the Established Church. The only bishop on the Royal Commission of 1905 was Denis Kelly, the Roman Catholic Bishop of Ross, Ireland, who was appointed late in the process to replace another Irish commissioner. Kelly's failure to represent a distinctive Roman Catholic viewpoint on the overwhelmingly Protestant panel was due, in McBriar's view, to the influence of the recently published anti-socialist Papal encyclical *Rerum Novarum*.[32] Two commissioners were both clergymen and members of the COS: the Rev. Thory Gage Gardiner and the Rev. Lancelot Ridley Phelps, professor of Classics and Political Economy at Oxford.[33] Phelps also had experience in poor law administration as Vice-Chairman of the Oxford Board of Guardians. The remaining clergyman on the Commission was the Rev. Prebendary H. Russell Wakefield, Alderman and former Mayor of the London Borough of St Marylebone. He served as Chairman of the Central Unemployed Body for London and considered himself a socialist in the mode of Canon Barnett. Although he was distrusted as a radical by colleagues like Helen Bosanquet, and did sign the Minority Report, he does not appear to have played any significant role in the Commission's work.[34] As was the case on the earlier Commission, none of the clerical members appears to have been an "effective" member.

Many Commissioners had been chosen for their experience in poor law administration. Sir Henry Robinson was Vice-President of the Local Government Board for England, while Sir Samuel Provis was its Permanent Secretary. J. Patten McDougall was Vice-President of the Local Government Board for Scotland. Frank Bentham, a prominent businessman, had served as Chairman of the Bradford Board of Guardians. T. Hancock Nunn, a member of the COS, was a member of the Hampstead Board of Guardians and had served on a number of "distress committees" over the years. Dr Arthur Henry Downes, the Senior Medical Inspector for Poor Law purposes to the Local Government

Board for England, was a firm supporter of the COS although not a member.[35]

Two Commissioners with experience in poor law administration were less conventional choices. Francis Chandler, former chairman of the Chorlton Board of Guardians, was also Secretary to the Amalgamated Society of Carpenters and Joiners; he was chosen, at his union's request, to represent the interests of the Trades Union Congress. He was "Lib-Lab" in politics.[36] George Lansbury, later a Member of Parliament, was an avowed socialist and member of the Independent Labour Party. At the time of the Royal Commission, Lansbury was a member of the Borough Council and Board of Guardians for Poplar, in which capacity he had long spoken for the interests of organized labor at national Poor Law Conferences of guardians. Somewhat surprisingly, Lansbury was also a member of the COS; he had joined only to harass the leadership from within the organization.[37]

Lansbury had grown up in London's East End, married young, and briefly emigrated to Australia looking for work. Upon his return to England two years later, he had begun a lifelong agitation against emigration schemes, harsh poor law administration, unfettered capitalism, and the unequal treatment of women.[38] Lansbury was certain that his radical evangelical mother, who had made him a devout Christian, would have become a socialist had she lived longer, and he inherited from her a strong dislike for "the Charity Organisation Society and all its works."[39]

The strong contingent of COS members was headed by Charles Stewart Loch, Secretary of the COS from 1875 to 1913 and its most prominent spokesman.[40] Born in Bengal, where his father was in the service of the East India Company, he had been educated at Balliol College, Oxford and served as Tooke Professor of Economic Science and Statistics at King's College, London from 1904–1908.[41] Loch was, as Vincent noted, the "indisputable head and dominant personality" of the COS; most would agree with Owen that Loch embodied "a fanatical belief in casework as a way of inculcating values of independence and self-help."[42]

Equally staunch in her belief in independence and self-help was Octavia Hill, a founding member of the COS and a member of its Central Council from 1875. Hill, the sole woman on the Central Council, was also a founding member of the National Trust.[43] She was the only member of the Royal Commission who objected in principle to any kind of public works to provide employment.[44] Her conviction that unemployment was always due to defect of character led her to question witness Richard Tawney quite persistently on the causes of joblessness among unskilled youths. Try as she might, she never shook him from his testimony that there simply were not enough jobs to go around.[45] She had made her reputation in the campaign to provide low-cost unsubsidized housing to the inhabitants of the London slums and thus was considered an expert on working-class housing. At the time of her appointment to the Royal Commission, Hill was already 67 and in poor health; this limited her participation in the panel's work.[46]

Age and ill health also limited the participation of Hill's friend Charles Booth and prompted his ultimate withdrawal from the Royal Commission in 1908.[47] Booth, past President of the Statistical Society, was chosen on the basis of his monumental survey, *The Life and Labour of the People in London.* By the time he was appointed to the Royal Commission, Booth's attention was engaged by his campaign for noncontributory old-age pensions, of which the COS heartily disapproved. In most other respects, however his views agreed with those of the Society, and he considered himself a supporter of the "principles of 1834."[48] Because Booth withdrew from the Commission a year before its conclusion, his name appears on neither the Majority nor the Minority Report.

Of the most "effective" of the Commission's "effective members," the least familiar name is that of William Smart, Adam Smith Professor of Political Economy at the University of Glasgow. Smart collaborated with Helen Bosanquet in writing most of the Majority Report, providing the required technical expertise in drafting detailed administrative proposals and utilizing statistics.[49]

Many accounts of the work of the Royal Commission portray it as a struggle between its two most active and "effective" members, Helen Dendy Bosanquet and Beatrice Potter Webb. The principal authors of the Majority and Minority Reports disagreed so consistently and so vehemently on nearly all matters great and small that the personal diplomacy of Lord George Hamilton as mediator was often sorely tested. Bosanquet and Webb appear to have disliked each other cordially at least by the end, if not at the beginning, of the Commission's work. Yet their differing political perspectives were probably as much to blame for their disagreements as their differing personalities and backgrounds.

Helen Dendy Bosanquet, like Octavia Hill, was the daughter of a man whose business had failed, leaving his children to support themselves as best they could.[50] Did this background contribute to their strident belief in self-support, independence, and paternal responsibility? Given her financial situation, Helen Dendy began her association with the

COS not as a volunteer but as a paid employee, rising quickly to the post of district secretary of the Shoreditch office at a time when few women held supervisory positions in the Society.[51] Given her education in economics at Newnham College, Cambridge, and her experience in social casework, she became one of the Society's chief theoreticians in these fields.[52]

Her late marriage to Bernard Bosanquet, a man of private means whose principal activities were philosophy and service on the board of the COS, was a result rather than the cause of her interest in Philosophical Idealism and in social work. He has been described as a "preeminent apologist and theoretician" of the COS and was certainly involved both in helping his wife to draft the Majority Report and in publicizing its findings, but it was Helen who was selected to sit on the Royal Commission in honor of her role in developing the practice of social casework.[53]

Although Helen Bosanquet took a very active part in the hearings of the Royal Commission, she was not aggressive in cross-examining witnesses, preferring to work behind the scenes.[54] In this she differed from Beatrice Webb, who irritated many of her fellow Commissioners with her persistent and effective questioning of witnesses; McBriar comments that "In another age, she might have become an eminent barrister..."[55] When it became obvious that no agreement on a single Commission Report would ever be reached, Bosanquet undertook principle responsibility for the Majority Report at the request of the Chairman, Lord George Hamilton. She wrote in its entirety the section on medical relief to children and, with the help of William Smart and Bernard Bosanquet, produced and revised most of the rest of the text.[56]

Students of Edwardian poverty offer wildly different views of Helen Bosanquet. She was, in the opinion of Ellen Ross, "a uniquely uncharitable interpreter" of the poor.[57] Ross McKibbon, on the other hand, pronounces her one of "the most accomplished Edwardian practitioners of a cultural sociology."[58] Paul Johnson seems to embrace both points of view in commenting that Bosanquet's observations on lavish working-class funerals show "her typical mixture of insight and disapproval."[59]

Bosanquet's counterpart and – to some extent – nemesis on the Royal Commission was Beatrice Potter Webb. Unlike the other two female Commissioners, she was the daughter of a very successful businessman who provided Beatrice a secure, even luxurious upbringing and bequeathed her a comfortable independent income. Like Helen Dendy Bosanquet, she married relatively late and, like both Bosanquet and Hill, was childless. Webb's childlessness, although sometimes a source of regret, was voluntarily chosen.[60] Before marrying Sidney Webb, one of the founders of the Fabian Society, she had begun her career as a social investigator by becoming a home visitor in Soho for the COS – work which she found very disagreeable.[61] Later she was involved in research on the sweated trades for Charles Booth's *Life and Labour*, even engaging in an early experiment in participant observation in an East End sweatshop.[62] By the time of her appointment to the Royal Commission, she had established a claim to expertise based on the detailed multivolume history of English local government in general, and poor law administration in particular, that she and her husband Sidney had compiled. Like George Lansbury, Francis Chandler, and Russell Wakefield, she was assumed to harbor radical opinions on poor relief; Sidney Webb's position as a leader of the Fabian socialists made this assumption inevitable. It would appear, however, that it was her persistent and aggressive questioning of witnesses, combined with an attitude of arrogant superiority toward her colleagues, which most alienated the other Commissioners and made a unified Report unattainable.[63] We shall return to the vexed question of just how much difference there was between the Majority and Minority Reports below and, again, toward the end of this study.

Beatrice Webb was largely responsible for the Minority Report, although Sidney did much of the actual drafting.[64] The Webbs already knew which remedies they intended to suggest; they picked through the evidence searching for details to support these remedies.[65] On the other hand, much the same might be said of the Majority Report. Over the course of this study, we shall see just how common this approach was in the social science of poverty.

Findings of the 1905 Royal Commission

Although many accounts of the findings of the Royal Commission have emphasized the differences between its two reports, and they were certainly seen by contemporary observers as nearly antithetical, the current consensus is that "the most striking point about the two documents is not their differences, but the distance between both of them and the Royal Commission report of 1834."[66] It is certainly true that both reports argued for changes in the existing system and that both envisioned a larger role for government than had their predecessors. Both reports acknowledged external factors like casual labor, low wages, and sickness that the earlier Royal Commission had entirely ignored. Both also discussed defects in the characters and family life of the poor, although the Majority Report is generally considered to have emphasized the defects, while the Minority Report is said to have emphasized the external factors.[67] Both reports criticized the quality of Poor Law medical and obstetrical services and the inadequacy of provision for the non-able-bodied poor.[68] Both had misgivings about outdoor relief but conceded, unlike the 1832 Commissioners, that it probably had to be continued in some form.[69] Thus even the Majority was unwilling to uphold "the principles of 1834" in their purest form, and even the Webbs attacked the harm done by "indiscriminate and spasmodic charity."[70]

One obvious difference was the recommendation of the Minority that the entire apparatus of the Poor Law be abolished and its functions taken up by specialized agencies dealing with health, employment, the elderly, and so on. This report was signed by only four members of the Royal Commission – Beatrice Webb, George Lansbury, Francis Chandler, and Russell Wakefield. Lansbury later commented:

> I have never pretended to agree with every detail contained in the minority report, but broadly speaking all of us who signed agreed with its main principles. We were unanimous that the present system had outgrown whatever usefulness it had ever possessed, and that the overlapping between the Poor Law and Public Health services should be got rid of, and so we plumped straight for the abolition of Boards of Guardians, workhouses, and all such institutions.[71]

Lansbury was less enthusiastic about the recommended provisions for services like infant clinics; his socialist principles disposed him to feel that "money must be spent on these things where the need exists, but there ought to be no such need."[72] In his view adequate income, not supervision, was the solution to nutritional deficiencies.

The Majority recommended transfer of some specialized services but had no appetite for what the Webbs called "the break-up of the Poor Law." They did, however, recommend administrative improvements, better provision for the non-able-bodied poor, and far more involvement of trained caseworkers in the administration of relief. Either approach would have been expensive. A majority of Poor Law Guardians, not surprisingly, did not want to be "got rid of" and vigorously contested proposals to do just that. In the end, despite a vigorous propaganda campaign by the Bosanquets and the Webbs to promote, respectively, the recommendations of the Majority and the Minority reports, neither resulted in legislation.

Instead, during the period before 1914 Britain began to move slowly toward social insurance on the German model, gradually removing populations like the elderly and the unemployed from the scope of the Poor Law. For reasons that will become clear over the course of this study, both the Bosanquets and the Webbs disapproved of this trend but were ultimately unable to halt it. The reasons for their disapproval were rooted firmly in the long tradition of English poverty research between the two great Royal Commissions. English poverty research, in turn, was rooted in a set of religious ideas so fundamental as to be virtually invisible to the researchers. It cannot be understood, therefore, without an appreciation of the Protestant view of poverty.

3
Protestant Paradigms in Victorian Poverty Studies

> Jesus said unto him, if thou wilt be perfect, go and sell that thou hast, and give to the poor, and thou shalt have treasure in heaven: and come and follow me.
>
> Matthew 19:21 Authorized (King James) Version

> To relieve distress of all kinds has always been accepted by the Christian Church as a duty peculiarly her own; and it was long before it was recognised that poverty is an evil so differing in kind from other misfortunes as to require very special treatment.
>
> Helen Bosanquet, *Rich and Poor*

Writing in 1898, Victorian poverty expert Helen Bosanquet saw it as a demonstrated truth that poverty is an inappropriate arena for the exercise of traditional "Christian charity." While she considered this recognition belated, in fact it reflected an attitude long established in the thinking of many English Protestants. The road from the monastic almshouse to the parish workhouse passed decisively through the Protestant Reformation.

Poverty in Christian and Protestant tradition

Max Weber, writing less than a decade after Bosanquet's observation, firmly identified puritan asceticism as the source of harsher treatment of the poor.[1] He noted that the Victorian legislation represented a marked change of attitude from that of earlier times, when "Medieval ethics not only tolerated begging but actually glorified it in the mendicant orders."[2] This change, he argued, was rooted in the rigid behavioral code of Puritans and in their Calvinist assurance that the elect and the damned are clearly distinguishable by their conformance, or non-conformance, to that code. Because they believed that hard work is a symptom of grace and, conversely, that "unwillingness to work is symptomatic of the lack of grace," the Puritans expected to see success in this life, and not just in the next, reward the elect.[3] This expectation was not unique to English Protestants of the Civil War era; John Wesley believed that vigilance must be maintained to avoid corruption among the faithful, since "religion must necessarily produce both industry and frugality, and these cannot but produce riches."[4]

If we assume that the elect work hard and attain success, can we therefore also assume that those who have not achieved success are lacking in grace? The answer to this question is not simple and lies in the realm of theodicy, the justification of God's goodness in the light of the existence of evil. For a Calvinist the answer is clear: God's decrees are unquestionable and are not required to make sense to men. His plan for mankind works itself out according to His will, and it can be assumed, without scruples, that men behave as they do in accordance with their assigned roles in that plan. Within the logic of this system, there is clear support for the Calvinist view that "The most hopeless forms of idleness and poverty could only be the products of fallen nature..."[5] For English Protestants who did not accept the doctrine of predestination, however, fairness was a real problem; we shall have occasion to address it many times and in many ways over the course of this study.

Might English thought on the moral status of the poor have taken this turn, whether or not the Reformation had occurred? English Catholicism in the nineteenth century has been described as "a church of the unskilled, where (unlike most Protestant churches) it was no disgrace to be poor and stay poor."[6] Not one person influential in the development of poverty policy in England during the time of this study was a Roman Catholic.[7] Without exception, all were raised in the Protestant faith; many, as we shall see, were Nonconformists. In view of the difficult social position of English Catholics during the eighteenth and nineteenth centuries, it is hardly surprising that they did not exert much influence in the field of welfare policy. But the Protestantism of all participants in this controversy must be kept in mind in assessing their appeals to "Christian" opinion.

John Bunyan and popular Protestantism: "The Lord of the Hill"

Certainly no account of English Protestant views can be complete without considering the enormous influence of John Bunyan. The arguments of pure theology, absorbing as they are for their participants, do not perhaps touch the ordinary believer very strongly. In the early Victorian era, a "popular Protestantism" transcended sect; Obelkevich is one of many who have seen Bunyan's *The Pilgrim's Progress* as "its most enduring expression." Widely read and widely influential from the time of its first publication in 1678, this "people's classic" communicated to many generations of English Protestant children its author's view of this life as a long and arduous journey through the hardships and temptations of this world to the better life that is to come.[8] Citing the Gospel of Matthew, the pilgrim Christian finds that he must avoid the ways that are "crooked and wide" and favor the only one that is right, "that only being straight and narrow."[9]

Progressing toward his goal, he is helped from the Slough of Despond and advances efficiently up a steep slope toward his goal before succumbing to the temptation posed by a comfortable way station. Awakening, he reproaches himself bitterly:

>...that I should sleep in the day time! That I should sleep in the midst of difficulty! That I should so indulge the flesh, as to use that rest for ease to my flesh, which the Lord of the hill hath erected only for the relief of the spirits of pilgrims![10]

A less scrupulous traveler might well assume that a way station has been placed on the path to facilitate rest, but Christian is too convinced of the virtue of industry, and too suspicious of physical comfort, to believe that any but spiritual refreshment is intended. This is the puritan asceticism of which Weber speaks, and it is a recurring theme in Bunyan's allegory. Mere physical hardship is meaningless in the soul's journey, except in the sense that it is conducive to spiritual attainment. Especially significant is Bunyan's use of the term "the Lord of the hill," here and in many instances throughout the story, to designate the Christian deity. Bunyan's is a God who will not make it easy for the believer to attain salvation; the struggle is meant to be difficult.

Samuel Smiles, author of a "people's classic" of the Victorian era, later echoed this theme when he noted that "The battle of life is, in most cases, fought up-hill; and to win it without a struggle were perhaps to win it without honour."[11] By the time Smiles wrote these lines in 1859, the notion had become a commonplace.[12] *Self-Help* is not a religious tract; it embodies the every-day moral common sense of the world that Bunyan had helped to make. Smiles has in mind what he calls "practical success in life."[13] And yet he sees the road to that success very much in terms of Christian's journey through the Valley of the Shadow of Death, where "the way was all along set so full of snares, traps, gins, and nets here, and so full of pits, pitfalls, deep holes, and shelvings..."[14] Likewise, in the view of Smiles, "The young man, as he passes through life, advances through a long line of tempters ranged on either side of him; and the inevitable effect of yielding, is degradation in a greater or less degree..."[15]

So thoroughly assimilated as to be more or less invisible, Bunyan's imagery of the moral journey of Christian has become the topography of the Victorian narrative of a life's progress. Also invisible is the assumption that virtue will be rewarded by success, while vice will result in failure. The battle of self-improvement, with success as its goal, is fought uphill.

Nonconformists, evangelicals, and social reform

At the start of the nineteenth century, English Nonconformists were for the most part members of the churches of the largely Calvinist "Old Dissent" – Congregationalist, Baptist, Quaker, and Presbyterian – or of the "New Dissent," sects which evolved during the evangelical revival of the eighteenth century.[16] Over time the situation became increasingly complicated by the weakening hold of the Calvinist doctrine of predestination, the Arminian controversy that resulted in the schism of the Unitarians, and the influence of evangelical thought on all denominations.[17] Despite the divide over predestination that separated Calvinists from others, Dissenters enjoyed a state of relative unity from 1830 to 1880, a period in which there was an observable Nonconformist consensus on matters of society and morality.[18] Not surprisingly, in view of the long struggle of Dissent for full legal equality, distrust of the state was a part of that consensus.[19] Also part of it was a view of human nature carried forward from the Calvinist past.

In 1846 the Evangelical Alliance, which included not only Nonconformist but Anglican evangelicals, drew up a statement of nine agreed principles that bridged their sectarian differences. The first point, predictably, was the Divine authority of Scripture. The third point was "The utter Depravity of human nature in consequence of the Fall."[20] Hilton sees this view of human nature as one of the essential beliefs of evangelicals, who felt that life constitutes "an ethical obstacle course" which depraved humans must struggle mightily to complete.[21] But evangelicals were not unanimous in their view of what roles, if any, the government and private charity should play in this process.

As the century wore on, some evangelicals undertook conventional feeding charities for the purpose of saving souls, combining the function of the monastery almshouse with the methodology of the revival. We shall have cause to consider this in more detail below, when the COS confronts the Salvation Army. Other evangelicals, like Ellen Ranyard's Bible women, aggressively pushed self-help along with the scriptures and were suspicious of any further activity on behalf of the poor.[22] Which of these approaches is representative of evangelical thought?

This disagreement has been explained as a division of evangelicals into "moderates" and "extremists."[23] Clearly these are loaded terms that should be used only with caution. Basically they resolve into a difference on how and how often God is seen as intervening in human affairs. The "moderates" did not believe that God actively intervenes often in the affairs of man. They "believed that ninety-nine of a hundred events are predictable consequences of human behaviour."[24] And just as God does not intervene, so neither should government; the only way to success in this life or the next is to struggle up the obstacle course alone. The "extremists," on the other hand, were pre-millenialists whose God frequently intervened in human affairs, rewarding the virtuous, punishing the wicked, and setting tests for the benefit of the tested. Soon this world would come to an end; in the meantime, the pre-millenialist evangelical had no problem with the idea that the government should intervene, as God intervenes, to punish the wicked and help the oppressed. Lord Shaftesbury, the great proponent of factory regulation and inspection, was of this school.[25]

These two views of divine providence underlay significantly different approaches to the problems of society. In the "general providence" view, God has set up the world to operate according to certain laws designed to promote happiness and salvation as long as they are followed – with misery and damnation the natural consequences of flouting them. Interfering with these laws would be unwise social policy. This view was the basis for the commitment of most evangelicals, and for that matter of most Nonconformists, to the ideas of freedom of choice and individualism.[26] In the "special providence" view, intervention by God often occurs, and intervention by a morally concerned state can easily be justified. While the two views suggest different attitudes toward what the state should do about poverty, they are not incompatible on the subject of why some people are poor in the first place. Poverty could be a consequence of not following the general laws (hard work, frugality, asceticism) conducive to success and grace, or it could be a specific punishment from God for bad behavior. Thus the general consensus among evangelicals at the start of the nineteenth century that the poor were generally to blame for their own poverty.[27]

The Protestant view of poverty and the Royal Commission of 1832

Lord Shaftesbury was what many of his contemporaries would have called a "religious enthusiast." Clearly even in the evangelical era not everyone was as thoroughly and transparently committed to religious values in public policy as he unquestionably was. But if we limit religious influence to conscious attempts to bring law into conformity with doctrine, we ignore the way religious concepts can shape modes of thought. Boyd Hilton has observed that in the period before 1850 "religious feeling and biblical terminology" essentially "permeated *all* aspects of thought (including atheism)" in Britain.[28] Gertrude Himmelfarb asserts that in the early nineteenth century "there was something like a moral consensus, a common view of what was moral and what immoral, and more important, of the primacy of morality in the formulation of the social problem and the making of social policy."[29]

Nassau William Senior, who with his colleague Edwin Chadwick firmly controlled the conduct of the Royal Commission and the writing of its official report, was not a religious controversialist. He was, however, an English Protestant of his time, who expressed in a published letter about the troubles in Ireland a hope that the cause of "Protestantism and civilisation" could be advanced in dealing with the uncivilized (and Catholic) Irish.[30] In a letter to the Lord Chancellor supporting passage of the Poor Law Amendment Act, he revealed himself to be a general providentialist when he identified the old poor law provisions as an interference in the way the world is designed to work. What can be expected but the disastrous state of affairs that the Royal Commission has discovered in the countryside:

> When a country has undertaken to repeal in favor of the bulk of its population the ordinary Laws of Nature, to enact that the Children shall not suffer for the misconduct of their Parents, or the wife for that of the Husband, that no one shall lose the means of subsistence, whatever be his indolence, prodigality, or Vice, in short, that the penalty, which, after all, must be paid by some one, for Idleness and Improvidence shall fall, not on the Guilty party or on his

Family, but on the Possessors of the Lands and houses infested by his settlement...[31]

Perhaps it is in this light that we should interpret R.K. Webb's observation that parsons were particularly active propagandists for the New Poor Law.[32]

Everywhere in the testimony of witnesses before the Royal Commission we encounter evidence of the assumption that the poor are poor as a result of their own faults. The witnesses frequently emphasize their allegedly dissolute behavior, especially but not exclusively in testimony regarding the bastardy provisions. Fairly typical is the testimony that "Pauper women are all gossips, the men all go to the ale-house...."[33] Underlying all of the testimony is the assumption voiced by the collector of the poor-rates in the parish of St Mary, Stratford-le-Bow: "The man who earns his penny is always a better man in every way than the man who begs it."[34] If the Assistant Commissioner who took this evidence, or the Commissioners who published the final Report, doubted the accuracy of the word "always," there is no sign of it. So vast a generalization is surely the hallmark of axiomatic thinking, not of empirical observation.

Over the years many commentators have noted the flimsy nature of the "evidence" gathered by the Royal Commission. Sidney and Beatrice Webb characterized it, not unfairly, as "picturesque details of the action of particular parish officers; and amusing anecdotes of their peculiarities."[35] That these anecdotes were never more picturesque than when the subject at hand was bastardy we shall see shortly in our examination of the role of Malthusian population theory in the thinking of the witnesses and commissioners of 1832. We shall also have occasion, when we take up the development of social science and its role in poverty policy, to consider in some detail how and why the testimony demonstrates what we might call an unscientific sense of the nature of good evidence. Perhaps the most fundamental insight on why the generalizations in the previous paragraph, and hundreds like them, were not challenged by the Royal Commission, lies in an observation of Harriet Martineau. Martineau was a supporter of – indeed a propagandist for – the New Poor Law. Never wavering in her opinions, Martineau, reports a biographer, spent her life "setting people straight."[36] Yet, in an uncharacteristic moment of introspection, Martineau once observed, "What we think probable we do not call severely for the proof of."[37] The testimony given matched the assumptions of contemporary English Protestants about the moral failings of the poor and therefore, to them, seemed quite probable.

A question of theodicy: Why are there poor people?

Poverty is problematic only in a society in which substantial numbers of people are not poor. Christian societies of preindustrial Europe were largely of the view that one's place in society is the result of God's will. For most people that means they were meant to be poor. This view of poverty as the normal human condition is reflected in Jeremy Bentham's definition, offered in the 1790s: "Poverty is the state of everyone who, in order to obtain subsistence, is forced to have recourse to labour… Poverty, as above defined, is the natural, the primitive, the general, and the unchangeable, lot of man."[38] To this natural state Bentham contrasts "indigence," the true inability to survive on available resources, which he sees as "the proper concern of the poor laws."[39]

This normal human condition was easy to reconcile with divine providence. A survey of Church of England sermons in the period 1830–1880 illustrates the continuation of this traditional Christian view in the preaching of the Established Church. A great many of the sermons sound the same theme: "the providence of God" has directed that most men will be poor, as a direct consequence of Adam's fall.[40] God's will is not always mentioned directly; rather poverty is often described as "the order of nature."[41] As we have seen, under the doctrine of general providence these are equivalent. That this was the prevailing treatment of poverty in Anglican sermons down to 1880 is a clear demonstration that, at least in the Established Church, traditional Christian views of poverty continued well into the century despite the moral opprobrium attached to indigence in Nonconformist and evangelical thinking.

These views were also heard on the floor of the House of Commons during the debate over adoption of the New Poor Law. Even Lord Althorp, as he introduced the Bill, exhibited considerable uneasiness in choosing between his religious convictions and economic considerations. On the one hand, he stated that probably any provision for the poor is "contrary to the more strict principles of political economy."[42] On the other hand, both "the feelings of religion" and the "dictates of humanity" require us to support those who are "really helpless, and really unable to provide for themselves."[43] How best to reconcile these divergent views? With the reformed administration now proposed, he declared, rather than with abolition of any provision for the poor.

We have seen how the Calvinist tradition made poverty morally problematic. As Britain's economy was transformed in the nineteenth century, the poverty previously the lot of most became the lot of fewer and fewer. "The natural order of things" was changing, and for those who did not accept the Calvinist doctrine of predestination poverty now required explanation. Lord Althorp still felt obligated to help the "really helpless," but the rest, in keeping with the rules of political economy he had embraced, were best left climb that hill alone.

It was Malthus, Gertrude Himmelfarb argues, who made poverty a moral problem when he attributed pauperism to a lack of moral restraint in poor people. It was he who convinced the government that helping the poor actually harmed them.[44] She is undoubtedly correct that "the gloom of the first edition" of the Malthus *Essay* (1798) pervaded all discussions of poverty for several generations and beyond.[45] Malthusian population theory, moreover, greatly influenced the aspects of poor law policy seen as relevant to it. Yet Malthus could never have achieved this influence if the ground had not already been prepared for him by the religious climate we have been exploring here. Malthus published his population theory at a time when Nonconformists and evangelicals, including the large number of evangelicals within the Church of England, already regarded the moral status of the very poor as highly suspect.[46] He wrote within the established context of the concept of general providence: God has established general laws that we ignore at our peril or follow as an aid to prosperity and salvation. This context had created a highly receptive audience for Malthusian population theory.

That Malthus did not agree with *all* of his contemporaries on the questions of the moral status of the poor and the doctrine of general providence was in fact the source of most of the negative reaction to the *Essay* in the author's lifetime. Many commentators denounced it, not because of lack of evidence, but on grounds of theodicy. How could a just God condemn the innocent to starvation and misery?[47] This question came up repeatedly in the debate over the New Poor Law, widely assumed to be based on Malthus.[48] One passage, in particular, was indignantly denounced by anti-Malthusians because of its seeming incompatibility with the concept of a caring God. Speaking of the laborer for whose maintenance his parents cannot provide and for whose labor there is no demand, Malthus declares:

> [H]e has no claim of *right* to the smallest portion of food, and, in fact, has no business to be where he is. At nature's mighty feast there is no vacant cover for him. She tells him to be gone, and will quickly execute her orders.[49]

Malthus removed this passage from all subsequent editions because of the storm of criticism it evoked, although critics of the *Essay* never forgot it.[50]

Many Christians, using the concept of general providence, could accept the Malthusian view without impugning the goodness of God. Prior to his appointment to the 1832 Royal Commission on the Poor Law, John Sumner, Bishop of Chester, wrote a treatise justifying Divine Providence while upholding Malthus. Sumner, a prominent evangelical, was a firm believer in general providence and saw no reason why God might not choose to advance the moral development of mankind through the law of population.[51] This Divine use of general laws to govern Creation makes religious belief entirely compatible with Malthusian population theory and, as we shall see, with Malthus's other great interest, Political Economy.

Temptation, transcendence, denial: religious threads in late nineteenth-century poverty studies

> Enter ye in at the strait gate: for wide is the gate, and broad is the way, that leadeth to destruction, and many there be which go in thereat:
> Because strait is the gate, and narrow is the way, which leadeth unto life, and few there be that find it.
>
> Matthew 7:13–14 Authorized (King James) Version

> It is little wonder that the less clear-headed amongst our people have got confused, that the clear voice of Nature has been drowned for them by the babel of philanthropic and political casuistry, and that they have turned away from the strait and narrow path to the broad path of indifference.
>
> Helen Dendy Bosanquet, *The Strength of the People*

One of the most striking aspects of late nineteenth-century poverty theory in Britain is the vigorous survival of religious ideas in the work of apparently secular thinkers. These ideas have been transformed into social scientific, rather than theological, concepts by the logic of the doctrine of general providence: the ways of God and the laws of nature are one and the same. This notional equivalence survived the waning of overt religious sanction for social policy and even, in the case of some of our social theorists, the waning of a personal belief in God.

With or without a Creator, the laws of the universe still required the Protestant variant of traditional Christian morality. This can perhaps be seen as merely a continuity of cultural metaphor and familiar phraseology. The habits of mind that accompanied these metaphors and phrases, however, had a definite impact on the shape of the emerging social science of poverty. For Helen Bosanquet "the voice of Nature," rather than the voice of God, calls the poor to the strait and narrow way. Yet her sense that voices offering them effortless comfort tempt them away from the rigorous struggle for salvation is strikingly reminiscent of Bunyan's tale of the pilgrim's progress. The Lord of the hill may be Nature, rather than the Puritan God, but Her policies are precisely the same.

This is very much in keeping with Owen Chadwick's observation that during the late nineteenth century, as adherence to religious doctrine declined, "nearly everyone, agnostic or not, assumed that the morality which they inherited was absolute and must be preserved, even though the creed linked with it might be dropped."[52] After mid-century, educated Victorians feared societal breakdown as a result of declining religious belief and therefore "were determined to make of morality a substitute for religion..."[53] Thus we find the agnostic Charles Booth listing among the causes of pauperism a high proportion of what had traditionally been classified as "deadly sins."[54] Booth was agnostic on grounds of theodicy: during a youthful religious crisis he had found himself unable to believe in a kind God who permitted so much human suffering.[55] Yet for Booth the wages of sin is still death – or at least a life of dire poverty. General providence can operate with or without God.

Helen Dendy Bosanquet, although never explicitly religious in her arguments, larded them with images drawn from English Protestant tradition and references to its classic works. Bosanquet was actively involved in the Philosophical Idealist movement, which will be considered in more detail below, and was disinterested in religious doctrine or practice. This makes all the more striking her frequent use of Christian and Protestant metaphors and ideas. Her review of the history of poor relief in Britain, for example, repeats the classic Protestant accusation that the monasteries created – rather than alleviated – poverty by distributing alms.[56] She also evokes Bunyan in identifying the bad habits she diagnoses among the poor as a disastrous "descent into the slough of self-indulgence."[57] Bunyan's Slough of Despond is

> such a place as cannot be mended. It is the descent whither the scum and filth that attends conviction for sin doth continually run, and therefore is it called the Slough of Despond; for still as the sinner is awakened about his lost condition, there ariseth in his soul many fears, and doubts, and discouraging apprehensions, which all of

them get together, and settle in this place. And this is the reason of the badness of this ground.[58]

We shall later examine the Public Health movement and its attention to the filth and scum that quite literally drained into slum neighborhoods, along with the spiritual filth associated with it. General William Booth, founder of the Salvation Army, explicitly labeled the capital's miserable slums "the great Slough of Despond of our time."[59] Bunyan's Slough has defied all attempts to make it a better place; it is meant to be an arena of moral trial. Christian is able to escape when Help appears to lend a hand; we shall see below how both the Salvation Army and the COS, each in its own way, attempted to provide this service for the denizens of London's slums.

General Booth was an evangelical activist whose work among the poor was always grounded in his desire to save souls. Helen Bosanquet, on the other hand, never explicitly used religious justification for her preferred policies. Tacit religious sanction under the doctrine of general providence, nonetheless, is nearly always present in her writings, sometimes quite close to the surface. Addressing future social workers, for example, she explains why it is a mistake to do too much for the poor:

> In the first place, we must put away the idea that we can save human beings – whether poor or rich – from the natural consequences of sin and vice and idleness; I do not say that we cannot with patience make them less sinful and vicious and idle, but where the seed has been sown the crop must be reaped, and any attempt to break the connection between moral failings and their natural punishment will retard our social progress indefinitely. We have not yet got beyond the wisdom of the law that if any man will not work neither shall he eat.[60]

Bosanquet's concern is with "social progress," not with salvation. Unlike General Booth, she does not quote scripture by chapter and verse, but she uses two well-known passages from the New Testament to underscore her view.[61] Sin, vice, and that most puritan of failings, idleness, do not incur divine retribution but rather have natural consequences; this is a direct result of "the law" (of unstated but biblical origin) that not working means not eating. For Bosanquet, as for Nassau Senior, the laws of God and of nature are one and the same.

In addition to their strong desire to uphold traditional Protestant views of morality despite their lack of adult commitment to religious faith, Charles Booth and Helen Bosanquet shared another attribute –

their Unitarian upbringing. Unitarianism strongly influenced the COS, both in its London center and in its provincial branches. Both Helen Dendy Bosanquet and Octavia Hill were raised in Unitarian homes, and it was influential Unitarian families, like the Rathbones in Liverpool and Manchester's Philips family, who dominated the provincial chapters.[62] Active supporters of the COS were often Unitarians or from "the senior echelons of the Established Church."[63] Influence in the COS translated into representation on the Edwardian Royal Commission, whose membership included Bosanquet, Hill, Charles Booth, and Beatrice Potter Webb. While the last was not a member of the COS, she too had been raised in a Unitarian family. In their adult lives Booth and Bosanquet were agnostic and thus disengaged from formal religion, while Hill and Webb were communicants of the Church of England. But the Majority and Minority Reports of the Royal Commission, written by Helen Dendy Bosanquet and Beatrice Potter Webb respectively, were both produced by women from a Unitarian background. Was this rather startling over-representation of former Unitarians a meaningless coincidence, or did it have some significance for their view of poverty?

Unitarians against the world

By the late twentieth century, many people in the English-speaking world thought of Unitarians as having almost no theology whatsoever, a tolerant sect with fluid boundaries and few doctrinal requirements. In its origins, however, Unitarianism is a direct descendant of the Calvinist churches, separated from the Presbyterian, Baptist, and Congregationalist sects by the Arminian controversy of the eighteenth century. The Trinitarian branches disapproved so strongly of this departure from what they saw as essential Christian doctrine that there followed, in the words of Clyde Binfield, a long period of "perpetual sniping between Unitarians and the rest."[64] Even after the Toleration Act of 1813 and the Dissenters' Chapels Act of 1844, this hostility within the ranks of Old Dissent continued. As a result, "the Unitarians formed a class apart" and endured frequent attacks from those who feared the demoralizing effects of "rational Christianity."[65]

Many observers have argued that Unitarians came to relish this role as persecuted upholders of truth. Harriet Martineau's biographer discerns in her works a recurring theme of "the high calling of the martyr" which he contends is quintessentially Unitarian.[66] Because of what they saw as their superior education, rationality, and willingness to withstand popular scorn in defense of their beliefs, "Unitarians thought themselves better fitted than anyone else resolutely to pursue and proclaim truth."[67] Determined as they were to rid themselves of the sentimental and superstitious beliefs of the less rational religious past, they were naturally inclined to the school of general providence, believing in "the inescapable working of natural law" and showing open contempt for the notion of "an interruptive providence."[68] Harriet Martineau was, therefore, representative of Unitarian opinion in seeking her natural laws in the realms of science and political economy, rather than in scripture, and in repudiating criticism from "misguided humanitarians" who favored a more paternalistic approach to social policy.

Some have argued that the abandonment of predestination led evangelicals to become preoccupied with sin and with missionary endeavors to save others.[69] Although the Unitarians, too, shed the doctrine of predestination in their pursuit of "rational religion," as a sect they replaced doctrine with a strong adherence to the concept of natural laws. "The principles of which they talked in every field were, to them, scientific truths, scientifically derived."[70] When we consider in detail the type of social investigation pursued by our Unitarians on the Edwardian Poor Law Commission, we shall see that this was indeed their vision of correct poor law policy. We shall also see that they staunchly defended their views against arguments they considered unscientific, sentimental, and contrary to natural law. Their critics, however numerous, must be wrong.[71] Widespread criticism only confirmed, rather than weakened, their views.

This commitment to general providence exercised through natural laws dictates, of course, a type of social action quite different from what would seem appropriate to the special providentialist evangelical. Hence the determined opposition of the COS to the activities of the Salvation Army in East London, described below. This struggle has always been depicted, ironically, as a conflict between the religious view of the Salvationists and the secular view of the COS. Although the Salvation Army was indisputably motivated by a religious concern for the souls of the poor, the policy of the COS had its own, less visible, grounding in religion of another sort. There was a broad consensus among the Victorians that certain types of behavior – hard work, frugality, sobriety, thrift – were of positive value to individuals and to society, the very essence of respectability. These norms were widely assumed in the early eighteenth century to have been required of man by the Protestant God. In the view of Calvinists, they would manifest themselves in the elect and be notably absent in the damned. In the view of the other Protestant sects, they would be rewarded with prosperity (and their absence would be punished with misery) by God in His special providence. Or God, in His general providence, had set up the world to operate naturally so that these virtues would be rewarded and these vices punished. The widespread consensus about the desirability of the Protestant virtues (and the undesirability of the Protestant vices) was so strong that it survived, in many cases, the lessening of certainty that God had any direct role in the system, or even that He had set up the laws of Nature in the first place. This is why Helen Bosanquet heard the "voice of Nature" calling the English people to avoid the easy way out offered by the false prophets of philanthropy. They must practice exactly the same virtues required by the Calvinist God, or remain forever mired in the Slough of Despond. The only way out is still uphill.

One advantage of this viewpoint is that it offers a neat solution to problems of theodicy. Charles Booth, it will be recalled, was unable to maintain his religious faith over the question of how a kind and merciful God could allow so much suffering in the world. He was hardly alone in this concern. The strong human tendency to personalize the supernatural makes even a Unitarian God who has set natural laws in motion impeachable for callousness and indifference. If the laws of nature have arisen on their own, however, rather than by divine invention, then there is no point in questioning them; they are what they are. Hence Charles Booth's view that the existence of poverty was due not to divine ordinance but "to the working of some 'natural' law whose nature it was the function of science to reveal."[72]

Temptation, motivation, and the attractiveness of evil

> They on the rock are they, which, when they hear, receive the word with joy; and these have no root, which for a while believe, and in time of temptation fall away.
>
> Luke 8:13 Authorized (King James) Version

> The great lesson, then, of the nineteenth century is this, that the English people is strong, but only when it is not tempted into weakness; that it easily succumbs to the suggestion of dependence, but that it responds nobly when called upon to assert its manhood.
>
> Helen Dendy Bosanquet, *The Strength of the People*

The concept of temptation recurs frequently in the late nineteenth-century literature of poverty. Often it can be found in the midst of an otherwise apparently secular consideration of social policy. It would be nearly impossible (and undoubtedly harmful) to strip a language of its longstanding cultural associations, even in writing what is intended to be precise, scientific prose. Habits of mind, however, often accompany habits of speech, and a close examination of the use of temptation in poverty theory often reveals problems that a mere change of terminology cannot remedy.

Consider, for example, a comment of C.S. Loch, head of the COS, very much in tune with Helen Bosanquet. Reviewing poor law history to justify "the principles of 1834" and protect them from unwise amendment, Loch states that the framers of the New Poor Law did not wish to allow starvation, "But they would not tempt the self-supporting to destitution. Therefore it was established under just but hard restrictions."[73] Since it would be overly generous parish officials, rather than the Devil, who would be tempters, temptation in the traditional religious sense does not appear to be at issue here. And yet it would be difficult, if not impossible, to recast this sentence in purely secular terms while conveying the same meaning. Why would anyone be tempted by destitution? In the next chapter, as we consider the contribution of Malthusian population theory to the New Poor Law, we shall gain some insight into the type of behavior Loch has in mind. Potential paupers would be attracted, not by destitution itself, but by the prospect of early marriage and comfort; these would lead, inevitably, to destitution. To say that people are attracted to reproduction and comfort is to say nothing new; to suggest that government can and should lessen or interfere with these attractions, however, is another matter. "Temptation" has unavoidably moralistic connotations. Its use, moreover, obviates the questions of motive that would naturally arise in a more skeptical reader. The term precludes any debate as to whether or not the behavior in question is harmful, or about the motives of those engaging in this behavior.

Temptation serves, therefore, not only as an indicator of moral judgment but also as a circumvention of difficult questions of motivation. The choice need not be tactical; Loch almost certainly did understand the situation in terms of temptation to do wrong. Having done so, however, he was unlikely to consider the motivation for the behavior in question problematic.

This theme recurs in the works of all of our late nineteenth-century poverty experts. Helen Dendy Bosanquet sounds it in her criticism of overly generous provision for the poor in the form of free school meals, boots, and dinner tickets:

This, then, is how we manufacture our "Poor". By our crude belief that the Poverty Line is a question of money, and that by merely putting money or money's worth into a man's hands we can raise him above it. By our ignorant meddling which robs human lives of far more than we give in return. By the standing temptation we place before every man and woman to barter their birthright of independence for a mess of pottage.[74]

Bosanquet's reference to a well-known Old Testament story[75] instantly telegraphs, to almost any English reader of her era, the notion of sacrificing one's long-term interests in favor of a moment's desire. When we examine the role of Social Darwinism in the poverty theory of the period, we shall see that this theme was central to Social Darwinist social science. (We shall also see how trading long-term advantage for today's food, as Esau does, need not be interpreted as avoidable fecklessness, although Victorian social scientists generally did so interpret it.) While Bosanquet here, as was her custom, uses a biblical metaphor, the passage does not deal with sin in the conventional religious sense. It does, however, employ the concept of temptation in the same way, and in the same context, as does C.S. Loch. Likewise Beatrice Webb:

> Unrelieved destitution and social misery is, in any Christian or in any civilised community, an infamy. But an indiscriminate relief of destitution, which tempts all those of weak will and idle disposition to become destitute, is not only infamous but also directly dangerous to the State.[76]

Obviously we are dealing, not with a chance turn of phrase, but with a major concern of our poverty theorists: poor relief must not offer temptation.

"If the object is to elicit the prevailing ideas and images of an age," Gertrude Himmelfarb has argued, "they might better be sought precisely where they are not the subject of conscious attention and reflection, where they reveal themselves inadvertently and unconsciously."[77] Thus the influence of religious ideas on the Victorian social science of poverty can best be seen in the context of discussions that do not overtly concern religion. Perhaps the best illustration of this is the heated controversy about the activities of the Salvation Army in slum neighborhoods. On the surface, our poverty theorists appear to address issues of social policy rather than of religion. On closer examination, however, they reveal deep undercurrents of religious thought.

Salvation Army social action was based on its theology, which General William Booth and his wife Catherine brought from the Methodist

New Connexion.[78] Its most distinctive feature, aside from unusually strong prohibitions against fancy clothing, drink, and entertainment, was its concept of sin: "Sin resided in the hearts of transgressors, and only the Holy Spirit could dislodge it."[79] This belief makes sense only in the context of special providence; Salvationists "envisioned God as ever-present in this world, intervening in the daily workings of human affairs."[80] As evangelicals of the special providence school, the Salvation Army represented, of course, everything that Unitarians despised in the "irrational" Christian sects. The COS, nevertheless, despite its heavily Unitarian leadership, did not engage the Salvation Army in religious debate. The COS was a secular organization concerned with social policy. Their determined opposition to Salvationist social action had, in theory, nothing to do with religion. But they opposed social action based on special providentialist theology for reasons derived from their own general providentialist view. Under the surface, the controversy was every bit as grounded in religious ideas on the COS side as on the side of the Salvation Army. Both groups, moreover, addressed their social programs to the problem of temptation.

For both Salvationists and the COS, man is by his very nature beset by temptation. General Booth regarded sinful behavior as the cause of much poverty: "[M]uch of the misery of those whose lot we are considering arises from their own habits. Drunkenness and all manner of uncleanness, moral and physical, abound."[81]

Much of his argument, however, is strongly environmentalist in its logic. Booth denounces "defects of the sanitary system" that result in unnecessary disease and

> firms which reduce sweating to a fine art, who systematically and deliberately defraud the workman of his pay, who grind the faces of the poor, and who rob the widow and the orphan, and who for a pretence make great professions of public-spirit and philanthropy...[82]

In General Booth's view, these conditions cause "many of our bravest and best to fold their hands in despair" and make the slum environment "the Slough of Despond of our time."[83] With so much misery and so little hope, how can the poor not fall into temptation? The Salvation Army, however, has not folded its hands in despair; like Help in Bunyan's narrative, its members will alleviate the sufferings of the poor and bring the presence of God into their lives so that they may be touched by grace.

Opposed to this overtly religious view was the COS view that the sins of the poor were, not an effect, but the cause of their poverty. Ignoring the natural laws of human behavior, the poor were reaping the consequences of their actions. Far from giving the poor a chance to experience religious conversion and renounce sin, the Salvationists were themselves tempting them to continue in their evil ways by removing some of the consequences of their behavior. Hence Helen Dendy Bosanquet's often-stated view that night refuges and soup kitchens cause vagrancy:

> The casual labourer throughout the winter now looks upon chance bowls of soup, paid for with odd half-pence or not at all, as the standard for himself and his children, instead of three meals a day provided out of his earnings. Formerly even a poor man included a settled home, however humble it might be, amongst his necessaries; now his standard has been lowered by charitable enterprise until he is content to pass his life in shelters, casual wards, and semi-charitable lodging houses. It is much cheaper than to maintain a home, and involves less work; so those men – of whom there is always a considerable number – who like to follow the line of least resistance, *i.e.* lead the easiest life, revert to the nomad type and have their standard permanently lowered.[84]

Although the concept of "reversion to the nomad type" is, as we shall see, a hallmark of Social Darwinism, the underlying assumption that people will be tempted to rely on the Salvation Army for subsistence merely because they can has its origins in the Protestant view of work and of poverty – given a chance to rest in the daytime, sinful mankind will be strongly tempted to do so, regardless of the consequences.[85] "There is no doubt," Bosanquet concludes, "that many people who, but for the shelters, would have had homes of their own, are now without."[86]

Recall Charles Murray's assumption, which we encountered in the Prologue, that "In the absence of countervailing influences, people will avoid work and be amoral." To Murray, writing nearly a century later, this statement is still an axiom that requires no proof. But is this truism, in fact, true?

Malthus, ironically, believed that much of what is worthwhile in human activity is aimed toward the support and enjoyment of family life: "The evening meal, the warm house, and the comfortable fireside, would lose half of their interest, if we were to exclude the idea of some object of affection with whom they were to be shared."[87] To Bosanquet, however, family life apparently has no inherent attraction, while idleness does. She argues even against helping the innocent wives and children of drunkards lest doing so create more drunkards.

> [N]ext door on either side are men with the same downward path so easy before them, and to a large extent restrained from entering it by the thought, "What will become of the children?" This restraining influence will break down much more rapidly for the knowledge that Smith's children are better cared for since he gave up the battle, and so the mischief spreads down the street like an epidemic.[88]

Elsewhere she makes the mechanism more explicit, claiming that "our lodging-houses and shelters have tempted thousands of men into a life of drifting who might have developed far higher qualities as heads of families."[89]

What is so tempting about a vagrant's life? Sometimes Bosanquet emphasizes the appeal of irresponsibility; sometimes, of drink. The Victorians realized that a large percentage of people sleeping in Salvation Army hostels and other night shelters were drunkards. But were they sleeping in night shelters because they were drunkards, or were they drunkards because they could sleep in night shelters? A contemporary observer, who had himself grown up in a Manchester slum, attested to the widespread problem of excessive drinking among his neighbors but attributed it to the insecurity of slum life: "Fear was the *leitmotif* of their lives, dulled only now and then by the Dutch courage gained from drunkenness."[90] He did not regard vagrancy as inherently attractive to the men of his neighborhood, recalling vagrants who deliberately sought arrest because they preferred prison to either homelessness or the workhouse.[91] He also noted that rising prosperity and employment had greatly reduced the number of vagrants in Britain.[92] Roberts wrote of the circumstances and motivations of people he knew, either in the Salford of his youth or in the Edwardian prisons where he worked as a literacy tutor. Bosanquet, on the other hand, was an outside observer who placed a substantially different construction on the lives of vagrants.

In a narrative of the life patterns of East London families, Bosanquet once again returns to her theme of the danger of the shelters:

> [A]s the children grow older the chances are that the burden of maintaining the family falls entirely upon the mother. It is so easy now for the father to disappear and to take up life free of responsibility in some of the many shelters or lodging-houses in London; to change

his name if necessary, but in any case to elude the necessity of feeding more than himself.[93]

Bosanquet offers no evidence that any substantial number of men has ever acted in the way she describes, only a few anecdotes which can hardly be said to establish a widespread pattern. In our examination of the practices of Victorian social science we shall gain insight into why she is so casual about evidence for her assertions. The issue here is why she considers it plausible that the men of East London find life in the shelters so tempting. Here she was certainly in agreement with her colleague Octavia Hill, who vehemently opposed the harm done by the Salvation Army's "indiscriminate almsgiving."[94] Hill's friend Charles Booth agreed, arguing in his Religious Influences series that the Salvation Army did more harm than good by confirming the patrons of their shelters and soup-kitchens in their shiftless habits.[95] Not surprisingly the Webbs, whose opposition to the temptation posed by indiscriminate relief we have already encountered, also weighed in against these institutions. In a critique of testimony offered to the Edwardian Royal Commission by an experienced East London poor law guardian, they note that his report failed to take into account the activities of the Salvation Army and the Church Army in his district. He refused to see that the strict policies of the Board of Guardians and the COS

> have been rendered entirely nugatory by the inevitable reaction which they have set up, in the form of undiscriminating provision of meals for the hungry and shelter for the homeless, good, bad, and indifferent, by those who take their Christianity literally.[96]

Had the typical patron of Salvation Army soup kitchens and night shelters made a decision to abandon family life because vagrancy is cheaper and easier? Had he become a derelict because he could obtain free, albeit minimal, subsistence from the Salvationists? Many modern social scientists consider such notions overly simplistic. About 70 years after the Edwardian Royal Commission, a report of the Royal College of Psychiatrists strongly asserted that "causes of excessive drinking are always multiple and interactive..."[97] One finding strongly recalls the non-specialist view of Robert Roberts: "Any environment which imposes continued stress on an individual can invite a risk of heavy drinking."[98] Considerations of this kind are unlikely to arise, however, in a mind that is comfortable with the model of temptation.

Helen and Bernard Bosanquet, McBriar has noted, exhibited "a puritan sense of the attractiveness of evil and of the strenuous effort needed to sustain good conduct."[99] In this they were not alone. The writings of all of our poverty experts, to varying degrees, demonstrate a strong if unconscious belief that idleness and vice are so tempting as to negate the desire for family life, normal comforts, and decency among the poor. So secure are they in this conviction that for the most part they show no curiosity about other possible explanations, no need to prove that temptation to idleness and vice actually motivates the poor. (Nor does their successor, Charles Murray, who confidently asserts that the welfare policies of the 1970s have "seduced" the poor "into long-term disaster.")

Anne Digby has identified "the theory of unstable moral equilibrium in the life of a poor man" as political economy's "most influential legacy in shaping the new Poor Law." This theory postulated that a poor man "might be tempted into pauperism or encouraged to retain his independence."[100] This was in fact the prevailing view of political economy, but it derives from the religious and cultural inheritance we have been exploring here. Political economists were content to set up a system in which the automatic mechanisms of a self-regulating system punish pauperism and reward independence. The Salvation Army tried to intervene, as God intervenes, by offering the poor a helping hand out of the Slough of Despond in the form of openness to grace. The Unitarian ethos of the COS suggested offering assistance only in forms compatible with the demands of nature's laws. None doubted for a moment the attractiveness of evil.

Philosophical idealism and the transcendence of circumstances by will

> These things I have spoken unto you, that in me ye might have peace. In the world ye shall have tribulation: but be of good cheer; I have overcome the world.
>
> John 16:33 Authorized (King James) Version

> [I]t is always the man in his selective activity who makes his circumstances, who chooses what his world shall be, even though he may let them afterwards mould his life by the habits they encourage.
>
> Helen Dendy Bosanquet, *The Strength of the People*

In his thoughtful examination of the long policy struggle between two influential couples – Bernard and Helen Bosanquet, and Sidney and Beatrice Webb – McBriar argues that Bernard Bosanquet's social thought is best understood in the context of his role as a professor of philosophy and leader, after T.H. Green, of the school of Philosophical Idealism.[101] His "insistence on the will's primacy over circumstances" connects his social policy with "his high-level metaphysical notion that the universe was structured by mind."[102] Helen Dendy, who met her husband at a gathering of the Ethical Society, was already convinced of the validity of Idealist philosophy before her first encounter with its foremost living exponent.[103] Philosophical Idealism, which Himmelfarb describes as a "secularized Evangelicalism," provided "a secular metaphysics in aid of a social ethics."[104] The fathers of the three most prominent figures in the movement, T.H. Green, F.H. Bradley, and Bernard Bosanquet, were all evangelical clergymen; in Himmelfarb's view, "they all transmuted that religious tradition."[105] As befits a secular metaphysics, Philosophical Idealism never claimed religious sanction. Its viewpoint, nonetheless, derives from a religious tradition of the transcendence of the spiritual over the material that was very much a part of the Victorian common culture.

Thus we find Samuel Smiles proclaiming, "It is *will*, – force of purpose – that enables a man to do or be whatever he sets his mind on being or doing."[106] Helen Bosanquet, daughter of a Unitarian rather than an Evangelical home, begins her book on "social economics" by quoting Oliver Cromwell on the primacy of character in human affairs: "The mind is the man. If that be kept pure, a man signifies somewhat; if not, I would very fain see what difference there is between him and a beast."[107] Bosanquet has no trouble finding support from Cromwell for the notion of the primacy of mind. The ethical imperatives she derives from Idealist metaphysics are indistinguishable from the moral requirements of the Lord of the hill – hard work, frugality, self-denial. Annie Fields, leader of the Boston branch of the COS, has been said to embody a fusion of "the Puritan's conscience and the Transcendentalist's idealism."[108] Much the same could be said of Helen Bosanquet.

Man makes his circumstances but the circumstances may then – if he permits – shape him in turn. This mixture of environmentalism and its implicit refutation through Idealism often recurs in the poverty theory of the late nineteenth century. Over time, as we shall see, accumulating evidence of the power of circumstance began to force itself upon the reluctant awareness of all poverty theorists. The primacy of mind and will over circumstance, however, provided a convenient mechanism for minimizing the importance of circumstance. Samuel Smiles supplies an unsophisticated instance of this thinking in his contention that children will turn out well if brought up in virtuous homes:

> On the other hand, if surrounded by ignorance, coarseness, and selfishness, they will unconsciously assume the same character, and grow up to adult years rude, uncultivated, and all the more dangerous to society if placed amidst the manifold temptations of what is called civilization.[109]

Smiles here serves up a rich stew of Calvinism, idealism, and environmentalism. Products of these homes are morally doomed by circumstances beyond their control, which mould them. Yet it is a sullied mind, rather than physical circumstances, which seals their fate. Society presents them, not with material limitations, but with manifold temptations. The mind is the man.

Helen Bosanquet, a far more sophisticated thinker than Smiles, also focuses on the mind of the individual rather than on his physical circumstances, which by implication are less important. Certain as she is that the individual "chooses what his world shall be," she does not pause to ask herself whether anyone chooses to be born in Mile End, to contract bronchitis or tuberculosis, to use an ash pit privy, to develop rickets, or to be the child of a drunkard. Such a person can, "by his selective activity," choose not to let his circumstances encourage him in bad habits, and that is what really matters. With the right mind, he can overcome the world.

It is probably difficult for a person whose culture takes for granted the primacy of the spiritual over the material to see how deeply this assumption colors the perceptions of its members. Not merely evangelicals and members of the Ethical Society, but a broad cross-section of late nineteenth-century England, viewed the world in this way, even regarding an interest in the physical as antithetical to progress. Beatrice Webb, for example, feared that social progress might be very difficult to achieve, "the average, sensual man not wanting to be improved!"[110] The increasing prosperity and decreasing vagrancy that Robert Roberts celebrated after World War I made far less of an impression on Helen Bosanquet, who argued that it was not the "world of things" but "the world of ideas" which "cries out for reconstruction."[111] She had consistently maintained the primacy of mind; true to herself, she continued to do so until the end. This viewpoint minimized the material aspects of poverty to such an extent that their very significance was implicitly called into question.

Denial: the poverty that is not poverty

And he lifted up his eyes on his disciples, and said, Blessed be ye poor: for yours is the kingdom of God.

Blessed are ye that hunger now: for ye shall be filled. Blessed are ye that weep now: for ye shall laugh.

Luke 6:20–1 Authorized (King James) Version

Riches are oftener an impediment than a stimulus to action; and in many cases they are quite as much a misfortune as a blessing.

Samuel Smiles, *Self-Help*

Victorian poverty experts do not appear to have taken poverty very seriously, as many historians have commented. To the early Victorians, "the critical social evil was not mass poverty but pauperism."[112] The Victorians, it appears, "were more worried about the allegedly corrupting effects of distributing even small amounts in charity than about the existence of poverty and the hardships suffered by the sick, the old or the workless."[113] In light of the cultural traditions we have been exploring, this attitude is not difficult to understand. Since our poverty theorists assumed that the mind and will can triumph over mere circumstance, how disabling could mere poverty be? The poverty theorists, accordingly, showed a strong tendency not only to downplay the importance of the hardships of poverty but even, in some instances, to count them as advantages rather than as handicaps.

In Bunyan's narrative of the *Pilgrim's Progress*, mere physical hardship is meaningless in the soul's journey, except in the sense that it is conducive to spiritual attainment. Thus it constitutes a positive good. This notion, sanctified by the sayings of Jesus, is ubiquitous in Victorian thought. In nineteenth-century English sermons, the idea that afflictions are good for people and will make the afflicted holier frequently recurs.[114] It is also evident in the popular works of Samuel Smiles:

Indeed, so far from poverty being a misfortune, it may, by vigorous self-help, be converted even into a blessing; rousing a man to that struggle with the world in which, though some may purchase by degradation, the right-minded man and true-hearted find strength, confidence, and triumph.[115]

Poverty, it would seem, is a blessing and wealth a curse. Later Smiles makes this conclusion explicit:

> The necessity of labour may, indeed, be regarded as the main root and spring of all that we call progress in individuals, and civilization in nations; and it is doubtful whether any heavier curse could be imposed on man than the complete gratification of all his wishes without effort, leaving nothing for his hopes, desires or struggles.[116]

The immense popularity of *Self-Help* indicates that Smiles must have struck a responsive chord in his large public. The book became standard reading for English youth and was used as a textbook in the Ragged Schools – thus reaching, if only passively, some of the children of the poor as well.[117] Its ideas were truly commonplace.

Helen Bosanquet sounds a similar note in a comparison of the fate of miscreants among the rich and the poor. The poor suffer more as a result of their "faults and follies" than the rich, because the economic consequences to them are greater.

> But if measured by any other consequences, it is from no callousness or lack of sympathy that I should maintain that the advantage is almost wholly on the side of the poor. For them, at least, the descent into the slough of self-indulgence is not, in a normal condition, made easy, and they have every inducement to escape before it is too late.[118]

From this standpoint, it is easy to see how Octavia Hill might believe "that poverty was not in itself a very serious evil."[119] So, too the conviction of economic historian and enthusiastic COS member Arnold Toynbee:

> No one wants high wages in order that working men may indulge in mere sensual gratification. We want higher wages in order that an improved material condition, with less anxiety and less uncertainty as to the future, may enable the working man to enter on a purer and more worthy life.[120]

Likewise, in the opinion of C.S. Loch:

> Increase in the means of living, unless there be at the same time a corresponding increase in thrift, foresight, and self-reliance, leads to an increase in the population without improving its quality... The destruction of the poor is not their poverty – it is their poor quality...[121]

On the Edwardian Royal Commission, not only the COS members of the Majority but also the author of the Minority Report, Beatrice Webb, shared this view. Along with proposed measures to be undertaken by the proposed Destitution Authority, the Minority Report offers this opinion: "The evil to be remedied is not the destitution of a day or of a month, but the continuous carelessness and ignorance bred of chronic poverty."[122] Mere physical hardship need not be an obstacle and may even help. Poverty is not poverty, and is therefore not in itself a matter of great concern.

> For what shall it profit a man, if he shall gain the whole world, and lose his own soul?
>
> Mark 8:36 Authorized (King James) Version

4
Political Economy and the New Poor Law

> The Poor Law Commission built the New Poor Law with the bricks of classical economics held together by the mortar of disdain for the dependent.
>
> Lynn Hollen Lees, *The Solidarities of Strangers*

> The effect of Malthusianism was immediate and dramatic. For half a century social attitudes and policies were decisively shaped by the new turn of thought. It was in this form, the form given it by Malthus and modified by Ricardo, that political economy took hold in the early part of the nineteenth century.
>
> Gertrude Himmelfarb, *The Idea of Poverty*

One of the longest-running debates about the New Poor Law concerns the role played by Malthusian population theory. Was the decision to overturn the existing system of outdoor parish relief in favor of the new workhouse system attributable to the influence of Malthus? James Bonar, an admirer of Malthus and of the New Poor Law, certainly thought so: "Malthus is the father, not only of the new Poor Law, but of all our latter-day societies for the organisation of charity."[1] Despite the frequent mentions of Malthus during the Parliamentary debate, however, Malthus's logic supports, not reform of the poor law, but its total abolition. The most ardent Malthusians among the members of the 1832 Royal Commission – Sturges Bourne, Bishop Sumner, and Bishop Blomfield – were therefore originally intent on abolition rather than on reform.[2] To understand why the Commission decided to reform rather than to abolish, we must view Malthusian population theory, not in isolation, but in the context of contemporary political economy.

The Political Economy Club and the men of 1832

The Political Economy Club, founded in 1821 by Thomas Tooke and James Mill, numbered among its members representatives of the most influential schools of social thought in Britain. Mill, a disciple of Jeremy Bentham, was among the most prominent of the Utilitarians.[3] Ricardo, too, was a member. Club members usually sided with him against Malthus on questions like underconsumption.[4] Yet Malthus was a member and seldom missed a meeting; whatever the nature of his theoretical disagreements with Ricardo, the two remained personal friends.[5] Another member who remained on terms of personal intimacy with Malthus, despite some disagreements on theory, was Nassau William Senior, Drummond Professor of Political Economy at Oxford. He was one of the two Royal Commissioners most responsible for the conduct of the 1832 inquiry and for its report.[6] Edwin Chadwick, Senior's colleague in the direction of the Royal Commission and in the publicity campaign for adoption of the New Poor Law, was admitted to the club later than the others.[7] Finally Lord Althorp, the evangelical peer who voiced his personal struggle between political economy and Christian charity as he worked to guide the New Poor Law through the House of Lords, was also an active member of the Political Economy Club.[8]

Clearly the framers and supporters of the New Poor Law shared a strong interest in political economy. Given the provisions of the bill, many observers have viewed the inquiry of the Royal Commission as a sham designed "to validate the dogmatic presuppositions of political economy."[9] But, with respect to the relationship of population and the poor laws, what *were* "the presuppositions of political economy"? On this question the members of the Political Economy Club were not of one mind. The nature of their differences underlay the debate over abolition versus reform.

Optimists and pessimists: Senior and Malthus on population

Not all political economists accepted Malthus's contention that population would always increase to fit the resources available. He himself incorporated into later editions of the *Essay* the possibility of the "prudential check" – voluntary limitation of births through late marriage – as a means of escaping famine and want. He was not hopeful, however, that many workers would adopt this strategy, because he regarded the desire to procreate as far stronger than the desire to better oneself.[10]

The logic of his view requires abolition of any support for the poor, since feeding them will simply increase the supply of eaters without increasing the supply of food. It will also increase the supply of potential workers and thereby decrease the wages available to each.[11] That is why Malthus himself favored abolition in principle, although he conceded that various customary, humanitarian, and political factors might make it difficult to achieve in practice.[12] Above all, Malthus felt, the poor must no longer regard public assistance as a right, although the government might feel the necessity of providing it. If it is a right, then laborers can count on its availability, and population will grow.[13]

Although Malthus was one of the founding fathers of political economy, others with equally good credentials disagreed with him on the prospects of the poor. Adam Smith was among the "optimists" who felt that the standard of living of the poor, most of whom were "sober and industrious," was bound to improve as more efficient applications of labor produced more wealth.[14] While it is often assumed that Smith favored abolition of the poor law on grounds of political economy, in fact he had no objection to the provision of relief to those who could not support themselves. It was to the Act of Settlement that he objected, because requiring the poor to apply for assistance in their own parish tied them to it, especially when they were unemployed, and thus inhibited the mobility of labor.[15]

Malthus's friend Nassau Senior was nearer to Adam Smith than to Malthus on this point. In his correspondence with Malthus, Senior accepted as demonstrated the mathematical thesis of the *Essay*: unchecked human reproduction did have the potential to double the population every 25 years. He doubted, however, that any society so enlightened as to be able to remove the negative checks to population growth – famine, war, violent crime, and so on – would be so unwise as to neglect the prudential ones.[16] Senior placed his faith in the human desire not just for the bare necessities of life but for the "decencies and luxuries" as well – what today we would call a higher standard of living.[17] Senior's belief in the good sense of the common man was not unequivocal. Loose administration under the old system, "the grand abuse of the English poor laws,"[18] had in his view encouraged irresponsible reproductive decisions. Thus "We have the poor laws to increase our numbers."[19] He told Malthus, however, that permanent improvement in the lot of the poor could be achieved if poor law administration encouraged them to aspire to it.[20] But how was it possible for government, short of abolition, to prevent abuse of the system without interfering in the free play of the market?

Utilitarianism: active government in a self-equilibrating system

Like his colleague Nassau Senior, Edwin Chadwick was an optimist on the question of improvement in the standard of living of the poor.[21] Chadwick had learned, as personal secretary to Jeremy Bentham, to postulate a positive role for government as a harmonizer of personal conflicts, thus bringing "greatest good to the greatest number."[22] Although individual initiative was always to be preferred, sometimes government had "to keep the ring clear" for it, making sure that the system worked as it should without hindrance from custom or vested interests.[23]

Jeremy Bentham long concerned himself with the poor laws and proposed elaborate schemes for their reform that are still to be seen today in the Bentham archives at University College, London, mercifully transcribed in the more legible hand of his secretary, Edwin Chadwick. Abolition of the poor law did not appeal to Bentham, despite complaints about its abuse. He specifically repudiated the idea of abolition, stating that no civilized community could permit people to starve, and that there would probably always be people in danger of doing so.[24] Bentham also noted that private charity would likely prove insufficient to provide decent maintenance for those unable to support themselves. Only public funding would suffice.[25] But care must be taken in any system of relief to make sure that the working poor are not attracted to a life of leisure at state expense, with "the destruction of society" as "the inevitable consequence."[26]

Such a catastrophe can be avoided as long as "the condition of persons maintained, without property of their own, by the labour of others" is not permitted to be "more eligible than that of persons maintained by their own labour."[27] This is the principle of "less eligibility," which administrators of the Victorian Poor Law saw as their guiding light; its mechanism was to be the "workhouse test." If assistance is available only in the workhouse, under conditions "less eligible" than those available to employed persons in their own homes, then anyone accepting aid must truly need it. Abuse is therefore impossible, and interference with the labor market is avoided. Although Bentham believed that the labor of those confined in the workhouse could provide sufficient income to pay for the expenses of the establishment, in reality workhouses never came close to paying for themselves.[28] But the requirement of labor from the able-bodied did have a function in the workhouse system as a component of "less eligibility," a protection from fraud and abuse. For this reason Chadwick enthusiastically incorporated the workhouse test into his proposal for the New Poor Law and continued to insist on its use when he served on the central authority administering the system. Chadwick admonished parish officers to avoid out-relief, work-creation schemes, and supplemental wages as an interference with the labor market:

> for where a parish has an efficient workhouse, either of its own or in union with other parishes, experience abundantly proves that a judicious application of the workhouse test, when the system is once fully established, renders any other test, by means of out-door employment, altogether unnecessary for the repression of pauperism.[29]

The workhouse system, therefore, represented government action designed not to interfere with the market. It fulfilled the moral obligation of society to prevent total destitution without violating the canons of political economy. It constituted a minimal intervention that government could make to restore the system, so it would work the way it was intended to work.

Was Malthus the father of the New Poor Law?

The New Poor Law resulted from a decision not to abolish the provision of relief, as Malthus believed desirable, but rather to reform it. In what sense, therefore, can he be seen as the "father" of the new system? Himmelfarb argues that the widely read theory of Malthus turned the tide toward blaming the poor for their own misfortunes. As we have seen, however, English Protestants were well prepared for such a perspective. "Malthus's case against the poor laws," as Himmelfarb notes, "consisted of equal parts of economics and morality."[30] Malthus was quite open in his belief that only the poor were to blame for their troubles; they must be made to understand "that they are themselves the cause of their own poverty; that the means of redress are in their own hands, and in the hands of no other persons whatever..."[31] The influence of Malthus is quite evident, moreover, in the emphasis on early marriage and bastardy in testimony before the Royal Commission and in its subsequent report.

Consider, for example, the testimony of Assistant Commissioner George Taylor, "an ardent Malthusian."[32] Taylor asserted that the existing system of family allowances placed "a direct premium on early marriages."[33] His remarks were entirely confined to the alleged effect of the allowance system on marriage patterns in his district, totally ignoring local courtship and marriage customs.[34] Taylor's testimony on the subject of "Bastardy and Improvident Marriages" raises the issue of precisely what constitutes an "improvident marriage." To this question Malthus offers a ready reply in an appendix to the 1806 edition of the *Essay*: "The lowest prospect with which a man can be justified in marrying seems to be, the power, when in health, of earning such wages, as at the average price of corn will maintain the average number of living children to a marriage."[35] Malthus biographer Patricia James, not surprisingly, was moved to describe this formula as "the *reductio ad absurdum* of prudential foresight."[36]

The reaction of Lord Byron demonstrates that doubts about the practical application of such an approach were possible without benefit of considerable hindsight. In the fifteenth canto of *Don Juan*, published in 1824, he describes Adeline as a follower of Malthus in the matter of suitable marriage:

> 'Tis not my purpose on his views to dwell,
> Nor canvass what "so eminent a hand" meant,
> But certes it conducts to lives ascetic,
> Or turning marriage into arithmetic.[37]

Byron, of course, based his view on common sense rather than on political economy. It would be unfair to imply that an interest in political economy automatically deprived its possessor of common sense. Nassau Senior, for example, was well aware that economic considerations might not be uppermost in the minds of people deciding to marry. In his writings on population he indicated that he regarded as obvious "the many sources of happiness connected with early marriage" and "the force of the passions which prompt to marriage."[38] Yet the proceedings of the Royal Commission show a frequent tendency to ignore such considerations. In testimony on the operation of the allowance system in the north of England for example, we learn that "At Dent... poor people, especially those who have become pensioners, marry early, more frequently under twenty years of age than above; they are induced to do this, no doubt, from a reliance upon relief from the poor rate."[39] Likewise D.O.P. Okeden testified: "In Dunstew, as in all the Oxfordshire parishes, the early marriage of mere boys is frequent, for the avowed purpose of increasing *their income*, by allowance for increase of children."[40]

Chadwick, too, in the circular from the Poor Law Commissioners cited earlier, commented that complete abolition of any family allowance system "would so far remove the incentive to early and improvident marriages, which the present practice has a tendency to encourage."[41]

A degree of confusion is evident here. Are the poor doing what comes naturally without the constraint of prudential considerations, or are they responding to the availability of payment for what they might not otherwise have done? The first of these two models is the argument of the Malthus *Essay*. The second, ignoring local customs and the proclivity of the human race to marry and reproduce under a wide variety of circumstances, seems to suggest a marriage decision made by Economic Man.

Economic Man – *homo economicus* – is an abstract concept of political economy. As John Stuart Mill observed, political economy does not take in the full spectrum of the mental life of man. "It is concerned with him solely as a being who desires to possess wealth, and who is capable of judging of the comparative efficacy of means for obtaining that end."[42] While the model has some utility in the study of a number of economic processes, Mill was well aware that its usefulness in analyzing more complicated human behavior is rather limited: "There is, perhaps, no action of a man's life in which he is neither under the immediate nor under the remote influence of any impulse but the mere desire of wealth. With respect to those parts of human conduct of which wealth is not even the principal object, to these Political Economy does not pretend that its conclusions are applicable."[43]

Would any of the men who gave or took evidence in the poor law inquiry have characterized their own decision to marry as a purely economic transaction with wealth its principal object? But then few if any were members of the social stratum about which the testimony was being offered. The young people so eager to marry who were described to the Assistant Commissioners were poor, and therefore already morally suspect. Their courtship customs were, as Henriques points out, totally ignored, and their behavior was interpreted according to the theoretical presuppositions of the observers. No less an authority than J.S. Mill was well aware, as the Royal Commissioners apparently were not, of the hazards of extending economic analysis beyond its proper sphere: "In these complex matters, men see with their preconceived opinions, not with their eyes: an interested or a passionate man's statistics are of little worth; and a year seldom passes without examples of the astounding falsehoods which large bodies of respectable men will back each other in publishing to the world as facts within their personal knowledge."[44]

Nowhere does Mill's observation seem more apt than in considering the proceedings of the Royal Commission with respect to the subject of bastardy.

Economic Woman has a baby: Maternal motivation in the Poor Law inquiry

> There are other sources of admiration and delight besides wealth.
>
> T.R. Malthus, *Definitions in Political Economy*

No subject considered by the Royal Commission provoked more heated discussion than the provisions governing bastardy. Patricia James notes that "It is perhaps impossible to contemplate the fundamental problems of population without some kind of emotional bias,"[45] and plenty of emotion was evident in the testimony and debate over this aspect of the proposed changes. Malthus himself had displayed some compassion toward unwed mothers, remarking in the first edition of the *Essay* that "so natural a fault" was easy to understand.[46] But much of the testimony before the Royal Commission reflects a far less charitable view. George Taylor, for example, insisted that women often used the bastardy laws to compel marriage.[47] His testimony did not offer a reason why they might be reduced to such measures, but he did, perhaps, suggest one: "If a girl, on finding himself pregnant, filiates the child, and fails in her speculation, by the putative father refusing to marry her, her next resource is the allowance for the support of the child…"[48]

The motive for such "speculation," clearly, would be financial. Taylor asserted that in pursuit of this goal false swearing of paternity was common.[49] C.P. Villiers made the same assertion: "The woman, therefore, learns that either by degrading herself originally she can obtain a husband, or by repeating the offense she can increase her income."[50]

This theme was so common in the testimony reproduced in the final report that Lynn Lees characterizes the Commissioners as "haunted" by "the image of women producing multiple bastards for profit."[51] Indeed Edwin Chadwick saw as one of the great defects of the old system its failure to contain bastardy: "The objects of the law respecting bastardy were to punish and check unchastity, and to prevent the state being burdened with the offspring of illicit intercourse. The effects of the law, as it was administered, were to add greatly to a wretched pauper population, and not only to license, but to give bounties for the promotion of the vice intended to be restrained."[52]

Harriet Martineau took up this theme in her efforts to provide publicity in support of the passage of the New Poor Law. While her didactic tales are admittedly works of fiction, in her preface to them she asserts their absolute accord with the true and deplorable state of the countryside: "I have unquestionable authority in the Reports of the Poor Law Commissioners; and the testimony of others who are occupied in the administration of parish affairs, for every parochial abuse and every pauper encroachment here exhibited; and I have taken no pains to select the worst instances of either that have come within my knowledge."[53] For the most part, Martineau portrays her country folk as good, simple people who are unfortunately susceptible to corruption by the parish pay system. But poor farmer James Beaver has paternity falsely sworn against him by the perfidious Jemima who, like her sister the Widow Brand, equates more children with more comfort, thanks to the generosity of the parish.[54]

In the testimony before the Royal Commission, even where false swearing of paternity is not alleged, blame tends to fall on aggressive women searching for husbands or for income. According to Edward Tregaskis, vestry clerk of Penryn St Gluvias, Cornwall, "We know and are satisfied from long and serious observation and facts occurring that continued illicit intercourse has, in almost all cases, originated with the females; many of whom, under our knowledge, in this and neighboring parishes, do resort to it as a source of support, taking advantage of the kindness of the provisions for the nurture of the offspring from their own inability to contribute, and thus receive the fixed weekly allowances from the parish officers..."[55] Mr Simon, testifying before the House of Lords in 1831, had gone further: "I know of many instances in which the mothers have themselves been instrumental in having their daughters seduced for the express purpose of getting rid of the onus of supporting them, and saddling them upon any unfortunate young man of the neighbourhood whom they could get to the house."[56] Mr Simon did not, apparently, see fit to expand his anecdote with a consideration of whether the "unfortunate young man" had consented to the extramarital activity that ensued; in any event, the reader is left in no doubt that female perfidy is to blame for the resulting pregnancy.

The remedy that the Royal Commission proposed was to place full responsibility for bastard children on their mothers, and at this proposal Parliament balked. While the bill's sponsors insisted that removal of liability from the father would reduce the number of bastards, other members were not so sure that this provision was either fair or useful. Mr Robinson found the proposal "monstrous" and doubted that making the mother liable would deter "persons who were seduced under promise of marriage."[57] Under the proposed system, moreover, there would be no financial deterrent to "licentious men," who could now "commit seduction with perfect impunity."[58] Lord Althorp, who apparently was more worried about the morals of women than of men, countered that under the present system false swearing of paternity was extremely common and that the allowance system tends to "hold out advantages to females of an abandoned character, and consequently to counteract that moral feeling which otherwise might preserve their chastity."[59] Mr Wolryche Whitmore apparently agreed, noting without further explanation that "The practice of giving public support to illegitimate children was a cause of their increase."[60]

But many expressed doubts. Mr Benet, speaking as an experienced magistrate, pointed out that the proposed change "proceeded on the principle, that women would perjure themselves for the small premium of 1s. per week," the sum usually allotted, which was merely sufficient to keep the child from perishing.[61] With this Mr Cobbett agreed, adding in characteristic fashion that it is not merely the poor who produce bastards; the illegitimate offspring of the nobility on the Pension List are supported "in splendor" at taxpayer's expense, while this proposal would deny any support to poorer bastards outside of the workhouse.[62]

Throughout the debate we see a clear divide between those who view the proposal as a cruel and unnecessary imposition on innocent women and children and those who see it as a way of preventing calculating hussies from cashing in at the expense of alleged fathers and the public purse. Mr Peter, for example, did not share Mr Benet's skepticism about the number of women willing to perjure themselves for a paltry sum; he was convinced that there were "numerous instances" in which a predatory woman will extort money from "a poor and perfectly innocent man."[63]

The argument continued in the House of Lords, where the Lord Chancellor insisted that the bastardy provisions of the old poor law gave a woman "little or no inducement (so far as law is concerned) to preserve her chastity."[64] The Bishop of Exeter, on the other hand, complained about the obvious bias of the Report with respect to bastardy; throughout, the putative fathers are described as "unfortunate," while the mothers are depicted as depraved. In his opinion there was no evidence to support this view, which rested on an assumption that lower-class women have no morals.[65] To this the Bishop of London replied that the Report's view of loose morals among lower-class women was, in fact, correct, due in part to the pernicious influence of the poor laws.[66] The deeply religious Lord Shaftesbury apparently was not convinced of this; he voted against the provision.[67]

While the debate over the bastardy clauses demonstrates significant support among legislators for the view of the Royal Commission that large numbers of poor women deliberately bore children out of wedlock for the purpose of gaining financial support (either from the parish or from the real or falsely-sworn father), in the end Parliament was not willing to change the existing system. Most of the members, unlike Mr Cobbett, were not inclined to compare the reproductive behavior of the poor with that of their social betters. Many of them, including those who opposed the change, were obviously quite comfortable with the assumption that the morals of the poor were very much suspect, but they did not agree as to whether it was the loose morals of poor women or of poor men that underlay the problem. Interestingly, the depraved men depicted in the debate are portrayed as merely looking for sexual gratification and unwilling to pay for its consequences. The depraved women, on the other hand, are depicted as acting for financial reasons. They are Economic Woman, unmoved by any consideration other than making a profit. Since the overhaul of the bastardy provisions, unlike the adoption of the workhouse system, was not carried, it would appear that a majority of members simply did not recognize in this model the actual women they knew.

The oversimplification noted by J.S. Mill is nowhere more evident than in the statement of the Lord Chancellor that the existing system of paternal liability left no inducement to the preservation of female chastity.[68] Is it likely that many women consider only financial aspects in deciding whether or not to enter into intimate relations with a suitor? Other claimants for a woman's consideration clearly could include her feelings toward him, her attitudes toward childbearing (with its attendant cares and risks), her religious views on sex and marriage, her family situation, and local customs and attitudes on courtship and illegitimacy. Might she not fear social disapproval, personal disappointment, perdition, death in childbirth, a life spent tied to an unsatisfactory husband? Witnesses and legislators who testified to the production of bastards for profit do not appear to have envisioned questions of this type. (Nor does Charles Murray, whose examination of the situation of "Harold and "Phyllis" focuses relentlessly on "what the incentives are.")[69]

Consider, for example, the conclusions drawn by Mr Cowell of Norfolk on the effects of allowance for illegitimate children:

> A bastard child is thus about 25 per cent more valuable to a parent than a legitimate one. The premium upon want of chastity, perjury,

and extortion, is here very obvious; and Mr. Sewell informed me that it is considered a good speculation to marry a woman who can bring a fortune of one or two bastards to her husband.[70]

Would Mr Cowell have considered bastard children an appropriate dowry to accompany a prospective wife? Would he have calculated their value? Might not a man willing to marry a woman with children have any other reason besides "speculation" for his choice? The Assistant Commissioner who took his evidence did not ask these questions, apparently satisfied, as Mill probably would not be, that financial considerations provide a full explanation of the behavior alleged by the witness. Considerations of property and income were not, of course, foreign to the matchmaking of members of the higher orders. Marriage was, then as now, about property and inheritance, not just about personal happiness. But bastard children would bring with them a considerable loss of respectability. And even if we assume, as the Royal Commission and many members of Parliament did, that financial incentives are uppermost in the minds of the poor in making reproductive choices, how precisely can these financial incentives be expected to operate?

Two economic models of reproductive decisions influenced by the Poor Law

If we choose to take seriously the idea that economic considerations played a major role in bringing about an increase in the pauper class under the old system, then there are two possible ways that these considerations could operate:

Model A: Left to their own devices, people would prefer to have a spouse and children, but not everyone can afford them. If relief is available, they will rely on it; they will marry and have children without fear that their circumstances might not support the expense of raising them to maturity. If relief is not available, then they will exercise prudence and restraint.

Model B: People are not inherently desirous of marriage or children, but they do want money. If the parish offers them financial rewards for having children, then they will have them. If no such rewards are available, then they won't bother.

Note that Model A is not a purely economic model, since it includes non-economic motivational factors. Model A is clearly the model behind the thinking of Malthus who, as we have seen, regarded the joys of family life as obvious and universal. (Malthus, himself the father of a large family, did however often appear to consider children the inevitable byproducts of sexual activity, toward which all men share an overwhelming impetus, rather than as desirable in themselves.) And on occasion Malthus spoke as if he were proposing Model B: "it is an acknowledged and much talked of fact that in many of the Southern parishes where the single man is paid much less than the married man, labourers have avowedly married for the express purpose of obtaining the allowance given for children."[71] Nevertheless, the clear import of his argument in the *Essay* is that marriage and reproduction are what people quite naturally want. In this he was speaking, of course, of a universal disposition of mankind rather than of the specific behavior of paupers.

It would appear that his friend Nassau Senior was of roughly the same mind, since he acknowledged "the many sources of happiness connected with early marriage."[72] Like Malthus he sometimes appeared to be using Model B when discussing the alleged effects of the Poor Law on population increase. There is no record, moreover, of his having challenged the abundant testimony on bastards-for-profit before the Royal Commission, much of which he published in the Report. Yet he does appear to have assumed that the attractions of marriage and family life were too obvious to require much in the way of economic explanation. The problem was to keep those who could not afford them from improvidently undertaking them. Again any inconsistency arises in addressing not the natural disposition of mankind but the specific behavior of the poor; again the speaker does not appear to recognize it.

Unlike Model A, Model B is a purely economic model, ignoring all other possible reasons for marriage and reproduction. This is the model we see in operation in most of the testimony on family allowances and bastardy before the Royal Commission and in most of the remarks from supporters of the New Poor Law in the Parliamentary debate. That this model underlies the assertions of reformers was by no means obvious to them; in fact, the debate contains many laudatory remarks about Malthus followed by claims that the poor marry, have children, and become pregnant out of wedlock for financial reasons – a claim that is inconsistent with the logic of Malthus's argument. But then, as we have seen, Malthus himself was not completely consistent on this point. Mankind acts in accordance with Model A, while perhaps those in actual or potential receipt of poor relief act in accordance with Model B.

The shortcomings of a purely economic model of reproduction – oversimplification, obliviousness to social and psychological dimensions, and the assumption of complete rationality[73] – are perfectly obvious to modern social scientists, although less so to poverty researchers than to others, for reasons we shall later address.[74] J.S. Mill was aware of the potential for trouble in this type of thinking, as he indicated in his comments on Economic Man. The rural magistrates who testified and the Assistant Commissioners who recorded their opinions, not surprisingly, lacked Mill's level of theoretical sophistication. But it must be noted that Model B poses an additional problem that could have been detected at the time of the Royal Commission. In fact it *was* detected by Mr Benet, who told the House of Commons that the customary allowance for a bastard child was a mere shilling a week, barely sufficient to keep it alive and "off the rates".[75] It was for this reason that he feared the effect of withdrawing support would be an increase of infanticide.[76] Model B presupposes not only that the decision to bear a child is economically motivated but that it is possible to make a profit on the child; otherwise the decision would make no sense in economic terms. How would it be possible to make a profit? Logically, a profit would be possible only if the allowance is greater than the cost of raising the child or if the child is grossly neglected and the money turned to other purposes.

Mr Benet, clearly, did not regard the allowance as lavish. No one on the floor of the House countered his assertion that the customary allowance was a mere shilling a week and barely sufficient to sustain life, but the subject was given no further attention as speaker after speaker echoed Edwin Chadwick's claim that the current system afforded "bounties" for bastardy.[77] Thus a subjective impression of profitability was created without any actual demonstration of it.

The other possibility for profit, of course, is the turning of the allowance to other purposes and consequent neglect of the child. Mr Wilson, in his testimony that many poor women in Sunderland deliberately bore bastard children in order to obtain the allowance, touched on this possibility, asserting that "They don't in reality keep the children; they let them run wild, and enjoy themselves with the money."[78] This claim, like Mr Benet's description of the meager size of the allowance, was neither contested nor supported. Negligent, carousing pauper mothers, like profiteering pauper hussies, seemed probable enough not to require empirical verification. In the end, though, it would appear that a majority of members of Parliament were less convinced of the widespread existence of such women than were the participants in the Royal Commission; the proposed change in the bastardy provisions did not pass. The proposed elimination of family allowances in favor of the workhouse test, however, was carried. Henceforth Economic Man and Economic Woman, in their manifestation as paupers, would no longer be encouraged (Model A) or bribed (Model B) to undertake independent family life.

A comment of Patricia James on the difficulties of population theory in the era of Malthus seems equally applicable to the testimony and debate on the behavior of pauper mothers. The problem "is not merely the complete absence of the statistics we take for granted today, but an attitude of mind which set a low value on ascertained facts."[79] As Mill noted, preconceived notions do not make a good substitute for facts. The New Poor Law, constructed on the foundation of the assumed moral depravity of the poor and the assumed economic motivations for their behavior, was the basic framework for a century of further pauper management that saw the development of increasingly sophisticated methods for investigating their circumstances and exploring their motivations. Over the course of that century the poor, and in particular poor mothers, came more and more under the scrutiny of the emerging social sciences.

5

From Political Economy to Social Science

> Just as there are iatrogenic disorders caused by the work that physicians do (which then gives them more work to do), so there are categories of persons who are created by students of society, and then studied by them.
>
> Erving Goffman, *Stigma*

During the nineteenth century, concerned observers developed new approaches to studying the problems of Britain's rapidly industrializing and increasingly urban society. They moved beyond a narrow focus on strictly economic questions, tackling both problems regarded as new and problems regarded as perennial. Reformers hoped to find solutions through individual, collective, and (sometimes) governmental effort. Each new approach left its mark on those following it. Each concerned itself, to a large degree, with the study of poverty. And each involved people who served as experts on the two Royal Commissions marking the span of the Victorian poor law. The development of social science in Britain and the study of poverty between the Royal Commissions are one and the same; neither can be properly understood without the other. Many of the experts chosen to review the status of the Victorian poor law in 1905 were selected on the basis of their contributions to Victorian social science.

The Public Health Movement and the disease of pauperism

Most accounts of the modern public health movement begin with the publication of Edwin Chadwick's *Report of the Sanitary Condition of the Labouring Population of Great Britain* in 1842. Almost invariably James Kay's earlier survey of Manchester, *The Moral and Physical Condition of the Working Classes* (1832), receives honorable mention.[1] While the rapid growth of cities in the early industrial era had steadily worsened sanitary conditions in the most heavily populated English cities, it was the cholera epidemic of 1831–1832 which shocked government authorities into action.[2]

Chadwick appointed Dr James Kay, along with Dr James Arnott and Dr Southwood Smith, to survey the health and sanitary conditions of the poor in order to establish the relationship between these conditions and pauperism.[3] Chadwick's famous *Sanitary Report*, a best seller in its time, reported the results of their investigations. It recommended improvements in drainage, better handling of sewage, and other measures to reduce the incidence of epidemic disease and improve the health – and thus the employability – of the laboring poor.[4] Although the *Sanitary Report* is sometimes presumed to reflect concern for the welfare of the poor, Chadwick's motive was not humanitarian. Since the sick could not work and the dead could not support their wives and children, he openly conceded "his narrow interests in keeping the poor rates down."[5]

Chadwick's recommendations on drainage and handling waste do not reflect a modern understanding of epidemiology. In an era before the widespread acceptance of the germ theory of disease, Chadwick and his colleagues envisioned cholera and typhoid not as water-borne bacterial pathogens but as products of the foul odors arising from accumulated waste. He was, in other words, a miasma theorist. He therefore proposed to flush this waste directly into the Thames, a procedure which made sense in the context of the miasma theory, however horrifying it may seem to modern experts on public health. Dr Southwood Smith, who served after 1848 at the General Board of Health and wrote many influential studies on sanitation and infectious disease, also subscribed to the miasma theory. They agreed with the best medical authorities of the day, who rejected quarantine and advocated sanitation to prevent epidemics.[6]

The equation of smell with disease clearly ascribes great importance to the value of cleanliness. Some policies derived from miasma theory, therefore, would clearly benefit public health, whatever the shortcomings of pouring raw sewage into the Thames, the main source of London's drinking water.

Chadwick was not alone in linking disease and pauperism, two of the great concerns of early nineteenth-century Britain. The metaphor of disease was often used in discussing vagrancy, pauperism, and other problems of poverty. Many a Victorian social theorist assumed the contagious nature of immoral behavior, particularly of the immoral habits that were assumed to underlie pauperism.[7] This tendency was certainly evident at the time of our first Royal Commission. Nassau Senior, for example, described pauperism in 1831 as a "disease" which "becomes every day more intolerable."[8] Chadwick, too, saw pauperism as a disease, "not disease of structure, but disorder of the functions."[9] The separation of various classes of paupers in the workhouse was intended not merely to make workhouse life less pleasant (and therefore less attractive to the poor), but to avoid contagion of the young with the presumed bad habits of their elders.[10] Reformers also assumed that removal of the impressionable young from the assumed "pernicious effects of family and neighborhood example" must prove beneficial.[11]

The creators of the New Poor Law, with its workhouse test for recipients of relief, wanted "to remove the poor from the fatal contamination of the pauper."[12] So did the physicians employed by the Poor Law Board. Dr James Kay, as a young physician, had conducted a survey of the poor of Manchester. He blamed a great many of the problems of the poor on the "the contagious example of ignorance and a barbarous disregard of forethought and economy, exhibited by the Irish."[13] Appalled by the squalid living conditions of the Irish, as well as by the contagion of their behavior, Dr Kay saw the immigrant as a vector of disease.

The problems of disease and pauperism were linked in the imagination of many Victorians, not only because the Poor Law Board sponsored the first well-known survey of public health but because the filth and smells of poor neighborhoods, so significant in the miasma theory of disease, were obvious to all. To many Victorians, moreover, disease and immorality were also linked. Boyd Hilton finds traces of Protestant theology in the medical theory of the early nineteenth century, with its assumption of the natural depravity of man and of the role of Providence in shaping nature to the benefit and instruction of humankind. An influential medical textbook published in 1843, *Lectures on the Principles and Practice of Physic* by Thomas Watson, serves to illustrate Hilton's point:

> It is ours to know in how many instances, forming indeed a vast majority of the whole, bodily suffering and sickness are the natural fruits of evil courses; of the sins of our fathers, of our own unbridled passions, of the malevolent spirit of others. We see, too, the uses of these judgments, which are mercifully designed to recall men from the

strong allurements of vice, and the slumber of temporal prosperity, teaching that it is good for us to be sometimes afflicted.[14]

Illness, like poverty, originates in immorality. Illness, like poverty, can be beneficial to Bunyan's Christian pilgrim in his uphill journey to salvation. Is it any wonder that poverty, like illness, is contagious? Or that illness should be so common among the poor, who are immoral? These ideas, rooted as they were in profound cultural assumptions, long outlived the miasma theory of disease. They recur in poverty studies undertaken by the more sophisticated social scientists of the late Victorian and Edwardian eras, including those who sat on the Royal Commission of 1905. C.S. Loch, for example, famously proclaimed that all relief must consist of "treatment" and that "Charity is the work of the social physician."[15] Helen Bosanquet predicted that, were public assistance given to the family of a drunkard, drunkenness would "spread down the street like an epidemic."[16] And the Webbs, considering the terrible conditions the very poor endured in slum environments, spoke of "a sort of moral malaria" that swallows up the next generation.[17]

The approaches to the study of poverty developed over the course of the nineteenth century retained key elements of the public health movement's view of the poor: a continuing preoccupation with dirt, a tendency to see the health problems of the poor as the results of their – or of their mothers' – immorality, precautions to prevent their contaminating others, and a desire to "treat" them for their own good and the good of society.

The Statistical Movement and the study of pauperism

Sociologist Philip Abrams began his classic study of the development of social science in Britain with the events of 1834, asserting that "1834 – the year of the *Report* of the Commission on the Poor Law and the founding of the Statistical Society of London – is about as rational a date for beginning a history of British sociology as one could hope to find."[18] The foundation in rapid succession of the Statistical Department of the Board of Trade (1832), the Statistical Society of Manchester, and the London society indicate a lively interest in the collection and analysis of empirical data.[19]

Much of the data that students of social phenomena require today was not available in the first half of the nineteenth century. The debate on Malthusian population theory, for example, took place in the absence of good information on whether the population of

Britain was in fact increasing at all – not to mention whether trends differed in areas where family allowance was common. Rickman's census of 1801 was the first ever attempted. Civil registration of births and deaths did not commence until 1837, when William Farr became the first chief statistician of the General Register Office.[20] The founders of the statistical movement were "policy-oriented political economists" who wanted an empirical basis for decisions that would affect the national economy.[21] Among the founding members of the Statistical Society of London were Edwin Chadwick and Nassau William Senior.[22]

The appointment of the 1832 Royal Commission on which Senior and Chadwick served has been said to reflect the ascendancy of a new interest in "fact-gathering" based on the rising prestige of the natural sciences.[23] The government selected "experts" to engage in the assembly and analysis of "facts" from "extensive empirical observations." Accordingly the commission's report was meant to be seen as empirically based and free of partisan bias.[24] We have seen how Harriet Martineau invoked the objectivity of the Royal Commission's findings as the basis for her Poor Law tales. We have also seen, however, that disinterested empirical observation had little to do with the proceedings of the inquiry.

Since the early nineteenth century, we have come to regard numbers and statistics as the only possible basis for sound social policy. Poovey recounts, for example, how the addition of numbers to the second and third editions of the Malthus *Essay* added greatly to its credibility and apparent factuality, even though the huge body of tables on food prices, mortality, and so on did not really address the weaknesses of his argument.[25] Yet the use of numbers, however convincing to the reader, does not preclude bias in selecting or interpreting facts. The members of the Poor Law inquiry, for example, often led witnesses with questions based on unexamined assumptions. Mr Wilson, in testifying to the false filiations common in his district, was asked, "Do you then attribute the rapid increase of the population very much to the effect of the Bastardy Laws in forcing early marriages?"[26] Mr Wilson agreed that he did, and his testimony became a datum supporting this theory. Had be been asked a more neutral question – "To what do you attribute the rapid rise of population?" – then he might well have volunteered other possibilities as well.

Edwin Chadwick understood how important it is to ask precisely the right question in order to obtain the desired answer. He observed to Nassau Senior that "It was only by personal enquiries made of witnesses on the spot, that I was enabled to deduce the principles which have been promulgated to the public…"[27] Chadwick was forced to do this himself, he told Senior, because the Assistant Commissioners had not asked the right questions.[28] When this procedure is followed, the principles are not "deduced," as Chadwick would have it, from the testimony. Rather they precede the testimony and shape it toward the desired conclusions.

Witnesses sometimes deployed numbers in matters that do not really warrant quantification, as in the testimony that "A bastard child is thus about 25 percent more valuable to a parent than a legitimate one."[29] This remark considers only the economic value of a child to its parent and makes the hidden assumption that economic value alone is relevant to the decision to bear the child. Even within this limited scope the figure of 25 per cent is unlikely to be very precise, ignoring as it does economies of scale, work lost due to childcare responsibilities, the child's potential wages, the child's life expectancy, and so on. But it looks very objective, because it is a number.

Problems with methods of obtaining information and the theoretical use of data plagued the statistical movement from the first. They are evident in both the literature of the public health movement and studies of poverty. James Kay, in his survey of the health of the Manchester poor, "never fixes the boundary between what he observes and what he assumes,"[30] – a difficulty we find both in the *Sanitary Report* and in the work of the Royal Commission. In organizing the statistical tables of the *Sanitary Report*, for example, Chadwick chose the place of residence as the significant locality and the mortality of women as the appropriate correlating statistic, since women spend more time at home than men. In so organizing his data, Chadwick dismissed all occupational factors, such as hazards posed by machinery or toxic by-products. He took women out of the non-domestic workplace and dismissed the time a man or woman spends outside the home as irrelevant to his or her health.[31]

To a large extent, therefore, the choices made in designing the survey predetermine its results, while the assumptions embodied in these choices are hidden behind a barrage of numbers that appear totally objective. In the same way the Poor Law inquiry chose to examine early marriage, bastardy, and family allowances, which they assumed to be significant, and chose to ignore all other factors in the economic and social life of the poorer districts. Late Victorian research on the health of the poor displays the legacy of Chadwick's choices: only that which takes place in the home is relevant to health.

A number of commentators have remarked on the fundamental ambivalence of the statistical movement, pulled as it was in two different directions by the underlying moralistic assumptions of its practitioners and the environmentalism inherent in large statistical surveys.[32] The derivation of an "average man" from a mass of data about large groups of people depersonalizes the social phenomena under study in a way that is hard to reconcile with the causal concept of individual moral defects.[33] This tension appears throughout the literature of the statistical movement. It is, as Abrams observes, evident within rather than between individual participants.[34] The literature of nineteenth-century poverty studies offers a flood of mixed messages from researchers who are torn between the facts in front of them and their moral assumptions.[35] This is particularly clear when we see Friedrich Engels, who certainly wanted to blame the terrible condition of the poor in Manchester on capitalist society rather than on individual failings, identify drink as the main problem of the Irish laborer. Engels mixes environmentalism and moralizing: "What else should he do? How can society blame him when it places him in a position in which he almost of necessity becomes a drunkard; when it leaves him to himself, to his savagery?"[36]

Other observers, less eager to indict capitalism for the plight of the poor, showed a similar ambivalence. Mayhew's survey mixed compassionate commentary on the urban poor with aspersions on their character.[37] Helen Bosanquet often wrote a few sentences blaming inadequate inspection of working and living conditions for much of the ill-health of the poor, then dwelt at length on the character defects of the invalid poor and their mothers.[38] Likewise, she could suggest several possible legitimate reasons why a man might be out of work "through no fault of his own" (keeping the phrase, every time she uses it, between quotation marks) but imply that character defects are really to blame because *there is always some reason* why the man who knows his trade cannot get employment..."[39] Sidney and Beatrice Webb, reviewing statistical evidence for voluntary limitation of births among the artisan classes, displayed similar ambivalence: "This change implies, on the part of both husband and wife, a large measure of foresight, deliberateness, and self-control, which is out of the reach of the less intelligent and more self-indulgent classes, and difficult for the very poor, especially for the occupants of one-roomed houses."[40]

We shall later examine why the Webbs saw precisely these characteristics as lacking in the very poor, as we consider the influence of Social Darwinism on poverty research. Once again, physical constraints are noted but then ignored. Character is assumed to be the main issue, although the numbers themselves do not justify such an inference. The mind is the man.

Even the more sympathetic surveys show traces of this ambivalence. Rowntree, who took such pains to document the difficulties of living within the means available to low-income working-class families, still separated poverty caused by moral defect from obviously undeserved "Primary Poverty." He ascribed "Secondary Poverty," the state of 28 per cent of the working-class population of York, to "Drink, betting and gambling. Ignorant or careless housekeeping and other improvident expenditure, the latter often induced by irregularity of income."[41] Rowntree found that objective circumstances cause most poverty, but that some of it is caused by bad character. Some of the activity that looks like bad character, however, is caused by objective circumstances.

Charles Booth, whose great survey preceded and inspired Rowntree's, displays the same tension. Booth, a member of the Edwardian Royal Commission on the Poor Law, served as president of what had by then become the Royal Statistical Society. Abrams places Booth at the apex of the statistical movement in terms of service, awards, elected positions, and good repute; Booth continued and refined the survey traditions of the movement.[42] His survey of the *Life and Labour of the People in London*, which took 17 years and thousands of pounds from Booth's personal fortune to complete, amassed staggering amounts of statistical data on the income and living conditions of Londoners. His desire to possess all of this detailed information reflected, obviously, a belief that the information was necessary for making appropriate social policy. Yet moral considerations everywhere intrude in the analysis and even in the structure of the data. When he discusses Class B, made up primarily of casual workers, Booth comments: "The labourers of class B do not, on the average, get as much as three days' work a week, but it is doubtful if many of them could or would work full time for long together if they had the opportunity. From whatever section class B is drawn, except the sections of poor women, there will be found many of them who from shiftless, idleness, or drink, are inevitably poor."[43]

Nothing about Booth's survey technique justifies such a statement. Nor did he have any factual basis for his assumption that prostitution is a manifestation of laziness because its practitioner "merely seeks her living in the easiest way open to her."[44] No prostitutes or casuals had been interviewed about their activities; their motivations are assumed. While Booth showed great sympathy for many of the poor and avoided the popular assumption that drink was generally the cause of their troubles, he showed little compassion toward the prostitute or the denizens of Class B. His attitude was rooted in moral assumptions that he brought to the survey, not in his data. Even as Booth exonerated many of the poor as prisoners of circumstance, he condemned others as deserving their fate. The poor drank because they were poor,[45] but the dockworker worked irregularly because he was lazy. Booth decided to acquire information about the poor, as he noted in the first draft of his project, in order to escape from "the *a priori* reasoning of political economy."[46] But numbers alone could not deliver him from his own unexamined (thus invisible) assumptions. Behind the statistics of *Life and Labour* lies the same ambivalence about environmentalism and individual character that marks all of the studies of the statistical movement.

Not all Victorians failed to notice the problems inherent in the movement. Charles Dickens was much amused by the mania for collecting facts. He parodied the movement to great comic effect in an article in *Bentley's Miscellany* published in 1837, purporting to be the minutes of a meeting of the British Association. The papers read at the meetaiing consist of a torrent of laboriously produced but meaningless facts, invariably followed by sententious comments on their ostensible moral significance.[47] (More sinister is Mr Gradgrind in *Hard Times*, who can always prove anything he wishes by appealing to volumes of statistics.) Within the statistical movement, growing awareness of the difficulty of proceeding from data to social policy led to the formation of the National Association for the Promotion of Social Science.

The Social Science Movement and the struggle against pauperism

Founded in 1856, the National Association for the Promotion of Social Science was variously known as the NAPSS, the Social Science Association, or the SSA. Its membership rolls included the most prominent social investigators and social policy makers of the time. Among the early members were Edwin Chadwick and Nassau Senior; Senior belonged to its Economic Section.[48] Other representatives of the world of public health, statistics, and poor law administration included Registrar William Farr, Dr Southwood Smith, and Dr Kay (then Kay-Shuttleworth), all active members. Many representatives of the local Boards of Guardians who administered the poor law were members and took part in the discussions. The Workhouse Visiting Society formed by Louisa Twining was one of the Association's constituent organizations.[49] Reform-minded politicians like Lord Brougham, Lord Shaftesbury, Lord John Russell, and Gladstone were likewise active members. The Association enjoyed a close working relationship with the Statistical Society and shared many members in common. Christian Socialists F.D. Maurice and Charles Kingsley, as well as a number of chambers of commerce, also took part.[50]

The SSA was an umbrella organization uniting a large and occasionally incompatible assortment of individuals and reform groups. Temperance organizations were active in its conferences, as was the COS, six of whose members sat on the Edwardian Royal Commission. While many of its members shared the Victorian passion for collecting statistics, members of the SSA were determined to find ways to use those statistics to inform social legislation. The SSA was the embodiment of the ameliorist impulse in Victorian public life, in that "the belief that held it together was that for every social problem there was an optimal ameliorating measure which could be scientifically arrived at by investigation and by patient discussion between all interested parties."[51] In keeping with this belief, the Association functioned not just as a forum for discussion but as a pressure group. It was particularly influential in the area of public health legislation.[52]

The Association was eager to bring together "all interested parties" for discussion, listening, for example, to the views of both temperance advocates and brewers on the problem of drink.[53] Yet its researchers do not appear to have felt the need to interview the poor themselves. Like naturalists studying Galapagos tortoises they talked about, rather than to, the objects of their interest.

The members of the SSA were eager to use statistics to suggest ameliorative legislation. We have seen in our consideration of the statistical movement, however, that the gathering of numbers could be theoretically problematic. The Association's membership contained numerous Fellows of the Royal Academy and of the Statistical Society; it also contained a large number of members whose sophistication and objectivity in the use of statistics were even less certain. A survey of its membership indicates that "Clergymen and doctors of medicine were the most numerous occupational categories."[54] Given the aims of the SSA, this is hardly surprising. Zeal for the improvement of society was common in these professions. Skill in handling statistics, however, was not.

The problems of the statistical movement are very much in evidence in the papers produced by the SSA. Papers read at the many SSA congresses held throughout Britain in the period of its greatest activity were not very scientific. "Statistics, when they were produced at S.S.A.

congresses, were nearly always used to underline a point, and seldom to point the way to one, and paper after paper is filled with *a priori* arguments."[55] Even when an author attempted to derive theory from the numbers, he almost invariably leaped from statistics to an over-simplifying conclusion that ignored all complicating factors in the interests of a policy recommendation.[56] Usually the oversimplifying conclusion rested on beliefs the researcher brought with him to the study. More often than not, the root of any problem facing the poor was found to be drink.[57] This was only to be expected, given the large number of clergymen in the Association and the participation of the larger temperance organizations, but it does suggest a less than objective approach to research. Charles Booth, who was sometimes unable to prevent his moral assumptions from influencing his survey, concluded that drink accounted for only a small percentage of destitution and may well have been more an effect than a cause of poverty.[58] Few members of the SSA had any such doubts. This relentless insistence that alcoholism was a moral rather than a social problem may explain why the first serious studies of the subject took place in Sweden rather than in Britain.[59]

The preconceptions that prevented disinterested study of alcoholism also precluded disinterested study of the poor. In the papers produced by members of the Social Science Association the causes of pauperism – bad character in general and drink in particular – are assumed. Numbers are used only to prove this point and to justify what the author sees as an effective remedy. Although facts and statistics decorate these studies, they do not in any sense inform them.

During the 1880s the coalition of forces making up the SSA began to break up. The consensus about what should be done to remedy social problems was lost, and some of the more academically-minded members began to suspect that the development of a sound theoretical science of society was being hindered by the SSA's relentless focus on policy.[60] But even as the Association began to lose influence and members, its legacy was carried on by one of its constituent groups, then near its apogee, the COS.

The Charity Organisation Society and the science of philanthropy

The COS is best understood by its original name when founded in 1869 – the London Society for Organizing Charitable Relief and Repressing Mendicity. The Society's name changed over time, but its basic assumption did not: the real social problem was not poverty but the wasteful and unsystematic distribution of relief that encouraged fraud, vagrancy, and parasitism. The Society sought to organize the activities of the many charitable foundations of the capital (and later of other cities) in order to prevent duplication of relief and distribution of alms to people unworthy of them. It also encouraged the local Boards of Guardians to tighten up the granting of public assistance. Its success was less than overwhelming. While the COS expanded to a large membership with chapters in many cities, including New York, it never achieved much success in gaining the cooperation of other charities.[61] A recent study of regional chapters makes a persuasive case that the COS claimed more influence than it actually enjoyed, that "their practical influence on rationalizing charitable disbursements across England was marginal."[62] Richard Titmuss, on the other hand, while conceding that the COS failed in its efforts to organize charity, held that it "became virtually a department of state."[63]

Perhaps there is less difference between these opinions than there appears to be. Research on the practical operation of the New Poor Law at the level of the local guardians would seem to indicate that there was a great deal of variation in their methods, with the "elevated principle and pragmatic penny-pinching" of the COS approach sometimes but not always in evidence at any given time or in any given instance.[64] Even if the COS lacked the dominance sometimes claimed for them, they were certainly not without influence, particularly in the constitution of the Royal Commission of 1905. The Society enjoyed, moreover, significant support from some sectors of the clergy: "Clerical support was mainly confined to the higher echelons of the established church and to some non-conformist ministers, particularly Unitarians. Work-a-day parish curates tended to join the majority of dissenting Protestants in shunning the COS's judgemental [*sic*] stance which many saw as being alien to commonly accepted ideas of Christian charity."[65]

For reasons we have already considered, this divide in clerical opinion makes a great deal of sense. The COS did enjoy the support of the "higher echelons" of church and society, as is readily evident in their sponsorship and membership lists. Queen Victoria was the Society's Patron; the Archbishop of Canterbury and many peers served as officers.[66] As Daniel Patrick Moynihan has remarked, poverty literature generally embodies "a discussion by individuals who are successful about individuals who are not..."[67]

One founder of the COS was Octavia Hill, granddaughter of Dr Southwood Smith and member of the Royal Commission of 1905. A member of the Central Council of the COS from 1875, she supported the Society vehemently in its protracted struggle with the Salvation Army.[68] Provision of low-cost housing for the poor under a strict regime of supervision and prompt payment of rent had made her reputation. In keeping with her strong belief in market principles, Hill encouraged private investment in such housing and insisted that rents be set at a level that would still permit a profit. Such flats provided very simple accommodation. Maintenance by the tenants was strictly supervised because, in Hill's view "in the long run it will be found ... that, without training these poorest people, no improvement in their houses will be of much avail.[69]

In the hard winter of 1869, Rev. W. Fremantle, rector of St Mary's Church in Marylebone and founder of a local chapter of the COS, asked Hill to administer relief in his parish under strict COS principles. Her approach to the problem illustrates not only the mentality of charity organization but how truly obtuse its proponents could be:

> Octavia's abolition in her district of coal tickets, free meals, and every form of monetary assistance, her insistence that any case of distress must be carefully investigated and the entire resources of the family examined before any dole could be given, her practice of offering work instead of relief and withholding relief if the work was not done, aroused bitter resentment, and for the first time in her life she found herself faced with the persistent hostility instead of the friendship of those she wished to help.[70]

Many Londoners had contributed funds for the free meals and coal tickets Octavia Hill despised, because they felt that widespread misery of a kind no Christian person could ignore existed in the poorer districts of the city. Hill, however, remained more concerned about harming the character of the poor by doling out possibly undeserved aid. Proponents of the COS view were certain they were right. The torrent of criticism that greeted Hill's administration of relief in Marylebone appears to have caused her no doubt; "The opposition she met only confirmed Octavia in her support of the Society. She had in her own work demonstrated the soundness of its principles and, remaining a staunch member to the end of her life, she fought more than one battle on its behalf."[71]

Given her unwavering views, it is understandable that when Charles Booth began to publish his monumental survey, *Life and Labour*, his friend Octavia Hill did not bother to read it. She already knew, she said, all that she needed to know on the subject.[72] Other members, however, did read Booth. The Society's official position was that Booth's study paid too little attention to "avoidable" poverty and was, therefore, misleading.[73]

Understandable, too, is the enormous antipathy that the COS aroused in its opponents and among the poor into whose circumstances they inquired. George Lansbury, a socialist MP of working-class origins who represented organized labor on the 1905 Royal Commission, warmly disliked the Society.[74] Lansbury's hostility dated back to his childhood in Whitechapel, where COS policy was "heartless and brutal."[75] COS supporters like Canon Barnett, he recalled, told his mother not to pitch in to help neighbors down on their luck, as was her custom, but rather to allow them to be sent to the workhouse. More sympathetic to his devout and compassionate evangelical mother's point of view than to that of clergymen like Barnett, Lansbury formed his own view of their attitude. "This message and my later inquiries made me a most bitter enemy of the Charity Organisation Society and all its works".[76]

The assumption of COS activists that they alone knew what was best for the poor seemed arrogant, and this arrogance probably played a role in the Society's failure to secure the cooperation of the numerous charities of late Victorian Britain.[77] The imperviousness to criticism which Octavia Hill displayed in her campaign against fraud and begging in Marylebone was common among COS activists. Humphreys attributes this to the fact that many of the most active and influential members of the COS were Unitarians. In his view, Unitarians had long since become used to defending truth against the fierce opposition of the outside world and in fact rather enjoyed it.[78] Octavia Hill, although later received into the Church of England, was raised a Unitarian, as was Helen Dendy Bosanquet. Many of the provincial notables active in chapters of the COS, like the Rathbone family of Liverpool, were also Unitarians.[79] Our study of religious influences on late Victorian poverty research suggests why this might be the case: Unitarians believed in natural laws, not in an intervening providence.

COS activists felt so secure in defending their position against attack because they believed that their approach to charity was "scientific." The COS based its claim to correct administration of charity on the findings of social science. The Society was, as we have seen, an active constituent of the SSA, and published research on the subject of poverty "in its journals and reports modeled on the official 'Blue Books.'"[80] COS principles included the "less eligibility" concept of the New Poor Law and an insistence that charity must help, not harm, the moral character of the recipient. The framers of the New Poor Law, who had borrowed the term from Bentham, intended "less eligibility" to act as a self-regulating mechanism to screen out people who did not really need assistance. C.S. Loch, long-time president the COS, insisted on its importance in 1895: "One maxim has been handed down to us, the fruit of long experience. It is the touchstone of the question. The condition of the recipient of poor-relief must not be made more eligible than that of the independent man who received none."[81] Staying true to "the principles of 1834," he insisted, "we shall be able to grapple well and sufficiently with times of difficulty, and we shall not have a Poor Law that will make our people less independent, self-reliant, and manly."[82]

Thus the COS claim to "scientific" administration rested not only on the Society's participation in the SSA but on the supposed objectivity of the inquiry of 1834, which had established its most fundamental principle. In the COS handbook for caseworkers, Loch recommended study of its report: "The reader who desires to get a grasp of the real issues depending on the administration of the Poor Law and of charity, cannot do better than study the Report of the Poor Law Commissioners, 1834."[83]

The distinction between appropriate recipients of poor relief and appropriate recipients of charity was fundamental to the COS approach. In the view of the COS, "the Poor Law existed for two kinds of person, both being in a state of destitution: those whose condition was their own fault, through laziness, improvidence, or misconduct, and 'chronic cases of distress, whether caused by illness or by age.'"[84] The deterrent Poor Law was the only appropriate recourse for the former and for the more feckless of the latter (since some provision should have been made against such a contingency). For truly undeserved distress, charity would be indicated.[85] Obviously, good administration would require a careful determination of each applicant's claim to being considered worthy of charity, so that the applicant could be either left to the parish Guardians or helped in the most appropriate way. The method of performing such an evaluation that the COS pioneered was another pillar of its claim to "scientific charity" – social casework.

Casework, the lasting legacy of the COS

One viewpoint common to both leaders and critics of the COS is that the Society based its "science of charity" on detailed investigation of the circumstances of applicants for relief, making receipt of such relief conditional on supervision by its trained staff. In so doing the COS gave birth to the profession of social casework, the foundation of public assistance in the English-speaking world today. Octavia Hill, as we have seen, made casework a vital part of her administration of relief in Marylebone and of her housing work. The two most active and influential members of the Edwardian Royal Commission, Helen Dendy Bosanquet and Beatrice Potter Webb, both began their careers as social investigators in this capacity. Webb was for a short time a volunteer rent-collector and visitor, while the less affluent Bosanquet was a long-time paid staffer for the COS. "The daily work of a District Office was partly done by volunteers – mainly women; but it is important to notice as one of the distinctive features of the C.O.S. that a paid staff was employed in casework from the first..."[86] The COS casework training school eventually became the Department of Social Science and Administration at the London School of Economics. Through it the COS strongly influenced the emerging practice of British social work.[87]

The Society developed casework as the appropriate means for separating applicants who could be suitably helped by charity from those who were best left to the Poor Law. The COS also considered casework the best method of making sure that charitable help was appropriate in both kind and amount. In theory the workhouse test made casework unnecessary in the administration of public assistance to the poor, because its built-in "less eligibility" mechanism prevented abuse. Outrelief, however, was more problematic. It appears that the practice of outrelief never entirely disappeared during the period of the New Poor Law, no matter how hard the central authority and the COS tried to end it. The Guardians seem to have worked harder at excluding able-bodied men and the Irish from the inadequate outrelief they offered than women with children and the aged.[88]

In the recommendations of the Edwardian Royal Commission, even the signers of the Majority Report were ready by 1909 to concede that some classes of the destitute were better kept out of the workhouse. They argued that the way to permit public assistance in the form of outrelief without bringing back the allegedly demoralizing effects of the Elizabethan system would be through the agency of social casework. Bernard Bosanquet, a long-time member of the COS board and its "preeminent apologist and theoretician," explained how this was to be done.[89] Bosanquet saw an imperative need to unleash an "army" of social workers trained in "the cure and prevention of social failure" to supervise recipients: "The whole of these proposals are founded on the conviction that there is a problem common and peculiar to the entire range of destitution or necessitousness, demanding a common and peculiar method of dealing with it."[90] Hence the need for "social therapeutics" to cure this problem which, as the Majority saw it, was "the failure of self-maintenance; the failure, that is, to maintain one's self and one's dependents at the standard prescribed by society."[91]

Superficially this social science view would appear to be quite different from the overt moralizing of the early nineteenth century. Bosanquet's elaboration of the theme, however, makes it clear that his secular terminology rests on the same old assumptions:

> The Majority proceed upon the principle that where there is a failure of social self-maintenance in the sense above defined, there is a defect in the citizen character, or at least a grave danger to its integrity; and that therefor every case of this kind raises a problem which is 'moral' in the sense of affecting the whole capacity of self-management, to begin with in the person who has failed, and secondarily, in the whole community so far as influenced by expectation and example.[92]

The Protestant sensibilities of this perspective are clearly evident, despite the fact that Bosanquet does not use religious terminology. Bosanquet was the son of an evangelical clergyman.[93] We have seen how the "secularized Evangelicalism" of the Philosophical Idealism that Bosanquet espoused contributed to the shape of poverty studies in the Late Victorian era.[94]

This metamorphosis of sin into "failure of self-maintenance" is very much in keeping with the observation that modernizing societies tend over time to develop "secular logics of evil." "The secular logics generally contain, in transformed or disguised forms, elements quite essential to them that have originated in the sacred mythologies of their civilizations or still older traditions. Most of the secular logics are neither purely 'secular' nor wholly 'modern.' Some of them only masquerade as 'secular.'"[95] Among these secular logics are "the liberal logic," which assumes that all sane adults possess rationality and are therefore capable of making responsible decisions, and "the therapeutic logic," which "tends to view everyone other than the 'professionals' as more or less damaged or childlike and in need of supportive aid and curative guidance."[96]

COS philosophy did not view everyone as "damaged or childlike," but it did view the destitute that way. Hence the need for "social therapeutics." This is why Octavia Hill's tenants required "training." It is why the Infant Welfare Movement of the turn of the nineteenth century was far more interested in "home health visiting" than in providing the wholesome food and access to contraception that the visited mothers really wanted.[97] It is why Helen Bosanquet wanted to make sure that a new public assistance authority, if created on the basis of the Majority Report, would take a casework approach to relief.[98] And it is why the Minority Report, chiefly the work of Beatrice Webb, recommends "*continuous* observation of the household both before and after birth" to ensure the health of children born in families under the supervision of their proposed Destitution Authority.[99] The recipient of assistance is always judged to be in some way "damaged," and the caseworker is assumed to know how best to treat the damage from a "therapeutic" standpoint.

There is an unmistakable element of class bias in this perspective. The educated, middle-class professional caseworker is presumed to possess qualities lacking in the poor, less educated recipient, who will benefit from the contact.[100] Even more problematic, however, is the assumption that a poor person must necessarily be "damaged." In Victorian poverty theory, the idea that there is a fundamental difference between the destitute and others was everywhere assumed, but on such a deep level that no one felt compelled to demonstrate its validity. This assumed difference, along with the religiously based assumption that mere physical deprivation is not necessarily a bad thing, made "pauperism" rather than poverty the concern of social science. So long as this difference is assumed, it does not really matter whether the difference is discussed in explicitly religious terms or in psychological ones, whether the clergyman or the social caseworker is delegated to the work of "social therapeutics." Hence the verdict of the "social control" school of poverty theorists that "If there is a real difference between the philanthropic and professional precepts that have variously justified relief practices, it is between invidious definitions of an essentially moral rather than a psychological kind."[101]

Thus in a fundamental way Gareth Stedman Jones was right in his observation that while writers like Woodroofe have tried to argue that the COS was reactionary in its ideology but progressive in its development of casework, the practice of casework cannot be disentangled from the ideas that sparked its creation. The COS itself regarded them as inseparable.[102] Decades of scholarly debate about individualism versus collectivism have, ironically, effectively obscured this unity from view. Humphreys notes in his excellent, detailed study of the influence of the COS that "Rather perversely for the COS, that part of their activities remaining of lasting application has been the methodological assessment of individuals which was so persistently the target of bitter contemporary hostility. Investigative techniques based on COS templates fabricated to retain rigid individualistic principles eventually became essential tools of the welfare state they had fought so determinedly to suppress."[103] If we shift our frame of reference from the question of individualism versus collectivism, long dominant in the discussion of Britain's march from 1834 to the Attlee government, and consider instead the context of Victorian social science in which casework was born, we can understand that there was nothing at all "perverse" about this outcome. Both the Majority and Minority reports of the Edwardian Royal Commission proposed a degree of government involvement in improving the lives of the poor beyond anything Edwin Chadwick would ever have contemplated, but both considered casework a vital component of that government involvement, because they assumed that the poor needed supervision and direction, not just income, in order not to be poor. They still saw "pauperism" rather than poverty as the problem. So there was no real need for the COS to survive as an institution. As the inventor of social casework, it had brought the assumption of the moral deficiency of the poor triumphantly into the era of "social therapeutics." The COS had won its war.

6
Ignoble Savages on Relief: Social Darwinism in Late Victorian Poverty Studies

If anatomy built the hard argument of recapitulation, psychic development offered a rich field for corroboration. Didn't everyone know that savages and women are emotionally like children? Despised groups had been compared with children before, but the theory of recapitulation gave this old chestnut the respectability of main-line scientific theory.

Stephen Jay Gould, The Mismeasure of Man

In this progressiveness of the human being we find one reason for those differences in the Standard of Life which we are trying to understand. Not all have yet worked out their freedom from the lower range of desires; for these, satisfaction of the appetites means only renewed opportunity for the repeated satisfaction of the appetites.

Helen Bosanquet, The Standard of Life

Social Darwinism in nineteenth-century Britain was too vast and too messy a phenomenon to lend itself to easy summary. Some form of it was espoused by thinkers on the right and on the left, by pacifists and militarists. Gertrude Himmelfarb has quite effectively demonstrated how "In the spectrum of opinion that went under the name of Social Darwinism almost every variety of belief was included."[1] It would, therefore, be difficult to demonstrate a clear line of Social Darwinist influence on social thought.[2] The most commonly discussed form of Social Darwinism is, of course, not Darwin's but Spencer's – the argument that natural selection, as a law of nature, dictates the least possible government intrusion into the lives of its citizens.[3] This is the form of Social Darwinism most often invoked in discussion of Victorian poverty theory, in keeping with the customary focus on the degree of government involvement as the key issue in the progress from 1832 to the welfare state. Spencer certainly helped to popularize the idea of *laissez-faire* as the state of nature, but in so doing he was responding to a strong and more diffuse tendency in British thought that both preceded and supported his ideas. Other aspects of this tendency were more influential than Spencer in the development of poverty studies in the Victorian era. This chaotic and illogical flow of ideas is perhaps best understood as a collection of appealing metaphors, almost infinitely plastic, that were used by social scientists and in turn shaped their perception of the problems they were studying. It was precisely the malleability of these metaphors that made them so useful to so many.

The concept of evolution was essential to all the uses to which these metaphors were put.[4] We can trace the influence of some of these metaphors on Victorian poverty theory; by and large they were the same metaphors that shaped Victorian anthropology. They are derived more from evolutionary biology than from Spencer, although the concept of societal evolution is very much a part of them. George Stocking prefers to call this influence "Darwinistic" rather than Darwinian, because it includes not only biological concepts but "metaphysical, moral, or ideological notions from other sources" that were invariably mixed in with them.[5] Consider, for example, how well Spencer's insistence on *laissez-faire* for purposes of natural selection fits in with the doctrines of political economy and with the Puritan requirement that the pilgrim struggle up that hill alone. A number of Victorian viewpoints worked very well together and transcended specific disciplines. Both Darwin and Wallace acknowledged the influence of the Malthus *Essay* on their theory of evolution by means of natural selection.[6] Even Samuel Smiles was inclined to think in vaguely evolutionary terms about the virtues he preached: "Economy also means the power of resisting present gratification for the purpose of securing a future good, and in this light it represents the ascendancy of reason over the animal instincts."[7]

It is not at all clear how the biological processes described by Darwin could produce, as their end result, self-restraint and economy. When we consider Victorian anthropology, however, we see more sophisticated thinkers than Smiles making the same inference of evolutionary causality. Beyond the imprecise use of biological concepts by social theorists, there is another good reason not to call the application Darwinian. Many Social Darwinists were more Lamarckian than Darwinian. They made little use of natural selection but did believe in the inheritance of acquired characteristics.[8] Helen Bosanquet, to give one example, complained about the lack of vocational training provided for the children of East London on Lamarckian grounds: "These are children of generations of woodcarvers, weavers, flower-makers, and engravers who have inherited a fineness of touch which none of the present training given in a Board School can improve."[9] We find more Lamarckian survivals when we consider some specific applications of Social Darwinist thinking to analyses of the slum environment of the very poor. But far more influential than the inheritance of acquired characteristics was the complex web of ideas derived from contemporary evolutionary biology in the concept of recapitulation.

Recapitulation in Late Victorian social thought

Because social theorists often applied biological concepts in ways far removed from their original contexts, we had best begin with their original meanings and then proceed to their later applications. To the developmental biologists who originated it, the theory of recapitulation was "the idea that higher creatures repeat the adult stages of lower animals during their own growth."[10] The idea had a wide currency in the biological sciences of the time:

> Recapitulation ranks among the most influential ideas of late nineteenth-century science. It dominated the work of several professions, including embryology, comparative morphology, and paleontology. All these disciplines were obsessed with the idea of reconstructing evolutionary lineages, and all regarded recapitulation as the key to this quest. The gill slits of an early human embryo represented an ancestral adult fish; at a later stage, the temporary tail revealed a reptilian or mammalian ancestor.[11]

The idea did not long remain exclusively in the province of biology. It immediately influenced psychology; both Freud and Jung were recapitulationists.[12] As many Victorian social scientists adopted the concept of societal evolution, the notion of recapitulation was useful in placing various societies and people on the evolutionary continuum. Thus "the assumption that the primitive, the infantile, and the pathological were alike" was "fundamental to evolutionist anthropology."[13] In no logical sense does such a use follow directly from evolutionary embryology, yet the appeal of the metaphor is obvious. Gould asserts that the concept of recapitulation was "irresistible" to "any scientist who wanted to rank human groups as higher and lower," postulating that the adults of inferior groups are like the children of superior ones.[14]

This process requires the classifier to make value judgments. Obviously, the value judgments precede, rather than follow, the classification. This point is particularly clear in the use of recapitulation in racialist thinking. When the theory of recapitulation came to be discredited by early twentieth-century biology, racists making biological claims suddenly found that whites are superior to blacks because they retain more, rather than fewer, juvenile characteristics.[15] It is for this reason, coupled with the lack of demonstrated fit between embryology and social development, that Stocking is inclined to the opinion that "the metaphorical extendibility of sociocultural evolutionism may have been more a matter of analogies of status than of process."[16] Invariably the populations to which the concept of recapitulation were applied were "inferior" – women, children, criminals, preindustrial people, as well as "beggars, paupers, madmen, and Irishmen."[17] Again and again, as we consider the role of recapitulation in late Victorian studies of the poor, we shall see how their characteristics are deduced from their status, rather than empirically established, and then identified as the cause of their poverty.

Retention of juvenile characteristics: the poor as children

Helen Bosanquet illustrates the assumption that the very poor are overgrown children as clearly as any poverty theorist of the late Victorian period. Consider her explanation for the lack of saving she observed in the poor of East London. Others might see insufficient income as the cause; Bosanquet blames the childish personality of the East Ender:

> Like many others, he argues from present to future, so makes no provision and is taken unawares. Even when the need of the future might be thought quite assured, as in season trades, the undeveloped mind refuses to grasp it; the combination of a large town and good money coming in makes a present so rich in possibilities, that the future fades before it and imagination shrinks from contemplating the barren meagerness of the six weeks when there will be no money, just as the child's thoughts will turn away during playtime from the dryness of the lesson hour.[18]

Seasonally employed adults are unlikely to be surprised, year after year, by predictable unemployment and its resulting hardships. Bosanquet, however, knows how children appear to behave and assumes that the poor, who are large children, behave the same way. So, too, she contends that the poor impulsively purchase on credit things that they do not really want, only to have them repossessed, because they "are like spoiled children with too many toys, always wanting something else."[19] Later in this study, we shall consider other possible interpretations of the spending habits of the poor. For now, suffice it to say that Bosanquet's interpretation does not consider other possibilities; it merely infers childish behavior based on the identity of the shopper.

Bosanquet's analysis of the young mother's (alleged) failure to save and plan for her expected baby once again depicts the poor as children. In Bosanquet's opinion, this lack of planning precludes much maternal interest: "And so the opportunity is missed, the interest lost, the baby when it comes is little more than a toy; the girl remains a girl, but without her buoyancy, and successive babies are merely successive occasions for calling in external aid."[20] Curiously, Bosanquet seems to regard the new baby in much the same light as the home improvements lacking in slum flats; she exhibits no awareness of a baby as a real person demanding sympathy and attention. (Bosanquet was herself childless. This fact may or may not help to explain her viewpoint here, but it certainly does come to mind.) In her analysis, once again the slum-dweller exhibits an undesirable retention of juvenile characteristics. In Bosanquet's accounts of the housekeeping and child rearing practices of poor mothers, this theme is often revisited, although not necessarily as explicitly as in these examples. Bosanquet's assumption of childishness can frequently be discerned, even when not openly acknowledged. Often it is paired with its twin, the assumption that the behavior of the poor resembles the behavior of primitive peoples.

Primitives as children, paupers as primitives

Bosanquet felt that the childish traits of impulsiveness, poor planning, and lack of self-control were observable in the behavior of the poor. These were also regarded by Victorian social science as characteristics of primitive people.[21] This line of thought preceded the 1859 publication of *On the Origin of Species* and thus was encouraged by, not created by, Darwinian theory. David Hume's Treatise *of Human Nature* (1737–1740) had postulated that "primitive man cannot see beyond his own interests and the gratification of immediate needs."[22] And Dr James Kay, as we have seen, was in 1832 inclined to describe the Manchester Irish as savages and beasts,[23] thus evoking vague notions of both social and biological evolution. Samuel Smiles contended that self-control is "the chief distinction between man and the mere animal,"[24] but Victorian anthropology was more often inclined to draw the self-control line not between man and the animals but between civilized man and the savages. Smiles himself reflected this view in his imaginative comments on the presumed spending habits of savages offered, significantly, in the context of an article on "Workmen's Earnings and Savings":

Wise economy is not a natural instinct, but the growth of reflection and often the product of experience. Prodigality is much more natural to man. Thus the savage is the greatest spendthrift, for he has no forethought, no to-morrow, and lives only for the day or for the hour. Hence the clever workman, unless he be trained in good habits, may exhibit no higher a life than that of the mere animal; and the earning of increased wages will only furnish such persons with increased means of indulging in the gratification of the grosser appetites.[25]

Samuel Smiles, while neither an anthropologist nor a professional observer of the poor, shared this equation of the poor and primitives with many serious social scientists.

Sidney Webb, for example, referred to the underclass of East London as "semi-barbarians" and as "degenerate hordes of a demoralized 'residuum' unfit for social life."[26] This equation of the pauper and the primitive was widely assumed among Late Victorian and Edwardian social theorists.[27] Himmelfarb traces the description of the poor as a "tribe" to the journalist Henry Mayhew, who often employed this term in his ethnographic description of the street life of the capital.[28] Undoubtedly Mayhew's widely read lurid accounts helped to popularize the notion of a deviant counter-culture (or, if you will, a "culture of poverty") among the poorer residents of the larger cities. Yet the influence of the idea is better understood in the widespread use of the concepts of evolutionary anthropology by the emerging developmental sociology of the time.[29]

From the 1860s British anthropology produced a stream of ethnographic accounts of "primitive" peoples, shaped by the evolutionary assumptions on which the discipline was built. These accounts were widely admired and emulated by social thinkers concerned with domestic problems.[30] The idea that self-control and repression of impulse are the key evolutionary developments that distinguish the civilized man from the primitive, or from the beasts, or from the child, was one of the most basic of these evolutionary assumptions. This idea was the foundation both of the evolutionary anthropology and of the social theory of the time; it held that "the repression of immediate impulse response was the essential mechanism of evolutionary progress in both the intellectual and the moral sphere."[31]

Stocking sees this idea as rooted in what he calls the ideology of the middle class.[32] Whether or not one agrees with this assessment, the religious background of the idea in the context of Protestant England is clear.[33] Certainly this view is in harmony with "the utter depravity of human nature in consequence of the Fall" postulated by evangelicals; and it stands to reason that a heathen, not in the state of grace, would not avoid snares and pitfalls as well as would a Christian. It is not really necessary to see Protestant theology as the direct cause of the image of the impulsive savage for the ready compatibility of the two concepts – sin and primitive self-indulgence – to be apparent. However derived, they work well together.

Obviously a representative of "primitive" humanity, so imagined, would be a far cry from Rousseau's "noble savage" – a fact of which Victorian social theorists were well aware. In his influential *Pre-historic times, as illustrated by ancient remains, and the manners and customs of modern savages*, published in 1869, the prominent anthropologist John Lubbock reflected:

> [T]he true savage is neither free nor noble; he is a slave to his own wants, his own passions; imperfectly protected from the weather ... ignorant of agriculture, living by the chase, and improvident in success, hunger always stares him in the face, and often drives him to the dreadful alternative of cannibalism or death.[34]

The evolutionary assumption would suggest that a nonagricultural society is "ignorant of agriculture," since mankind is presumed to be passing through a series of developmental phases in a set order as they are variously achieved. This assumption of primitive ignorance will recur, as we shall presently see, in discussion of the economic habits of the poor of East London and elsewhere. Although improvidence is hardly the most plausible interpretation of cannibalism, Lubbock was certainly not alone in this analysis. Edward Burnett Tylor, considered the founding father of British anthropology, held much the same view. Tylor led the movement to establish an anthropology section in the British Association for the Advancement of Science and was its first president. He achieved the presidency of the Royal Anthropological Institute, a knighthood, and a Fellowship of the Royal Society.[35] His discussion of the subject of cannibalism in the 1877 "Scholar's Edition" of the *Encyclopaedia Britannica* begins well, mentioning famine, hatred, and a variety of religious and magical practices as causes of cannibalism. But in his elaboration of famine, he suggests another cause:

> The records of shipwrecks and sieges prove that famine will sometimes overcome the horror of cannibalism among men of the higher nations. Thus it is not surprising that savages, from their want of food adapted for storing as well as from their reckless improvidence, should in severe climates be often driven to this extremity.[36]

The current edition of *Britannica* does not list "reckless improvidence" among the possible causes of cannibalism. That Tylor thought to do so tells us more about the unexamined assumptions of Victorian social science than it does about the South Sea islanders. Tylor's analysis is axiomatic, deriving claims about behavior from theory rather than deriving theory from observed behavior. Tylor operated in the tradition of Victorian "armchair anthropology" and had never visited the Pacific. His own fieldwork was done in Mexico and at a Zuni pueblo in the United States.[37] In neither location did he encounter cannibalism. Tylor derived his information on the Pacific islanders from a regular correspondence with observers in the field who volunteered information and answered his questions. Many of his most active correspondents were Protestant missionaries, "only a few of whom," as Stocking notes, "were able to respond to native religion in a relatively unethnocentric way."[38] Anayzing their accounts, Herbert finds exceptional moments of real understanding but in general "a piling up of monotonous rhetorical formulas which clearly exert a strong determining influence upon all their so-called empirical observation."[39] These missionaries had left England prepared to find the depraved behavior of unsaved humanity, and find it they did.[40] Likewise Tylor, operating in the context of an evolutionary social science that saw "impulsiveness" and "improvidence" as the defining characteristics of primitive man, never questioned what were to him very plausible observations.[41]

Thorstein Veblen's attempt to stand Social Darwinism on its head, *The Theory of the Leisure Class* (1899), produced an outrage that is both amusing and enlightening. Veblen skillfully assaulted the comfortable assumptions of contemporary social science and, with great delight, asserted that the upper strata of society were the least evolved, not to mention the least industrious. Tracing the origins of upper-class pastimes in tribal societies, Veblen proclaimed that "the characteristic feature of leisure-class life is a conspicuous exemption from all useful employment."[42] (Veblen was not alone in his unwillingness to take pious invocations of the work ethic seriously; Marx and Engels had earlier noted that in English bourgeois society, "those of its members who work, acquire nothing, and those who acquire anything, do not work.")[43] Veblen delighted in equating the practices of high society and of primitive man, incorporating under the rubric "conspicuous consumption" all "costly entertainments, such as the potlatch or the ball."[44] Also deliberately outrageous was his assertion that bad character is an adaptive trait in evolutionary terms: "Freedom from scruple, from sympathy, honesty and regard for life, may, within fairly wide terms be said to further the success of the individual in the pecuniary culture. The highly successful men of all times have commonly been of this type..."[45] Veblen's evolutionary logic is unimpeachable; it is the rich, not the poor, who hold society back from advancement. Because they are "sheltered from the stress of circumstances," they can retain "atavistic traits" that retard the development of the masses who emulate them.[46] Like Dr Kay's slum Irishmen, they are a bad example to others.

Interestingly enough, the writings of Helen Bosanquet, who vehemently upheld the work ethic but found it lacking at both ends of the social ladder, echo this assertion. She often remarked that there is also a "wealthy section of the Residuum" which shares significant characteristics with the very poor:

> There is the same insuperable aversion to work, the same self-indulgence, the same eager devotion to trifles and absorption in the interests of the moment. All that they need to complete their likeness to their poorer brethren are the dirty homes and squalid surroundings, and if they were left for only a week to their own exertions there can be little doubt that these also would appear.[47]

Perhaps for Bosanquet only the middle class was truly virtuous.

By and large, however, Helen Bosanquet concerned herself far more with the lapses of the poor than of the rich. Certainly she was very comfortable with the assumption that the poor behave in improvident, self-indulgent ways that are the cause of their poverty. In a strict logical sense, it should be noted, Bosanquet's observations on the "wealthy section of the Residuum" call into question the assumption that it is laziness and bad behavior that cause poverty. These wealthy miscreants behave like the poorer ones but are quite effectively protected by wealth from the consequences of their behavior. In other words, vice creates poverty only if you lack a reliable income, so income does matter. But then it would appear that Bosanquet did not examine this discrepancy in a strict logical sense. Like most British social scientists of her time, she was far more disposed to look for evidences of poor character and for atavistic traits that retard the advance of society at the bottom of the social ladder than at the top. And it is on the foundation of this widespread consensus that the inspired mischief of *The Theory of the Leisure Class* rests.

The eugenics movement and the survival of the least fit

The variant of Social Darwinism known as the eugenics movement played only a minor role in the development of poverty studies during the late Victorian and Edwardian period, yet occasional traces of its concerns turn up in the writings a few of our poverty experts. They are particularly evident in the work of Sidney and Beatrice Webb. Sidney Webb remarked in 1907 that recent trends in the British birth-rate were cause for concern, because it is "the Irish Roman Catholics and the Polish, Russian and German Jews, on the one hand, and the thriftless and irresponsible – largely the casual laborers and the other denizens of the one-roomed tenements of our great cities – on the other" who are freely reproducing.[48] Citing as an authority Karl Pearson, mainstay of the eugenics movement, Webb added, "This can hardly result in anything but national deterioration; or, as an alternative, in this country falling to the Irish and the Jews."[49] Beatrice Webb reflected on the need to "endow motherhood" to avoid producing the "myriads of deficient minds and deformed bodies that swarm in our great cities."[50] Reacting to the Russo-Japanese War, she commented on the need for "scientific methods" in the "international struggle for existence."[51]

Such terminology and worries definitely evoke and probably reflect the contemporary notoriety of eugenic arguments. The Webbs, however, in general are not concerned with genetic inheritance as much as with transmission of undesirable savage characteristics – whether through the Lamarckian inheritance of acquired traits or through the contaminating example of bad behavior. The problems which they occasionally discuss in eugenic terms can be explained either by the contagion of bad behavior or by the survival of atavistic tendencies in the less evolved. In this as in so many aspects of the social theory of their time, all of the components work so well together that it is both difficult and, in a sense, unnecessary to sort them out. Their use is metaphoric, rather than logically strict, and is therefore vague.

Evidence on infant welfare before the Royal Commission of 1905–1909 occasionally employed the language of eugenics. Usually, however, the speaker was concerned not that the children of the poor will inherit the physical ailments of their parents but that their health will be undermined by the savage practices of primitive childrearing. When we examine the depiction of slum mothers in Edwardian social science, we shall see little concern for the inheritance of intelligence, but much concern about the transmission of bad habits of mind. Mother is the source of trouble, not as a source of bad genes but as an Ignoble Savage.

Some policy implications of the recapitulationist view of the poor

This view of the poor as undeveloped minds, as children, as savages, powerfully reinforces the "therapeutic logic" of casework. No less a proponent of individual liberty than John Stuart Mill could justify interference in the lives of the incompetent. "Despotism is a legitimate mode of government in dealing with barbarians, provided the end be their improvement, and the means justified by actually effecting that end."[52] Besides paupers, Gertrude Himmelfarb points out, the other large categories of Victorian people disenfranchised by status were criminals (who forfeited their right to vote when convicted) and women, children, and the insane – all assumed to be mentally incapable of making good use of the vote.[53] Bernard Bosanquet, in his defense of the Majority Report of the Edwardian Royal Commission, asserted that "less eligibility" did not have to mean harsh treatment of the poor, but it did necessarily involve "the surrender of self-management" by the pauper.[54] This logic also prompted Beatrice Webb to object to unemployment compensation or workmen's health insurance in the form of unsupervised payments.[55] "I cannot," she observed, "dismiss my rooted prejudice to relief instead of treatment."[56]

While some degree of supervision of the incompetent is not difficult to justify, supervision becomes far less defensible if incompetence is inferred from status rather than empirically verified. As we have seen, the authority of nineteenth-century social science was the basis for Poor Law policy made by experts. As we have also seen, there is considerable ground for suspicion that the "observations" of these experts were shaped to a significant degree by their unexamined assumptions about the poor. This raises an important question: on the subject of poverty, just how "scientific" was Victorian social science?

7
Science and Pseudoscience in Victorian and Edwardian Poverty Studies

> The Commissioners set themselves first to collect evidence from all over the country in great detail; and in 1834 they presented the report from which we have quoted – a report which is classic not only for its masterly handling of a mass of evidence, but as being the truly scientific basis for the greatest social experiment ever tried.
>
> Helen Dendy Bosanquet, *The Strength of the People*

> Scientists needn't become explicit apologists for their class or culture to reflect these pervasive aspects of life.
>
> Stephen Jay Gould, *The Mismeasure of Man*

Helen Bosanquet's remarks about the work of the Royal Commission that preceded hers raise the two most important questions we can ask about late nineteenth-century poverty research. Why did Bosanquet, despite the obvious defects of the 1832 inquiry, see it as a "scientific basis" for poor law policy? And, for that matter, why did Bosanquet *want* a scientific basis for social policy?

The second question is easier to answer than the first. Many late Victorians hoped that social as well as technological problems could be solved by using the methods of the prestigious physical sciences. It has been said that "faith in science" and a concern for morality were the two defining characteristics of Victorian philanthropic enterprises.[1] Ameliorist reformers and social scientists aspired to improve social welfare by using "scientific, rational, organized means," creating many societies and publications toward that end.[2] Beatrice Webb saw the London School of Economics as a way to fill the "urgent necessity of a concrete science of society implemented through historical research, personal observation, and statistical verification."[3] This science would, she hoped, counteract the prevailing influence of political economy, "the so-called Manchester School, of its unverified deductive reasoning and abstract generalisations, of its apotheosis of the 'economic man', exclusively inspired by the motives of pecuniary self-interest, and of its passionate defence of the rights of property as against the needs of humanity."[4] Sidney Webb, much attracted to the evolutionary sciences of geology and biology, hoped to use their concepts by analogy in social science.[5] This attraction to science was hardly surprising. "In every age," C. Wright Mills once observed, "some one style of reflection tends to become a common denominator of cultural life."[6] In late Victorian Britain, that style of reflection was Darwinian biology.[7] As we have seen, however, Darwinism meant many things to many people, and some social theorists strayed far from the original meanings of the biological terms they employed.

The type of "analogical inference" that Sidney Webb wanted to make is problematic because it may not be valid outside the context of the original science in which the concept arose. In fact even *in* its original context the concept may prove to be wrong, as recapitulation in the end proved to be, because the natural sciences have conventions of verification and falsification. The "analogical inferences" of a social science that borrows biological concepts are much less clearly defined and therefore even more prone to error, especially if the social science makes no effort to subject its hypotheses to empirical testing. Herbert Spencer, like the late Victorian anthropologists, frequently used (and misused) metaphors from the prestigious physical sciences.[8] Using scientific terminology does not make a theory "scientific," but it can make the theory *look* scientific. Likewise, abandoning the concept of Economic Man does not in itself deliver social theory from the "unverified deductive reasoning and abstract generalisations" which Beatrice Webb so disliked in political economy. When we examined recapitulationist anthropology and poverty research, we saw how "social scientists" defined personality characteristics by deductive reasoning from their religious and Social Darwinist assumptions, without recourse to economic concepts. Their approach was still *a priori*, nonetheless.

To invoke the rigor and objectivity of science is not to emulate them. Victorian social science was eager to do the former and often quite unable to do the latter. The "mass of evidence" before the 1832 Commission whose handling Helen Bosanquet so admired was, as Lynn Lees observes, largely anecdotal, passed through the filter of middle and upper-class male Protestant observers, selective in its focus, and dressed up with numbers to appear objective.[9] Helen Bosanquet's inability to comprehend the failings of this inquiry, and her willingness to see it as "scientific," alert us to the problems we shall encounter in the work of the experts who staffed the Royal Commission of 1905. Every problem of the statistical movement and the social science movement recurs, often, though not always, invisible to the social investigator. And the most fundamental problem is just the type of "unverified deductive reasoning" that Beatrice Webb so disliked.

Use of *a priori* reasoning without testable hypotheses

Probably very few people today take Harriet Martineau seriously, but R.K. Webb has observed that she is useful to historians because "she reflected and magnified some powerfully symptomatic contemporary concerns."[10] Martineau's preconceptions prepared her, for example, to accept uncritically the view of bastardy presented by the 1832 report. Her popular political economy tales, J.S. Mill remarked, "reduced the whole science to absurdity by carrying it out logically to all its consequences."[11] In the same way Samuel Smiles often serves to illustrate the weaknesses of the viewpoints he popularized, because his unsophisticated transparency makes his assumptions obvious. Thus in his widely popular book of 1871, *Character*, Smiles attributed mental illness to lack of self-discipline:

> The importance of strict domestic discipline is curiously illustrated by a fact mentioned in Mrs. Schimmelpenninck's Memoirs, to the following effect: that a lady, who with her husband, had inspected most of the lunatic asylums of England and the Continent, found the most numerous class of patients was almost always composed of those who had been only children, and whose wills had, therefore, rarely been thwarted or disciplined in early life; while those who were members of large families, and who had been trained in self-discipline, were far less frequent victims to the malady.[12]

The provenance of this information is, to say the least, rather vague and indirect, although not much more so than some of the testimony presented to the Royal Commission of 1832 on the subject of bastardy. Are only children actually overrepresented among lunatics? Even if we accept, on such slender hearsay evidence, that only children do in fact predominate in the asylums, serious problems with the theory still remain. We cannot deduce the strictness of upbringing, as Smiles assumes we can, from family size alone. We have no evidence about the childrearing practices of these families. Perhaps only children are raised *more* strictly than others, as their parents have less work and more time for their supervision. It is possible that lunatics with siblings to care for them are less likely to end up in the asylum. But for Smiles accurate information about the numbers and the facts – not to mention other possible interpretations – are superfluous. The "facts" in question arise directly from theory and not the other way around. Smiles is so sure that lack of self-discipline causes insanity that any set of observations, from any source, will do to "prove" his preconceptions correct. Harriet Martineau's comment on our disinclination to seek proof of what we consider probable is very relevant here.

Samuel Smiles never claimed to be engaged in serious social science. He wrote a number of widely read didactic biographies and popular books of advice, all of them advancing the view that hard work, self-restraint, and good conduct could overcome any barrier on the road of life. Unfortunately, many of the social investigators of his time, who shared his assumptions and did claim to be engaged in serious social science, were guilty of precisely the same faults. Like Smiles, they based theory on unexamined assumptions, sought evidence only to prove what they already knew, and failed to imagine – much less to seek – alternative explanations or potentially disconfirming data.

When we consider the ancestry of Victorian poverty research, a tendency toward this type of *a priori* thinking is clearly evident. Keynes, who greatly admired his predecessor in the development of under-consumption theory, pointed out that the Malthus *Essay* is essentially "*a priori* and philosophical in method" despite attempts in the later editions to dress the theory up with facts and numbers.[13] The facts and numbers were sought after the publication of the thesis, in an attempt to bolster the argument; the theory is in no sense derived from them. Engels observed in a letter to Lavrov that Darwin translated Malthus from mankind to nature – a fact which, as we have seen, Darwin freely acknowledged – and then the Social Darwinists translated it back to mankind from nature, declaring it proven.[14] Papers read before the SSA and published in its journals regularly used statistics to "prove" *a priori* arguments rather than as a source or critique of theory.[15] This was also true of the contemporary work of New England charity reformers. The American counterparts of the COS did not need statistics to prove their assumptions, because "their assumptions were never in doubt," but they did use them to "impress the community with the reformers' truths."[16] When statistics are sought only as proof of theory, rather than as its source, and no attention is given to the possibility of error, we are in the realm of propaganda, not of science.

To protect *a priori* theorizing from criticism, it helps to define its focus in such a way as to preclude unwelcome evidence or points of view. Economic analyses of social issues, Diana Strassman points out, accomplish this by narrowing the focus to individual choices: "Although choices are directly influenced by background circumstances and constraints, the emphasis on choice over constraints leads to the tendency to direct attention toward choice instead of toward the constraints that direct and underlie choices."[17] We have seen how Edwin Chadwick narrowed the focus of his public health survey to purely local factors in choosing the home, rather than the workplace, as the locus of concern. We shall see, in our examination of the housekeeping and childrearing practices of slum mothers, how a relentlessly narrow focus on the behavior of these women is used to imply that they are to blame for most of their children's problems.

In the end, as its focus narrows to accommodate theory and terms are manipulated to the same end, *a priori* social theorizing of this type tends inexorably toward tautology. Strassman demonstrates how this occurs in economics, as all observed forms of giving are reconceptualized as manifestations of "self-interest."[18] Exceptions are reinterpreted as confirmation. Much the same can be said – and often has been said – about the "culture of poverty" approach to the study of low-income populations. If the pathological behavior of the poor is both the cause of, and an effect of, their poverty, then this circular reasoning leaves cause and effect "hopelessly tangled."[19] Such was Rowntree's delineation of the causes of "secondary poverty." We shall see more of them.

Poverty research, by venerable tradition, both constructs such circular tangles and ignores the problems they cause. The dean of twentieth-century poverty research in the United States, for example, sets up a table of four boxes with arrows linking them in a loop: "Poverty," "Cultural and environmental obstacles to motivation," "Poor health, and inadequate education, and low mobility limiting earning potential," and "Limited income opportunities."[20] The second of these categories is not logically necessary as a mechanism. Its existence has not been demonstrated empirically, although it has long been assumed to be true, and its sole function is to make poverty self-perpetuating and therefore, at least in part, the fault of the poor themselves. A century of precedent, dating back to the SSA, makes Moynihan feel secure in his *a priori* construction.

From anecdote to generalization

The Webbs correctly labeled much of the evidence on bastardy before the 1832 Royal Commission "picturesque anecdotes."[21] The Commissioners, however, were following in the footsteps of Malthus, who sought supporting data only after publishing his theory and provided it, in the later editions, in the form of "anecdotal examples which neither verify nor disprove his ideas."[22] Analysis of the work of Helen Bosanquet, Margaret Loane, and Florence, Lady Bell – "probably the most accomplished Edwardian practitioners of a cultural sociology" – shows that "nearly all of their writing" was drawn from anecdotal evidence.[23] Anecdotal evidence is, of course, only as valid as it is typical.

Among Helen Bosanquet's many anecdotes of slum life in *Rich and Poor* (1898), probably the most striking is the story of "Mrs. B.," a widow living with her mother and five children in "a miserable garret."[24] Bosanquet approves the COS caseworker's decision to investigate Mrs B.'s circumstances thoroughly and to recommend improvements, rather than take the easy path of giving her money. But Mrs B. did not respond enthusiastically to the suggestion that she send some of her children to live in the schools the Guardians ran for pauper children:

> She did not know much about the school, she said, and did not care about parting with the children; she had never realized how greatly it might be for their benefit, and like so many of her class she would go on starving and toiling in the old well-known mechanical routine for years, without thinking of making the necessary effort to break through. The visitor represents the advantages and explains how and where application should be made, but is not very successful. Perhaps there is a lingering hope in Mrs. B.'s mind that the 5s may still be forthcoming, if she can hold out..."[25]

In this rather appalling anecdote, the unfortunate Mrs B. gets no credit for wanting to keep her children, a desire that Bosanquet attributes not to maternal love but to ignorance and, perhaps, greed. Bosanquet's perspective is ironic in view of the long-standing opposition of the COS to Dr Barnardo's Homes for orphans and foundlings, whose very existence, it claimed, encouraged the poor to abandon their children.[26] The notion of a woman wanting to keep her children only in the hope of five shillings raises the specter of Economic Woman producing bastards for profit and with it all the same questions. Could she really make a profit by keeping them for so little money? Might she not desire their company for some other reason?

There is no evidence that Bosanquet, comfortable in her view of the poor, considered such objections. The caseworker eventually wore down Mrs B.'s resistance and talked her into parting with some of her children, sending them off to a less contaminating atmosphere:

> And so matters are fairly in train for getting several of the children away into the parish schools, where they will have good air, plenty of food and warm clothing, and for giving the others at least a chance of doing well. Much more trouble, of course, than giving 5*s*, but how infinitely more worth while![27]

Of course the children could have had better food and clothing at home, without the loss of their mother and grandmother and siblings, had the caseworker seen fit to take the easy way out and simply give the family money. (Parish outrelief, of which the COS disapproved, would also have permitted the children to remain at home.) No neglect or abuse is charged; why was it so important to remove these children from their home?

Mrs B.'s failure to realize that it might be "greatly to the benefit" of her children to be parted from their mother recalls Charles Dickens's satirical observation about using the principle of "less eligibility" to keep the workhouse from becoming too "attractive" to the lazy poor:

> The members of this board were very sage, deep, philosophical men, and when they came to turn their attention to the workhouse, they found out at once, what ordinary folks would never have discovered – the poor people liked it! It was a regular place of public entertainment for the poorer classes… a brick and mortar elysium, where it was all play and no work.[28]

Once again, as in the formula of Malthus for the minimal prospects of prudent marriage, when common sense is at war with theory, theory wins hands down.

Rich and Poor, like most of Bosanquet's work, abounds in anecdote. From anecdote she quickly progresses to generalization, even though she has not established the typicality of the anecdote. Her conversation with a local coroner on infant deaths, for example, leads her to the sweeping conclusion that "Improper feeding is a far more potent cause of starvation among the children of the poor than insufficient feeding."[29] Later, our detailed examination of the childrearing practices of slum mothers will reveal other factors, here never considered, which contributed to the high mortality of slum children. Bosanquet is constructing a grand theory out of rather slender evidence. On the basis of a few cases, she concludes that "there is hardly a child in East London which gets a fair start into life without its digestive organs being seriously impaired."[30]

Anecdotes are usually available to illustrate nearly any point of view, including contradictory ones. Maud Pember Reeves, a more sympathetic observer of the life of the poor than Helen Bosanquet, surveyed the health of infants and mothers from a lying-in clinic in Lambeth over a period of several years for the Fabian Women's Group. (We shall take up this survey later in the chapter in an examination of bad and better social science of the Edwardian era.) Reeves tells the story of Mrs S., who "is an excellent needlewoman, and makes nearly all the children's clothes. She is also a wonderful manager, and her two rooms are as clean as a new pin. This had not prevented her from losing five children when these particular budgets were taken. She soon after lost a sixth."[31]

While Helen Bosanquet sees the infants of East London as dying because of bad mothering, Maud Pember Reeves sees the children of Lambeth as dying in spite of good mothering. Which anecdote tells the true story? Neither writer can be said to prove her own theory on the basis of one anecdote. Neither disproves the other's theory. Have all poor babies who die been killed by bad mothering? Have all poor children who die been killed by circumstances beyond the control of their mothers?[32] Neither writer formulates her generalizations in quite such absolute terms, so the anecdotes reveal, rather than prove or disprove, her preconceptions. The more sweeping a generalization derived from anecdotal evidence becomes, however, the more vulnerable it is to counter-example. This vulnerability should, of course, make the generalizer especially sensitive to apparently disconfirming evidence. Even if we take for granted the veracity and good faith of both Helen Bosanquet and Maud Pember Reeves – and certainly there is no good reason not to do so – in a sense neither Mrs B. nor Mrs S. ever really existed as a pure piece of evidence. We know them only as they come to us, filtered by the interpretive narrative of the writers who present them. It would be a fascinating experiment to have Helen Bosanquet visit Mrs S. and to have Maud Pember Reeves visit Mrs B., to see how if at all their anecdotal accounts of these women would differ. Unfortunately such an experiment can never be undertaken.

Sidney and Beatrice Webb recount a clear example of the dangers of relying on anecdotal information from one informant. Mr Crowder, long a member of both the COS and the St George's in the East Board of Guardians, testified to the Edwardian Royal Commission that strict application of the principle of less eligibility in his area had markedly improved the self-reliance of the poor, who now seldom applied for out-relief.

> What Mr. Crowder did not tell the Poor Law Commission, and what, in fact, he refused to see, is that, during these very years the Salvation Army and the Church Army, and various charitable agencies acting on similar impulses, have been freely and indiscriminately giving the relief that Mr. Crowder's Board of Guardians and Mr. Crowder's Charity Organisation Society were refusing; and that, accordingly, any such inference as he drew from the diminution in the number of paupers or of Charity Organisation Society cases, is entirely unwarranted.[33]

While the decrease in applications for out-relief in St George's parish was empirically verifiable, the value of Mr Crowder's evidence, however sincerely presented, was diminished by his disregard for other possible explanations.

The typicality of anecdotal evidence is always problematic, as is the question of how the narrator's point of view may have shaped the narrative. There is a tendency to remember events not as they happened but in the form of "canonical stories," unconsciously selecting from the events that occur those which make sense from our own frame of reference. This tendency leads us "to cram the real and messy complexity of life into simplistic channels of the few preferred ways that human stories 'go'."[34] The photographs used by Dr Barnardo to raise funds for his orphanages were not strictly documentary, but rather conformed to the type of the "evangelical true narrative" in "representing truths transcending the details of any individual case."[35] Harriet Martineau's "didactic view of fiction," her biographer observes, was intended "to show not actuality but potentiality."[36] Allegory is, however, a less defensible approach to serious social science than to fiction. Scientists, therefore, must take care not to fall into "canonical stories."

On the subject of fiction, Victorian social novelists like Mary Gaskell, Charles Dickens, and Benjamin Disraeli took a very different approach to "the social problem" from the one used by scientifically inclined social theorists. "As an explicit alternative to the abstract aggregations with which political economists appealed to readers' rational judgment, novelists deployed a mode of representation that individualized characters and elaborated feelings in order to engage their readers' sympathy."[37] The COS preferred individual case studies to "abstract aggregations," amassing in its social work practice the voluminous information from which Bosanquet's anecdotes are drawn. In the social theory supported by these anecdotes, it can be argued that characters are individualized in order to prevent abstraction, and imputed feelings (like Mrs B.'s implied greed) are elaborated in order to *disengage* the readers' sympathy. This suspicion is only reinforced by instances of anecdotes involving characters whose existence is so vaguely established as to approach the ideal type.

Use of ideal types as evidence

The sketchier the characters depicted in anecdotes, the more they appear to be not actual people but ideal types constructed from theory. In her essay on "The Children of Working London," Helen Dendy Bosanquet details the circumstances of four "families of children who lend themselves fairly well as specimens of different types."[38] The word "specimens" makes this sound scientific, as does her statement that the information before her is from "a survey," but the reader is not informed as to how the survey was conducted, or by whom. Nor is the typicality of these "specimens" established empirically. Convention would compel a modern sociologist to reveal her methods and sources. Bosanquet, whose work preceded the development of such conventions and who knows that she is speaking truthfully from the files before her, simply expects to be believed.

While the terminology gives this paper a scientific aura, it contains no facts or figures. What we have is anecdotal evidence of unproven significance and unknown provenance. Precisely because each of the families illustrates in its own way a positive or negative point that Bosanquet wants to make, the modern reader is left wondering how much reality may have been lost in fitting the families into the intended molds, or indeed whether these families actually existed. They are undoubtedly "representative" in the sense that they represent what Bosanquet considers to be important distinctions, but are they in fact representative of the lived reality of large numbers of people?

Thus Bosanquet details what she claims to be the typical path of the marriage of a working girl in East London:

> As the children grow older the chances are that the burden of maintaining the family falls entirely upon the mother. It is so easy now for the father to disappear and to take up life free of responsibility in some of the many shelters or lodging-houses in London; to change his name if necessary, but in any case to elude the necessity of feeding more than himself. Or if he carries his ideas of irresponsibility

still further, he may – as many indeed do – dispense with the trouble of seeking new quarters, and falling back upon the plea of "no work," remain at home an idle loafer, living upon oddments of charity and his wife's poor earnings. There is no depth of selfishness to which they may not sink when once they have come to this.[39]

Bosanquet never claims that this is the story of a specific person, but she does represent it as typical, implying that many such real persons exist. How many? Bosanquet offers no evidence that any substantial number of men have ever behaved in this way, much less that the motives she imputes to her hypothetical irresponsible father are a sufficient explanation of his behavior. Nor does Bosanquet explain why not having to work would make a life lived on such pittances or in a shelter attractive to many men. (As we have seen, however, it is likely that the notion of temptation to idleness shapes her thinking.) She feels no need to explain why this hypothetical father has no emotional attachment to his wife and children. In the end, the reader must accept the typicality of such behavior on her authority as an expert, not on any kind of proof that she is correct. If her account appears plausible, then the reader presumably will ask for no proof. If her account appears implausible, then the reader may well suspect that Bosanquet has constructed an ideal type out of her theoretical preconceptions, not out of anyone's observed behavior. To understand why this model seemed plausible to Helen Bosanquet, and to the many contemporary readers who accepted her expertise, it helps to recall the passionate war between the Salvation Army and the COS for the soul of East London.

Perhaps the single most extreme example of this type of argument is provided by Bernard Bosanquet; it is here quoted in its entirety: "I have heard of a lad who was morally murdered by benevolent ladies who gave him little casual jobs one after the other, and kept him hanging on and on in expectation till the time and spirit in which he could have fitted himself for an industry had left him and passed by."[40] Without any further information, how are we to believe that this lad, if offered a good post, would have turned it down in favor of odd jobs? In fact, we have no compelling reason to believe that this lad ever had any better prospects than those offered him by the morally murderous ladies of this anecdote. The details and provenance of the anecdote are so vague, and its suitability to the author's argument that make-work and doles are demoralizing is so obvious, that we need a great deal of faith in Bernard Bosanquet's veracity to escape the suspicion that there never was any such lad. Was he merely an ideal type – the entire creation of ideas, rather than of flesh and blood? (This suspicion can only be increased by the knowledge that Bernard Bosanquet was a major figure in the school of Philosophical Idealism.) Bosanquet here proves nothing in a scientific sense, although by the use of anecdote he creates a vague impression that his theory is based on empirical findings rather than on speculation.

This style of argument has proven remarkably durable in poverty studies unsympathetic to the recipients of relief. Charles Murray, for example, in his influential book *Losing Ground* (1984), sustains his argument from highly questionable statistics by considering the plight of an admittedly hypothetical couple, Harold and Phyllis. They are in a very real sense the centerpiece of his brief against AFDC support. Phyllis has become pregnant, and Murray has them consider their options in order to decide whether or not to marry. In the end they decide against, since high welfare benefits make marriage and low-wage employment a poor economic decision.[41] How many people decide whether or not to marry in this way? This uncritical use of an ideal type creates the impression that many do. Harold and Phyllis, however, are Economic Couple, with all the problems of oversimplification that J.S. Mill noted long ago. Like Bernard Bosanquet's lad and Helen Bosanquet's irresponsible fathers, they come to us equipped with only those details and motives that the author selects to make a didactic point. Throughout Murray focuses relentlessly on the choices that Harold and Phyllis make with respect to the welfare system, largely ignoring the nature of outside constraints on those choices. Whatever this may be, it is not science.

The process of reduction to stereotypes, Michael Katz explains, is nearly inevitable even in quantitative social science, since theory inevitably involves generalization. Real people are too complicated to fit neatly into the abstractions of social scientists, "who impose a grid constructed without reference to the lived experience of the people they study."[42] If this problem exists even in social theory drawn from data, then it can only be worse in social theory derived from preconceptions that selects data only to illustrate its points, not to test them. If the proof consists of anecdotes, filtered through the same "grid" between lived experience and theory, then the problem is worse still, as the anecdotes become indistinguishable from the theory they are meant to prove and move inexorably toward ideal types.

There is nothing inherently wrong with the use of ideal types in social science. Max Weber argued that the interpretations of any scientist, social or physical, probably stem from an underlying value system. The use of ideal types can easily be justified by submitting them to empirical testing.[43] While a perfect realization of the ideal type will not be found in reality, the type can and should be compared to the actual behavior of real people to see how well the type does, or does not, describe reality.[44] The ideal type, therefore, is not evidence; it is an explanatory device whose usefulness must be determined by empirical testing against available evidence. When an ideal type is presented as an accurate representation of behavior, without any demonstrated correspondence to observable phenomena, it does not prove anything. "On the other hand," as Weber observed, "such presentations are of great value for research and of high systematic value for expository purposes when they are used as conceptual instruments for *comparison* with and the *measurement* of reality."[45]

This is not to suggest, however, that numbers alone can save social science from the problems we have noted in argument from anecdotes and ideal types.

Problems of data selection and use

From our discussion of the statistical movement and the social science that followed it, we understand that the use of numbers to establish or prove social theory can also be problematic. Mr Gradgrind was not the only person who had a gift for making numbers appear to say whatever he wanted them to say. In his discussion of the attitudes of the French Left toward contraception in the second half of the nineteenth century, for example, Angus McLaren notes that most parties freely acknowledged the statistics showing that the French birth rate was in fact declining after 1850 but "attributed the decline to whatever aspect of contemporary society they considered most noxious and therefore most likely to result in sterility," whether the favored cause be capitalism, bicycling, or tobacco.[46] Much of the criticism of Charles Murray's *Losing Ground* has concerned his careful choice and interpretation of statistics; his "trends" in family disintegration and their relationship to the welfare system are the result of carefully chosen statistics, carefully interpreted to yield the desired results.[47] We have already seen how the presence of numbers made the later editions of the Malthus *Essay* seem more convincing. Gertrude Himmelfarb says much the same of Charles Booth's survey. "Just as Malthus's theory, a century earlier, seemed to have all the authority and certainty of the multiplication tables, so Booth's schema – the classes of A, B, C, etc. – appeared to be as natural and indisputable as the alphabet itself.

And his findings seemed as precise and unequivocal as numbers and decimals could make them."[48]

Himmelfarb is not trying to discredit Booth's work; on the contrary, she titles the first chapter in her section on *The Life and Labour* "Charles Booth: A Man of Property and Conscience." She is merely pointing out aspects of his presentation that made his findings more plausible to his contemporaries than they might otherwise have been. Numbers often look more impressive than anecdotes. But, as Mary Poovey points out, even numbers are "interpretive, for they embody theoretical assumptions about what should be counted" as well as about how the numbers should be interpreted.[49]

Economist and sociologist J.A. Hobson indicated just how important these assumptions about what to count can be in his critique of the then recently published book *Aspects of the Social Problem,* edited by Bernard Bosanquet, several of whose studies we have considered. Hobson found the book all too typical of what he saw as the narrow vision of the COS: "Professing to be devoted lovers of 'facts', and to be the exclusive possessors of the facts relevant to the study of poverty, they confine themselves wholly to facts in their bearing on individual cases, ignoring those facts which consist in the relation of individual to individual, or in other words, 'social facts.'"[50] From the COS point of view, for example, the details of the work history and character of an unemployed person are of interest, but the overall rate of unemployment in London is not. C. Wright Mills called this type of focus "psychologism," which he defined as "the attempt to explain social phenomena in terms of facts and theories about the make-up of individuals."[51] As we have seen, "psychologism" works well with the Protestant attitude toward poverty and the individualistic concepts of political economy. Its product is, as Hobson observes, a style of poverty research that ignores any phenomenon outside the individual case and therefore counts some things and not others – a selectivity which must be kept in mind in evaluating the numbers thus produced.

Consider the case of Alexander McDougall of the Manchester Poor Law Board, who claimed in an 1884 study that in Manchester "51.24 per cent" of pauperism was "brought about by causes directly arising from drinking habits."[52] This is, to put it mildly, an amazingly precise figure. Of course this precision depends on the accuracy of classification by the people who compiled his data and had to decide which causes did and did not arise "directly from drinking habits." If a man drinks and is a pauper, is there necessarily a causal relationship? And if so, which is cause and which effect? A classifier who assumes, as most reformers of the time did, that drink is a principal cause of poverty, will place more cases in this category than will a classifier who does not. McDougall, moreover, does not define problem drinking. Charles Booth, who believed that drink was just as likely to be an effect of poverty as a cause, estimated the incidence of destitution caused by drink much lower than did McDougall.[53] All we have really learned here is that a Manchester pauper of this period had a 51.24 per cent chance of having his situation blamed on drink. When we examine presently the statistical survey undertaken by the New York chapter of the COS on the causes of poverty, we shall see a deliberate attempt to eliminate classification bias of this type. In the confident proclamation of the Manchester figures, we see no awareness that such bias is even possible. Numbers are numbers.

The 1832 Royal Commissioners used leading questions to obtain data that fit their preconceived theories. This technique was still alive and well when later committees attempted to find the right facts to publish. The members of the 1904 Inter-departmental Committee on Physical Deterioration, Jane Lewis notes, were already convinced that "education was the only solution to the problem of infant mortality" because they assumed that bad mothering was the source of the problem. "All witnesses were asked whether they felt that educating girls and mothers in infant management was a good idea, yet when a witness indicated that poverty rather than ignorance might be the reason for the use of canned milk, for example, the point was never pursued."[54] As a direct result of this interview technique, the Committee found and reported that an overwhelming majority of the witnesses favored the education programs its members wanted to institute, and did not report that significant numbers of witnesses had advanced other, less welcome, solutions. When such self-confident and uncritical procedures are followed, the ultimate findings are predetermined by the design of the inquiry.

Bias and its sources

The subject of where Victorian poverty researchers obtained their information is an important one, not only because we need to know whether the information was altered (or invented) in order to prove a point, but also because even an honest reporter can find himself collecting some facts, and not others, on the basis of his preconceptions. "Facts are not pure and unsullied bits of information," biologist Stephen Jay Gould reminds us; "culture also influences what we see and how we see it."[55] By determining survey design, preconceptions can influence the result of an inquiry without any conscious mis-representation on the part of the inquirer. Sidney and Beatrice Webb point out one of the difficulties facing the honest practitioner of social science:

> It is a law of the mind that, other things being equal, those facts which seem to bear out his own preconceived view of things will make a deeper impression on the student than those which seem to tell in the opposite direction. We notice these facts much more easily than we see any others, and they remain more firmly in our memory.[56]

The Protestant view of poverty, the ideas of political economy, the various schools of social science, and Social Darwinist typologies all helped to shape the thinking of the men and women who undertook Victorian poverty studies. Another source of bias, as the Webbs knew, was the difference in social class between the poor and the people who studied them. "And, to put the issue more generally, can the invest-igator, coming from one social class, ever accurately analyse the dynamic force and the specific direction of the feelings of another social class?"[57] Their concern was valid; class bias is evident in much of the poverty research of the era. The Webbs themselves, aware as they were of the problem, were not immune to it. Consider their assertion that while artisans had begun voluntarily to limit family size, the self-control this required was "out of the reach of the less intelligent and more self-indulgent classes."[58] Poverty researchers were, overwhelmingly, middle-class; the information they gathered passed through the filter of their understanding of the lives of the poor. This is why observers like Malchow have argued that the views of Victorian poverty researchers tell us more about the people who held them than about the poor.[59]

The facts about the poor gathered by the Royal Commission of 1832 passed through male Protestants of the upper classes on their way to the Report. So, too, Charles Booth acquired the information for his great survey primarily from middle-class informants rather than directly from the poor. "It did not occur to him," Himmelfarb notes, "to take the observations from the people themselves" – an approach which neither Beatrice Webb nor any other prominent social scientist of the time criticized.[60] We shall see that Booth was aware of the poss-ibility of class bias among his middle-class informants and that he con-sciously attempted to take it into account. Booth's approach was far more sophisticated than that of many of his contemporaries, who showed no such concerns. The Edwardian Royal Commission heard evidence on the subject of "The Condition of the Children who are in receipt of the various forms of Poor Law Relief in England and Wales" from three female professional experts, one of them a doctor. Their evidence was gathered partly from personal interviews with poor mothers but mostly from "relieving officers, school teachers, and others."[61] The witnesses classified the mothers of these children by "character and intelligence," comparing those who were "really above the average" to those who were "the really bad mothers,"[62] apparently oblivious to their dependence on other people's judgments. No one thought to ask the mothers or the children to explain their lives in their own terms.

A deep vein of prejudice runs through middle-class accounts of poor people throughout the period of this study. This basic yet unself-conscious attitude is exemplified by the remark of Samuel Smiles, always master of the commonplace, that the ancestors of the explorer Livingstone were "poor but honest."[63] Edwin Chadwick dismissed the claim that proponents of the Ten Hours bill were concerned about the health of their children; obviously, said Chadwick, they had no such concern but merely wanted to protect adult jobs.[64] Chadwick's biographer probably spoke for most people who have spent much time studying Chadwick when he remarked of his subject that "It is doubtful whether he ever understood a human being."[65]

Helen Bosanquet, who never doubted her superiority to the girls of East London, once remarked of their expenditure on finery that this "leads for the most part, of course, to mating..."[66] This remark recalls, by its terminology, the recapitulationist comparison of the poor to animals and savages. Would Bosanquet have described the wedding of a friend's daughter in this way? Middle-class assumptions about the moral inferiority of the poor were even embedded in English law in "the differential treatment meted out to debtors from different classes;" the middle-class debtor was assumed to be making an honest effort to pay, while the poorer one was not. The high cost of filing for bankruptcy prevented the latter from availing himself of the opportunity afforded the former to start over.[67]

This confidence of superiority often manifested itself in the notion that associating with middle-class visitors and professionals was in itself an elevating experience for the poor. Helen Bosanquet, making the recapitulationist argument that custom and tradition have prevented the very poor from escaping "the lower circle of desires and satisfactions which we share with the brutes," hoped that these less evolved citizens could be spurred on to progress by emulating the example of the more evolved people just ahead of them, "who have pointed the way."[68] Unless her reader shares the assumption of primitive ignorance, it is not entirely clear why anyone would have to point out the advantages of not living a hand-to-mouth existence; perhaps this might be true of piano ownership, but surely not of escaping the squalor Bosanquet describes.

Octavia Hill believed both that she was training her tenants to lead more civilized lives and that she was their friend.[69] In the end, it was always Hill's view that prevailed, and Hill could (and did) evict her tenants if they failed to follow her rules.[70] It is difficult, therefore, to imagine how she could reconcile the lack of reciprocity in these relationships with the concept of friendship, unless she saw it as only natural that the superior should command and the inferior obey.

Not surprisingly, the poor resented this attitude of superiority on the part of their supposed betters. George Lansbury, for example, was not impressed by the achievements of Toynbee Hall, which was intended to benefit the poor by placing earnest young middle-class people in their midst to help them. "In any case, my sixty years' experience in East London leaves me quite unable to discover what permanent social influence Toynbee Hall or any other similar settlement has had on the life and labour of the people."[71] The settlement did, however, benefit the inhabitants of Toynbee Hall, who in Lansbury's view learned nothing significant about their neighbors but were afterwards able on the basis of the project's reputation to get "very fine appointments" as "experts on social affairs."[72]

Lansbury's employer permitted him the flexible schedule necessary to serve as a member of the Poplar Board of Guardians – a role nearly impossible for working-class people because the meetings were deliberately held at a time of day when most laborers had to be at work.[73] Class barriers, Lansbury felt, made it difficult for the overwhelmingly middle-class Guardians to understand the circumstances of the people whose fate they held in their hands, much less to make rational decisions on policy. He noted that many local Boards favored stone-breaking as an element of the workhouse test for able-bodied men. Lansbury tried for years to explain, as one who had done it, that stone-breaking was not only brutally hard work but also skilled labor. His fellow Guardians, inexperienced at the task, did not believe him.[74] In his account of a visit to one of the better London workhouses with Lord George Hamilton, Chairman of the Edwardian Royal Commission, Lansbury relates that he responded to Hamilton's praise for the institution by saying, "What is not good enough for you and me is neither clean nor comfortable enough for others."[75] Nor did Lansbury subscribe to the common view that accepting public assistance was disgraceful. "I could never see any difference between the pension of a widowed queen and outdoor relief for the wife of a worker."[76]

This recalls Cobbett's comment about aristocratic bastards on the pension list and points up one of the most bitter criticisms of the COS – its double standard for judging the behavior of the poor and the behavior of the well-to-do. Hobson enjoyed pointing out these inconsistencies. In his review of *Aspects of the Social Problem*, Hobson noted that the COS dislike doles because they are not the result of work, failing to notice that neither are ground rents or increases in the value of stocks.[77] Shaw once observed that the middle-class regards pimping and prostitution as immoral but has no objection to so underpaying young female employees that they are driven to prostitution.[78] Shaw made clear his unwillingness to accept the moral superiority of the well-off in the character of Alfred P. Doolittle who, when asked "Have you no morals, man?" replies, "Can't afford them, Governor. Neither could you if you was as poor as me."[79]

There is much evidence that the poor, who had so little, were far more generous to each other than the authorities or the COS were to them, because they knew how easy it was to fall on hard times.[80] George Orwell admired the refusal of the poor to conform to middle-class notions of prudent marriage: "Take, for example, the fact that the working class think nothing of getting married on the dole. It annoys the old ladies in Brighton, but it is a proof of their essential good sense; they realise that losing your job does not mean that you cease to be a human being."[81] Unlike Orwell, few middle-class observers were willing to consider the possibility that the standards of their own class might not be universally valid. Victorian observers of female factory operatives, Margaret Hewitt found, were "extremely biased, judging the working classes by the rules of conduct of the middle and upper classes to which they themselves belonged..."[82] As we shall see, Victorian and Edwardian social theorists judged the shopping habits and parenting skills of the slum mother by middle-class standards, invariably finding them wanting.[83] The staff of infant welfare clinics were obsessed with regularity of feeding, then the favored strategy of medical providers and of the middle-class mothers who took their advice, but not of the poor mothers who used the clinics.[84] This insistence on a strictly regulated feeding regimen reflected middle-class concerns about learning self-discipline, rather than any objective understanding of the needs of infants.

The belief that there is only one correct way to raise children – the middle-class way – clearly underlay the somewhat astonishing assertion of the 1909 Minority Report that "The Local Health Authority found the bulk of the poor mothers – those in receipt of Outdoor Relief no less than the others – totally unaware of how to rear their babies in health."[85] In view of this, the Minority advocated education, in the form of "some properly trained and tactful visitor" to the home, since "very few of the mothers in the working classes have either the time or the ability to understand books or leaflets on the management of children."[86] Apparently time-honored techniques learned from one's own mother just wouldn't do, at least in cases where this source of advice was herself poor. The class bias of this viewpoint is also evident in the Minority's strong recommendation that the Local Health Authority send visitors to all mothers in receipt of relief to provide needed information and to see that such a mother is not "free to neglect her infant, to endanger its life by irregular hours, and even to let it starve quietly to death if she chooses."[87]

Middle-class observers, Paul Johnson has pointed out, had a strong tendency to label attempts by the poor to maintain their status extravagance, while regarding middle-class status concerns as perfectly reasonable.[88] He suggests that they saw practices like high expenditure on funerals and outings in purely economic terms because they did not understand the cultural context in which working-class people valued them.[89] Of course the outrage that greeted Thorstein Veblen's *Theory of the Leisure Class* suggests that members of the higher orders were reluctant to view their own purchases as "conspicuous consumption," preferring to view them as amenities of civilized life. As we have seen, Veblen was inclined to regard extravagance as most characteristic of the highest strata, percolating down through the others by example and imitation.

Insistence on doing things the "right way" involved not only a smug assumption of class superiority but ignorance of the details of lower-class lives. Criticism of female factory operatives by the contemporary researchers studying them, Hewitt found, reflected profound ignorance of the conditions under which they lived, prompting repeated campaigns to get them to adopt standards of housewifery that were literally impossible in their dwellings.[90] We shall see more of this phenomenon when we consider the housekeeping practices of the slum mother in detail. Middle-class observers, in Johnson's view, failed to recognize instances of thrift among the working-class because this thrift took forms so different from the ones to which they were accustomed.[91] Perhaps the best summary of the effect such ignorance could have on the views of middle-class observers was offered in 1913 by Maud Pember Reeves: "Experience shows how fatally easy it is for people to label all poverty as the result of drink, extravagance, or laziness ... They see, or more often hear of, people whose economy is different from their own. Without trying to find out whether their own ideas of economy are practicable for the people in question, they dismiss their poverty as 'the result of extravagance' or drink."[92]

Victorian social novelists, Gertrude Himmelfarb has observed, could rely on their middle-class readers' ignorance of working-class life to protect them from charges of implausibility. "They could feel free to create characters sharing their own values and feelings, on the assumption that all human beings were essentially the same; or they could create characters with exactly the opposite values and feelings, on the assumption that they were, after all, alien creatures belonging to another nation or race."[93] The latter technique is evident in much of the published poverty research of the late Victorian and Edwardian era. We have seen the many sources of a strong belief that the poor were indeed "alien creatures," and the ways in which their values and motivation were inferred. Himmelfarb notes, in passing, that perhaps the same criticism could be made of Blue Books and sociological studies of the time.[94] It can, indeed; here, too, readers' ignorance of the lives of the poor assisted the plausibility of the narrative.

Sidney and Beatrice Webb realized that class bias had the potential to distort serious research into the lives of members of other social strata and yet were unable entirely to avoid it themselves. There is little evidence of any such concern on the part of some of their contemporaries, much less of conscious attempts to guard against it. Social researchers differed in their levels of willingness to recognize and eliminate bias, as well as in their understanding of the methods of science, thus producing a range of more and less successful studies of poverty in the late nineteenth and early twentieth centuries.

Bad science and better science

In examining the problems of the nineteenth-century social science of poverty, we have seen that this influential research displays *a priori* reasoning without testable hypotheses, argument from anecdote, use of ideal types as evidence, and a tendency to predetermine the outcome of survey results through decisions made in the design and classification phases, as well as unwillingness to recognize bias or guard against its effects. Helen Bosanquet exemplifies both the aspiration to scientific status for social research and the inability to conduct research in a scientific way. Recall, for example, the study previously discussed in which she speaks of a "survey" of East London children as "specimens" but offers nothing other than anecdotal evidence to support her argument.[95]

In *The Strength of the People,* published in 1903, Bosanquet begins – interestingly enough – with a quotation from Cromwell to establish the primacy of character in all analysis of human behavior: "The mind is the man. If that be kept pure, a man signifies somewhat; if not, I would very fain see what difference there is between him and a beast."[96] This takes her fairly efficiently from Puritan values to recapitulationist Social Darwinism. Within five pages she has traveled from Cromwell to modern experimental psychology and its findings on the satisfaction of physical wants. Modern science, Bosanquet acknowledges, sees no "total difference in kind" between man and animal,[97] thus establishing the possibility of making comparisons between the poor and the lower animals, if not the relevance of doing so. (Under the assumptions of Social Darwinism, the relevance is obvious.) While the subtitle of her book is "A Study in Social Economics," it contains at least as much Social Darwinism as political economy. "The Tyranny of Instincts" reviews some findings of experimental psychology and then argues that in order to progress, man must plan for himself and escape from instinctive drives. She cites Darwin to the effect that it may have been to man's advantage "to have sprung from some comparatively weak creature"[98] but then develops the concept in a spiritual sense which she admits, in passing, was not the one intended by Darwin.[99] Where Darwin spoke of physical attributes, Bosanquet speaks of the development of character. Evolution, therefore, becomes a metaphor used in an analogy assumed – but not demonstrated – to be valid.

Bosanquet considers several hypothetical poor families and the decisions they make, using ideal types as if they were evidence and focusing narrowly on choices rather than on constraints. She concludes with this sweeping generalization: "There is no one so wedded to habit, and so swayed by likes and dislikes, as the untrained, undisciplined woman."[100] While this assertion fits in well with Bosanquet's theme of progress through escape from instinct and development of self-control, it constitutes an elaboration of theory, not an empirically demonstrable (let alone demonstrated) phenomenon.[101] She follows with a stream of admittedly hypothetical cases and anecdotes about the alleged recklessness and childishness of slum mothers. Bosanquet offers no hard evidence for any of the anecdotes or to support the typicality of the hypothetical cases, all of which are predictable from her recapitulationist assumptions.

In "Progress During the Nineteenth Century," Bosanquet decries the Elizabethan Poor Law, accepting at face value every claim made by the Report of the 1832 Royal Commission as to the allegedly demoralizing effect of outrelief and its tendency to increase the pauper population. Her sweeping conclusion: "The effect of allowance is to weaken, if not to destroy, all the ties of affection between parent and children."[102] Are "all the ties of affection between parent and children" based on financial support? If so, then this is Economic Family, with all of the consequent problems of oversimplification. Bosanquet presses on, implying on the authority of the Report that families of this type were quite common in England before the New Poor Law:

> The neglect which was perhaps most serious for the future of the people, as well as most fruitful of misery at the time, was that of childhood. If the agricultural labourer regarded his children as a means for deriving an income from the Poor Law, the town-dweller found still more profit by putting his to work in the mills while they were still infants.[103]

Did laborers of the eighteenth and early nineteenth centuries view their children as capital goods? Was it really possible to make much of a profit on them? Or was it merely necessary to turn to the Poor Law in order to feed them? In view of the testimony offered before both Royal Commissions on the general inadequacy of child allowance, this claim is highly questionable. To Helen Bosanquet, however, it was so obviously true as to require neither explanation nor empirical proof.

In the end, the reader is asked to accept these anecdotes and *a priori* conclusions from unproven assumptions on the strength of Helen Bosanquet's status as an expert: she has spent many years inquiring into the circumstances of the poor, therefore she must have had experiences that justify her beliefs. This is not science; it merely invokes science and then proceeds not to practice it. It is an argument from authority.

Some practitioners of Victorian and Edwardian social science *were* concerned about the potential for bias and error. Charles Booth, as we have seen, did allow his preconceptions to influence his research. He was, however, also aware of the problem of possible bias and went to some trouble to avoid it. The very scale of his enormous survey was in itself some protection against the possibility of mistaking a few anomalous cases for widespread phenomena. He carefully acquired as many sources of information about the neighborhoods he studied as possible to guard against bias in any one source. Although he did not, as we have seen, interview a significant number of the poor to obtain their view of themselves, he did live for short periods in some of the neighborhoods under study, boarding with poor families, in order to observe for himself what life was like for their residents.

Booth tried to counter possible bias in the reports of the school visitors by comparing any available statistics from the census and other sources; he likewise sought information for his industry series from trade unions as well as employers.[104] Beatrice Webb, a cousin of Booth's wife Mary, involved herself in the collection of information for the industrial series both as a reader of statistical abstracts and as part of an early experiment in participant observation, working as a "plain trouser hand" in one of the sweatshops of the East End.[105] This employment, undertaken in an appropriately dressed-down manner in the spring of 1888, was intended, like Booth's temporary lodgings, to provide the real flavor of experience which mere statistics cannot give.[106]

Booth's street-by-street survey of the residents of East London neighborhoods consists primarily of anecdotes passed through the school visitors who provided his information, yet they differ in some significant ways from those offered in Helen Bosanquet's many books. While they involve value judgments and assumptions about the people discussed, many of them are far more detailed than the anecdotes we have previously considered. The house at No.18, Shelton Street:

> has eight rooms. The parlours and the first floor have been occupied by a shifting set, usually a low class of costers whose wives and children sell watercresses or flowers in the streets. On the second floor lived Mr. and Mrs. Park with five children, and were there for at least eight years. The Parks were English Protestants; the man, now about forty-eight years old, served in India as a soldier, and was discharged in ill-health suffering from pains in the head and loss of memory due to fracture of the skull and sun-stroke. His drinking habits also stand in his way. He does house-painting when he can get it, which is rare. The mother works hard for her children and attends every mothers' meeting she can, as well as every mission-hall if possible. This brings her soup three or four times a week and sometimes a loaf of bread, and so the poor woman keeps her little room, and the children with bread. At Christmas she may contrive to get two or three Christmas dinners from different places. The room here was

full of rubbish – all in it would not fetch 10*s*; the dirty walls covered with little pictures never taken down; vermin abounded and the stench was awful. These people have had seven children, but about eight years ago two of them, aged nine and eleven, going to school in the morning, have never been heard of since.[107]

The next paragraph goes on to describe the family upstairs.[108] This account, while not uniformly impartial or sympathetic, supplies much more detail than Helen Bosanquet's anecdotes. The school visitor who supplied it appears to have been at least as interested in getting his facts straight as in drawing conclusions. In response to all this detail, we are inclined to believe that we have some sense of the Parks as real people.

To Booth's credit, he understood the possibilities for error and the importance of convincing the reader of the accuracy of his survey:

It will be readily understood that I have no proof to offer for the accuracy of the foregoing statements. I have no means of checking them or any of the descriptions which will follow. The greatest care however was taken to make the account of each street complete, and I am satisfied that none of my informants had any wish but to tell their stories truthfully.[109]

Nowhere in Helen Bosanquet's voluminous writings does she acknowledge that error is possible or that she bears the burden of proving her assertions. Booth's understanding of these issues led him to search out other sources of data that might corroborate, or call into question, the information supplied to him by his informants.[110] This enabled him to present his survey results with confidence, not of personal infallibility, but of methodological care.

There is another way in which Booth's understanding of the study of social problems was more sophisticated than that of many of his contemporaries. In some complicated human behaviors, he realized, cause may be confounded with effect, rendering interpretation difficult even when correlation has been established. In the Final Volume, Booth presents much testimony from "the clergy of the Church of England, Nonconformist ministers, and schoolmasters" about the prevalence of drinking among the poor. He remarks on their consensus of opinion that "while there is more drinking there is less drunkenness than formerly, and that the increase in drinking is to be laid mainly to the account of the female sex."[111] Booth notes the near unanimity of this opinion as well as the "teetotal bias" of some of the persons offering it.[112] And yet, after discussing the large body of opinion supporting the idea that intemperance causes poverty, Booth is inclined to set it aside:

> But I think it will be seen even from these extracts that it is not really possible to isolate drink as a cause of poverty. It plays a part, and a great part, but it is only as the accompaniment of idleness, extravagance, incompetence, or ill-health that it is fatal.[113]

Drink, in Booth's view, can cause poverty, can combine with other factors to worsen poverty, or can be caused by poverty. A reader inclined to environmentalist explanations for poverty is unlikely to be pleased by Booth's list, citing as it does only one item that can be seen as outside the control of the poor – ill health.[114] And yet, judgmental as he may at times have been, Booth had some sense of the complexity of social phenomena and the difficulty of sure attributions of causality in matters of behavior.[115]

Helen Bosanquet's reaction to Charles Booth's multi-volume survey is instructive. Octavia Hill, as we have seen, did not even read it, believing that she already had all the facts she needed. Helen Bosanquet did read it, or at least some of it, to enter the widespread popular discussion of Booth's finding that "almost one-third of the population of London was poor."[116] The COS, as might be expected, disagreed, its publications contending that Booth had distorted the picture by understating "avoidable" poverty and thus implying that lack of money, rather than lack of character, caused the problem.[117] To estimate earnings, Booth had gone to some trouble to compare the figures provided by the school visitors with figures on the going rates he obtained from employers, trade unions, and other sources. He found a significant number of families for whom earnings were simply insufficient to provide adequate food, clothing, and shelter. Helen Bosanquet dismissed this finding out of hand:

> I speak confidently, and with full knowledge of all the difficulties of a small income, when I say that there are comparatively few families in London through whose hands there had not passed in the course of the year sufficient money and money's worth to have made a life free at any rate from hunger and cold, and with much in it of good.[118]

In the first of two footnotes appended to this sweeping assertion, Bosanquet immediately qualifies it by observing, "I speak here of the normally constituted family. A reservation is necessary where we have to do with the question of women's wages; where, that is (from illness or death of the man), the woman is the wager-earner."[119]

Whether or not we accept Bosanquet's assumptions about what constitutes a "normal" family, families with female breadwinners certainly made up a higher proportion of the impoverished population than her relegation of them to a footnote might suggest. Booth found, in his East London survey, that among the roughly 100,000 people in Class B ("casual earnings") there were 6,500 widows. "Widows or deserted women and their families bring a large contingent to this class," he noted.[120] In Classes C and D combined, he found that 13,325 of his families (14 per cent) consisted of "female heads of families with young children."[121] In Rowntree's survey of York, 15.63 per cent of the families living in "primary poverty" were in this situation "due to death of chief wage earner" and 5.11 per cent "due to illness or old age of chief wage earner."[122] In Rowntree's Class A, "the poorest people in the city," he judged that "in the case of 1295 persons, or almost exactly two-thirds of the whole, the immediate cause of poverty is the removal of the wage-earner by death or desertion, or the inability to earn wages through illness or old age."[123] The Majority Report of the Edwardian Royal Commission, primarily written by Helen Bosanquet, would report six years after the publication of her critique of Booth that "By far the greater number of children who are dependent, or partially dependent, upon the Poor Law are those who live at home with one or both parents; for the most part they are the children of widows."[124]

In her second footnote to the claim that genuine insufficiency of wages is "comparatively" rare, Bosanquet adds, "I am aware that this is contrary to Mr. Booth's opinion."[125] She then quarrels, vaguely and briefly, with some of his data, observing that "he takes the income for five weeks only" and that Booth's data might be inaccurate.[126]

That Bosanquet "speaks confidently" no one would deny, but the grounds on which her confidence stands are less secure. When we examine how Edwardian poverty theorists viewed the spending habits of the slum mother, we shall see that Bosanquet did not really possess the "full knowledge of all the difficulties of a small income" she claimed. Her vague objections to Booth's data are not so much a meaningful critique of his methods as an assertion that his information must be wrong because his conclusions, in her view, are wrong. Nor does she share her reasons for objecting to the use of five weeks' wages. (Familiarity with Bosanquet's work on poverty prompts this writer to believe Bosanquet is suggesting here that far more money was earned at previous times but not saved against adversity by the feckless workers whose short-term wages are recorded in the tables of *Life and Labour*.) "Mr. Booth's opinion" is the result of an enormous survey whose findings were cross-checked against other sources of information on earnings, yet Bosanquet feels secure in refuting it by a mere assertion of her expertise, an appeal to authority.

We have already met briefly with the survey conducted by the Fabian Women's Group that is the subject of Maud Pember Reeves' classic *Round About A Pound A Week*, published in 1913. The researchers wished to study "the effect on mother and child of sufficient nourishment before and after birth."[127] They visited 42 families in Lambeth whose names they obtained from the local lying-in clinic, following up with repeated visits over several years. Eight families participated only briefly for reasons Reeves explains. Four of the children were born prematurely and died after only a few hours.[128] The participating families were trained to keep detailed budgets for the investigators' inspection; in a few cases the husbands or children of illiterate women kept the accounts for them.[129]

While the sample size is small, full details of methodology are disclosed, as are the preconceptions with which the investigators began. Reeves notes the committee's original assumption that families of "men earning over 26*s* a week were likely to have already sufficient nourishment," while wives of those earning less than 18*s* would be likely to share the supplemental food around rather than reserve it for themselves and the new baby, thus skewing the results of the study.[130] She adds that after two years of inspecting the budgets, the researchers realized their initial estimate was too low and therefore raised the upper limit to 30*s*.[131] This openness about assumptions and about the discovery that they are incorrect is refreshing after reading Octavia Hill and Helen Bosanquet; it permits greater confidence that the survey results may produce new information, not merely reinforce old notions.

In the published results the researchers carefully note that the extra nourishment afforded to mothers and infants in the study is not included in the budgets, lest the reader be misled about the condition of families of similar income not receiving such assistance.[132] Reeves also notes that the budgetary information from the household accounts has been verified by the visitors "from the study of rent-books and of insurance-books, from the sellers of coal, from the amount taken by the gasman from the meter," from the boot-clubs and clothing-clubs.[133] Like Charles Booth, the Fabian ladies saw the need to avoid relying on one, possibly unreliable or biased, source. The COS's caseworkers were also in the habit of verifying information given to them by applicants for relief. They questioned employers, landlords, local tradesmen, and even neighbors in a way deeply resented by the applicants, to make sure that no fraud was being perpetrated and that relief was not being obtained from multiple sources or by disreputable people.[134] Probably because of their commitment to "psychologism" and to moral theories of poverty, however, they do not appear to have felt it useful to compile this information in any way other than case by case, nor did they offer it as evidence in their studies of poverty to support their anecdotes and hypothetical families.

In her account of the Lambeth survey, Maud Pember Reeves offers a great deal of detail on the cooking and storage facilities of the homes in the survey, information which we shall discuss later in our look at the housekeeping and childcare practices of slum mothers, which is entirely absent from the accounts of slum life given by writers like Octavia Hill and Helen Bosanquet. This makes possible a better-informed examination of the eating habits and food-shopping practices of the subjects than can be made from disparaging but vague comments about "inappropriate feeding" and "extravagance." Likewise her observations on the cleanliness of the homes, and the reader's evaluation of them, are informed by details on the provision of water to the houses and the amount of money available for soap. The book does include a number of illustrative anecdotes, one of which we have considered earlier on the subject of "Mrs. S," as well as some value judgments on the wisdom of large expenditures for burial insurance and the drinking habits of some husbands. But it also offers enough detail to enable the reader to make his own judgments as to the worth of the evidence presented. The survey makes a serious attempt to proceed from evidence to conclusions, rather than to search out data to confirm existing assumptions.[135]

On the basis of the data, Reeves postulates a vertical stratification of health in the low-rent homes of London; health was worst in families living in the basement and improved with each floor higher. This could be due to properties of the rooms or to income, since rents in the basement were lower.[136] Likewise first babies were found to be the best fed, the least overcrowded, and in the best health.[137] In view of the survey results, Reeves argues, "It is not necessary to invoke the agency of drink to make 20s a week too small a sum for the maintenance of four, five, or more, persons. That some men in possession of this wage may drink does not make it a sufficient wage for the families of men who do not drink."[138]

These observations are all what J.A. Hobson would call "social facts" and not, therefore, the type of fact with which the COS was concerned. Helen Bosanquet reviewed *Round About A Pound A Week* soon after its appearance, and not long after the furor over the differences in the Majority and Minority Reports of the Edwardian Royal Commission. Bosanquet's reaction was significantly less negative than her earlier response to Charles Booth's great survey although, characteristically, she showed no interest in the survey methodology. The budgets, Bosanquet agreed, contain very little margin of elasticity in any area except food. As she freely admitted, "The amount is lamentably small for a family with children to maintain."[139]

Bosanquet, however, then dismissed some of the survey evidence out of hand. Reeves had declined to endorse the strictures against early marriage that had been universal among critics of the poor ever since Malthus, noting that the cost of living in a boarding house made being a bachelor no cheaper than marriage – merely less comfortable.[140] Bosanquet accused Reeves of being "rashly dogmatic" and asserted, without presenting any supporting evidence, that even by waiting to marry until the age of 25 a young man could save up, without difficulty, a substantial sum.[141] Likewise Bosanquet agreed with Reeves that the rents on slum housing are actually higher than those on lodgings elsewhere, and that overcrowding produces ill health. She dismissed, however, the idea that these factors are outside the control of the poor. The problem is not in the housing or in its cost, but in its inhabitants: "The chief difficulty lies in the lack of mobility in this class of the London poor. They have lost the courage to move even so far as across London, to say nothing of migration or emigration."[142] In Bosanquet's view, "Such lack of enterprise would lead to congestion and unemployment in any rank of workers."[143]

Bosanquet has not actually demonstrated any lack of courage or enterprise on the part of the inhabitants of Lambeth, merely inferred it from their place of residence. Many of the casual laborers of East London worked at the docks, making nearby residence vital in a city lacking affordable mass transit; rooms across town would not be within walking distance of jobs in the neighborhood. Moving to a new area would mean having no dependable web of credit in the local shops, no long-term friends and neighbors to help in times of crisis. Migration to another city or country would make the distance from these supports even greater. (Indeed, Young and Willmott found that families in their Bethnal Green study were still reluctant to move away from the neighborhood in the 1950s because of the safety net represented by relatives. In their view, "These bonds, important still, probably counted even more in the earlier days of factory industry, when the mother-centered kinship system served to give working-class women some security in a life beset by its opposite.")[144] Bosanquet considers none of these practical problems. Poverty must be the result of a defect of character; therefore there must be some way to interpret apparently independent factors, like high rents, in a way that demonstrates poor character. An exception – a "social fact" – has been reinterpreted as confirmation, with no evidence needed.

One further example of "better" science in the study of poverty was produced, ironically, by the COS – not of London, but of New York. The New York chapter of the COS undertook in 1908 a large survey of the families on its rolls, presenting the results in a book by General Secretary Edward T. Devine.[145] Devine and his colleagues studied 5,000 families on the books of the district committees of the COS during the two years preceding September 30, 1908.[146] In the manner characteristic of the Society's casework, large amounts of information had been gathered about applicants for aid. The New York chapter made the uncharacteristic decision to aggregate this information in order to find out more about the causes of poverty. Also unusual for the COS was the researchers' desire to avoid biasing the outcome of the survey by prejudging which factors were important. They made an effort, therefore, to cull the files and list *all* factors present in each case without assuming their importance or causal role.[147] The result of this procedure was, not surprisingly, "social facts."

Devine immediately realized that a striking number of the impoverished families were "partial families" missing one or both parents through death, widowhood, or desertion. He also noticed the preponderance of children; nearly half of the 9,172 individuals encompassed by the survey were children under the age of 14.[148] These are circumstances highly correlated with poverty, rather than characteristics of individuals. The book contains a great many charts and graphs showing how the various factors tabulate and, to some extent, cross-tabulate. When the factors are taken individually the top five, in order, are physical disability, unemployment, defect of character, widowhood and desertion, and overcrowding.[149]

This list, of course, allows a much smaller role for "defect of character" than the one generally assigned to it. Moreover, Devine observes that classification bias has probably inflated the level of "defect of character":

"Defect of character" has been interpreted very broadly in order that there might be no ground for inferring that its full weight was not being given. Every family in which there was a wayward child, or a woman with a bad temper or a disposition to beg, or any one who was lazy, has been counted in, though in many of these cases there may be physiological or external reasons for what seem to be faults. In every case of desertion it has been assumed that something was wrong with the character of the deserter, even when nothing definite is known except the fact of desertion... Every unmarried couple also is included. Even with this rigorous interpretation of the term, however, we find that defect of character sufficiently noticeable to be recorded is present, to our knowledge, in only a little over two-fifths of all the cases, while over three-fourths of them are physically or mentally handicapped, in some way or in numerous ways, at the time of application.[150]

The researchers were so concerned about being accused of ignoring character defects that they chose to err on the side of overcounting them. This is eloquent testimony to the overwhelming dominance of the personal defects theory of poverty in British and American social thought. And yet they had the intellectual integrity to gather the facts in as unbiased a manner as they could devise, to examine them for clues, to disclose their qualms about their methodology, and to stand by their unexpected results. They also pondered whether some of the phenomena they found were causes or results of poverty, regarding the establishment of causality as problematic. Devine wondered, for example, whether "defective personality is only a halfway explanation, which itself results directly from conditions which society may largely control."[151] At the very least, he was open to the possibility and capable of imagining it.

Devine's account is not without preconceptions and bias. Although he questions the COS premises, arriving at some interesting conclusions that we shall consider later, he often sounds very much like a middle-class man of his time and a member of the COS. After presenting a largely environmentalist analysis of poverty, for example, Devine abruptly notes that: "No doubt we do encounter instances in which in this life individuals who suffer are but paying penalties for their own misdeeds. Passion and indolence do have their consequences."[152] He argues, likewise, that "We are far too lenient with our criminals," with the confusing addendum that "social failure" from preventable conditions is probably the root of much crime.[153] He also blames much of the ill health of the poor on "ignorance and the continuous neglect of the elementary rules of personal hygiene."[154] Two pages later, however, we find him commenting that "polluted water, infected milk, and dirty food" are largely to blame.[155] Such confusion, as we shall see below, pervades nineteenth-century poverty literature and probably reflects the uncomfortable friction of disagreeable evidence against strongly held preconceptions. Edward Devine and his colleagues, however, were at least willing to examine their biases, to gain enlightenment from facts, and to transcend their preconceptions – in short, to pursue genuine social science.

Confusion and mixed messages

Perhaps the most striking commonality in nineteenth-century British poverty studies, after the personal defects theory, is the ubiquity of ambivalence and confusion about personal and environmental factors. We saw this ambivalence in the Statistical Movement. It characterized every writer we have considered, from the most environmentalist of them to the least. Even Edwin Chadwick eagerly offered the "counter-attractionist" view that if the poor were to be made more sober they would have to be given things other than beer to drink, places other than pubs in which to spend their time.[156] His argument that the poor rates could be kept lower by improvements in sanitation and public health implied a significant role for illness from environmental causes in the genesis of pauperism.[157] Yet he explicitly claimed, in another context, that the Commission of 1832 had proven "most pauperism was due to personal faults."[158] C.S. Loch, that staunch defender of the "principles of 1834" who long headed the COS and who sat on the Edwardian Royal Commission, managed to assert the primacy of char-acter defects while, in the same sentence, tacitly acknowledging that environmental factors might be their cause: "The recklessness of the poor as to whether they keep in work (caused, it must be remembered, in great measure by the conditions under which they have to work) is amazing."[159] Loch evinces no awareness of self-contradiction. This is the circular reasoning to which Katz refers in his critique of "culture of poverty" arguments, which leaves "cause and effect hopelessly tangled."[160]

This confusion increased as the nineteenth century wore on. Some-times, like Chadwick, the researcher made different and conflicting claims in different contexts. Thus we have Charles Booth arguing in connection with his great survey that heavy drinking might be a result, rather than the cause, of poverty[161] and yet asserting, as he advanced his case for old age pensions, that drunkards, prostitutes, and criminals should be left to their own devices because their suffering is deserved.[162] Booth likewise argued that early marriage and the high birth-rate of the poor are probably products, rather than causes, of poverty.[163] Yet later, in his campaign for old age pensions, he showed little sympathy for those guilty of "early marriages and recklessness in the bringing of children into the world" as compared to the elderly who deserved, in his view, state pensions.[164]

Helen Bosanquet frequently remarked on the inadequacy of women's wages to support a family. This never led her, however, to try to estimate the number of families whose sole financial support was female, let alone to discuss the low wages of women as a cause of poverty. (Her footnote argument with Booth, discussed above, is a case in point.) Often her excursions into environmentalism take away with one hand what she bestows with the other. Considering the problems of slum children, for example, Bosanquet writes eloquently of the bad practices of landlords and local officials that perpetuate squalor. She lists recommendations that address problems beyond the control of the poor family but then reduces their importance: "more stringent enforcement of existing sanitary regulations, stricter supervision against overcrowding, and most important of all, better training of boys and girls for the responsibilities awaiting them: little more than this is needed to make a healthy life for children as possible in poor London as in rich."[165] Why is training the most important of her recommendations? Bosanquet never explicitly answers this question. After a detailed examination of the horrors of the slum environment beyond the control of its inhabitants, she returns to the comfortable ground of deficiency of the poor. She sees no need to explain her decision; all that she has written before, and will write hereafter, explains it for her.

In the same way Bosanquet offers an anecdote about a child with an apparently tubercular "hip-disease."[166] The child's suffering seems to make a case for undeserved misfortune, until Bosanquet goes on to recount various instances of the "thriftless" behavior of the child's relatives. (Just how this behavior could be seen as relevant to the child's tuberculosis Bosanquet does not explain.) Bosanquet blames – at some length – inadequate inspection of housing and working conditions for some of the illness she chronicles in the family but seems more interested in their alleged bad character. There is plenty of blame to go around. "I believe the same to be true of thousands of the little invalids who are now looked upon as the necessary victims of town life. They owe their lot to nothing so impressive as an inherited doom, but to a very commonplace carelessness and stupid selfishness on the part of the family and community into which they are born."[167] Clearly this conclusion admits the relevance of environmental factors; the community has been negligent in not stepping in to enforce decent working and living conditions. Yet much of the narrative is devoted to a catalogue of the perceived character flaws of the child's relatives. The possibility that low income is to blame for any of this misery is nowhere considered.

Bosanquet, as we have seen, was quite willing to see the faults of members of the "residuum" – fecklessness, aversion to work, self-indulgence – in some wealthy citizens as well. Here she makes a recapitulationist argument for the importance of these faults: "This absence of the economic virtues is, of course, only one aspect of a very strongly marked type of character; it accompanies a low order of intellect, and a degradation of the natural affections to something little better than animal instincts."[168]

We have seen how well the Protestant view of poverty and the ideas of political economy work together; thus there is a great deal of interest in the phrase, "the economic virtues." Inevitably, Bosanquet argues, "this type of character" must result in destitution since "no artificial social arrangements can alter the fact that the man in any rank of life who is not self-supporting is an economic failure."[169] (Apparently Bosanquet has now entirely forgotten about the "wealthy members of the Residuum" she had discussed a few pages earlier; obviously the "artificial social arrangement" of inherited wealth protects them quite effectively from destitution.) She does, however, volunteer the observation that her model does not cover all cases of destitution. The exceptions, she says, are those "who fall from the ranks of independence through merely temporary misfortune; they owe their failure to the accident of circumstance alone, and not to any inherent defects. It is unfortunately true that long-continued misfortune is only too likely to develop these defects, but until this has taken place there is always hope."[170]

These exceptional cases sound very much like the sort of cases the COS staff were looking for as they sifted through large numbers of applicants, looking for the few worthy of help. Although Bosanquet thus offers some allegedly exceptional cases in which poverty is not caused by personal defects, she hazards no estimate as to the relative proportions of the deserving and undeserving. She also muddies the waters with her minimal concession that some of the character defects may be "developed" by, rather than causes of, long-term hardship – a concession which she neither emphasizes nor explains.

A similar muddle occurs when Bosanquet tries to take on the possibility of environmental factors in that favorite target of critics of the poor – drink. After acknowledging that malnutrition is the most probable explanation for the finding of the school authorities that boys in the industrial schools run by the Guardians are significantly shorter than average boys of their age, she adds this qualification: "Moreover we are told that there is a direct physiological connection between malnutrition [*sic*] and the craving for alcohol, which goes far to explain the prevalence of drinking amongst the very poor. The provoking part of the matter is that the money spent on alcohol would often be enough, with good management, to supply a really sufficient diet."[171] Just *how* often would the money spent on drink be sufficient to supply a good diet? Bosanquet does not say. We have seen that the Fabian Women's Group inspection of household budgets yielded a contrary conclusion with regard to the large number of families they found to be attempting to survive on 20 shillings a week or less.

While the notion of the "prevalence of drinking amongst the very poor" is nearly everywhere asserted in Victorian and Edwardian poverty studies, it is nowhere proven.[172] Certainly the assumption is plausible. In the absence of data on the drinking habits of higher strata of society, however, it cannot be valid to base a claim that the very poor drink more than others on any figures that could be discovered or estimated about the drinking habits of the poor alone. Since "we are told" that malnutrition somehow predisposes the poor to drink, we are in a sense given an environmentalist explanation for the alleged heavy drinking of the poor. Yet Bosanquet also tells us that the poor could avoid malnutrition by spending their money, "with good management," on food instead of drink. Malnutrition causes drinking, which causes malnutrition, which causes drinking.

Earlier, in our discussion of the Statistical Movement, we saw that Rowntree's survey of York produced a tangle of cause and effect in the matter of Secondary Poverty, which Rowntree estimated to include 28 per cent of the working-class population of York or 18.51 per cent of the whole population.[173] Rowntree found over 15 per cent of the working-class population, or nearly 10 per cent of the whole population, to be living in Primary Poverty, defined as income insufficient "to maintain a moderate family (*i.e.* not more than four children) in a state of physical efficiency."[174] None of the "immediate" causes he listed for Primary Poverty inherently involve defects of character, although he indicated that the fourth of them might:

(1) Death of chief wage-earner.
(2) Incapacity of chief wage-earner through accident, illness, or old age.

(3) Chief wage-earner out of work.

(4) Chronic irregularity of work (sometimes due to incapacity or unwillingness of worker to undertake regular employment).

(5) Largeness of family, *i.e.* cases in which the family is in poverty because there are more than four children, though it would not have been in poverty had the number of children not exceeded four.

(6) Lowness of wage, *i.e.* where the chief wage-earner is in regular work, but at wages which are insufficient to maintain a moderate family (*i.e.* not more than four children) in a state of physical efficiency.[175]

Note that in only one cause does Rowntree insert a comment implying that defect of character might be at fault in some instances. He does not indicate how often this interpretation might be justified, merely suggesting that it may be in some cases.

From the perspective of the personal defects theory, the same list would yield far more suggestion of character defect than Rowntree implies. We have seen, for example, how much stress critics of the poor placed on their failure to save against contingencies like the ones numbered 1 through 5 on this list. We have also seen Helen Bosanquet suggest that "there is always some reason why the man who knows his trade cannot get employment,"[176] which would imply that Cause #3 is particularly suspect. We have seen and shall see a tendency to blame the ill health of the poor on their own behavior, and one of the major preoccupations of poverty studies after Malthus was to criticize the poor for marrying young and having large families. These perspectives would place Causes #1, 2, and 5 more firmly on the character defect list as well, leaving only #6, the lowest on the list, as a purely environmental cause. Clearly Rowntree saw it as such, arguing on the basis of his data that "the wages paid for unskilled labour in York are insufficient to provide food, shelter, and clothing adequate to maintain a family of moderate size in a state of bare physical efficiency."[177]

Rowntree has allowed the facts from his survey to tell their own story, inserting the possibility of a moralizing interpretation into only one of his causes. Only in the matter of Secondary Poverty does he encounter real difficulties, suggesting causes not from quantifiable phenomena like wages or death of breadwinner but from value judgments about the household budgets. He produces a list with entries like "ignorant or careless housekeeping, and other improvident expenditure," and then observes that "irregularity of income" may be responsible for them.[178]

After a discussion of the "predominant factor" of drink, however, Rowntree offers another environmentalist interpretation: "Though we speak of the above causes as those mainly accounting for most of the "secondary" poverty, it must not be forgotten that they are themselves often the outcome of the adverse conditions under which too many of the working classes live."[179] Rowntree, a Quaker and a temperance advocate, was even able to argue that the monotonous hard work and lack of education characteristic of lower working-class life probably produce a degree of boredom that contributes to excessive drinking.[180] All things considered, Rowntree did a remarkable job of trying to prevent his preconceptions from biasing his work, and his sympathy for the poor of York is unmistakable. He did, however, fall into the pit of circular reasoning by entangling cause and effect in his discussion of "secondary poverty," where income is less obviously insufficient and alleged character defects are therefore more likely to be invoked.

Sidney and Beatrice Webb were, as we have seen, aware of the dangers of bias and of the importance of good methodology in social research. This did not, however, prevent their offering arguments that manifest the same sort of confusion and mixed messages that we have seen in other social theorists of the time. Consider, for example, their argument for school feeding in response to the findings of the Physical Deterioration Committee in 1905.[181] The Webbs concede that the measure is controversial but consider it necessary since education is wasted on "hungry or starving children."[182] They argue that "insufficient income" is not always to blame for child malnutrition, since "poverty may bring with it ignorance, unsatisfactory home conditions, lack of parental control, and absence of influences favourable to nutrition."[183] The Webbs do not offer any evidence for these problems, nor do they explain what they mean by the suggestion that poverty "may bring with it" the problems they list. Does poverty cause these problems? Is poverty caused by these problems? Is poverty sometimes accompanied by these problems? This is a classic "culture of poverty" loop, with no basis for differentiating cause and effect.

Although the Webbs assert that "The working-class woman is as devoted to her children as any other mother,"[184] they also indicate that overwork and insufficient income combine with the physical hazards of the slum in such a way that the necessary "watchful care" of the mother "almost inevitably declines."[185] This sounds like a purely environmentalist argument, but it is immediately followed by the statement that "the influence of the elementary school" has been "raising the standards" of working-class mothers and increasing their "parental responsibility."[186]

The slum mother is devoted but irresponsible; she is prevented by her circumstances from providing proper care but can be influenced by the school to provide it anyway, thus transcending her circumstances by act of will. The closest we can come to a coherent argument here is to posit a mother whose circumstances cause character defects reversible by moral means, without change in her circumstances. Is it the slum mother's "standards" that are to blame, or is it her environment? Or is it both, in an endless causal loop?

Similar confusion as to the importance of environmental and personal factors sometimes led the Webbs, like Edwin Chadwick and Charles Booth, to make significantly different claims in different contexts. Perhaps the most striking instance of this can be seen in *The Prevention of Destitution*, written to create publicity for the recommendations of the Minority Report of the Edwardian Royal Commission. The Webbs present a largely environmentalist view of the causes of extreme poverty:

> As a matter of fact, we find five well-trodden paths along one or other of which the vast majority – we might almost say all – of the three or four millions have gone down into the morass of destitution. At least one-third of them are sick or prematurely broken down in strength, and would not be destitute but for their sickness or infirmity. Then we have the army of widows with young children on their hands, who have been suddenly plunged into destitution by the premature death of the breadwinner. Of the total, indeed, one-third are infants and children; who are destitute not on account of any characteristic of their own, but merely because their parents are dead, or for one reason or other unable or unwilling to fulfill their parental obligations. A large contingent have fallen into destitution merely as the result of the infirmities of old age; whilst another large contingent are in the same condition plainly because of their imbecility, lunacy, or congenital feeble-mindedness. Finally, we have to recognise the able-bodied person whose destitution comes obviously from his prolonged inability – it may be incapacity or unwillingness – to find sufficient employment at a sufficient rate of pay to provide him and his dependents with the necessaries of life. All of these roads run in and out of each other, creating what we may accurately describe as a vicious circle round about the morass of destitution...[187]

While this list does suggest that failure of parental support may be due to unwillingness and that unemployment could be due to laziness, the list is predominantly environmentalist. It resembles the list offered by

Edward Devine of the New York COS; in fact the Webbs shortly afterwards recommend Devine's book as further evidence that most poverty is caused not by personal failure but by failure of social institutions.[188] And yet 35 pages later, after a discussion of the eugenics movement, the Webbs sound an entirely different note, indicating that while acquired characteristics may not be inherited in the physical sense:

> there is such a thing as social inheritance, as well as biological. Even if each generation of babies inherited nothing of the physical degeneration of its parents, of which we can by no means feel confident, there is certainly a very potent family tradition and "class atmosphere" of slovenliness, physical self-indulgence, and irresponsibility – it may be actually of "parasitism" – which is quite unmistakably transmitted from one generation to the next. To put the case more generally, we cannot afford to leave unchecked the influences that produce, not death alone, but even more widely slums and disease, physical starvation, mental perversion, demoralisation of character, and actual crime, however convinced we may be that the evil characters acquired in such an environment are not and will not be physically transmitted from parent to child.[189]

What logical relationship might there be between the "five well-trodden paths" to destitution and the catalogue of moral depravity depicted here? The wording of their qualms about inheritance does suggest the possibility that they contemplate Lamarckian, rather than Darwinian, processes at work. Since the Webbs have postulated no mechanism by which "slovenliness" or "self-indulgence" might produce widowhood or old age, we might speculate that these defects are the products, rather than the causes, of destitution. But then surely their transmission to the next generation causes *its* destitution, since these characteristics are said to "produce" slums and disease. We appear to be entering a circular "culture of poverty" loop here, with cause and effect endlessly confounded. The presence of these defects is nowhere demonstrated, merely assumed. The list, moreover, is entirely predictable, on the basis of recapitulationist theory, religious assumptions, and class bias.[190] Despite the generally environmentalist presentation of the "five paths," the Webbs in the end do assume character defect to be present in a way that has not been demonstrated and cannot be logically derived from the factors listed.

They do not seem particularly sympathetic toward these impoverished people, whom they had previously identified as mostly invalids, young children, widows, and the elderly. In the tradition of the public health movement, they make them sound more like plague-carriers than like victims of circumstances beyond their control. This harsh tone – reinforced by the use of the term "parasitism" – completely undermines the import of their previous environmentalist argument.

Apparently evidence about the identity of the destitute was not enough, in itself, to conquer deep-seated assumptions about their character. As increasing accumulations of data from studies like those of Booth, Reeves, and Rowntree indicated ever more forcefully that poverty might very well be the result of circumstances beyond the control of the poor, it became more and more difficult even for theorists like Helen Bosanquet to ignore the evidence. But how could it be reconciled with the well-established tradition of assuming the poor to be morally inferior to others? In our consideration of religious threads in late nineteenth-century poverty theory, we have seen how the notion that the mere physical circumstances of poverty are not very significant, because they can be overcome by sheer force of character and will, makes it possible to downplay the role of forces beyond the control of the poor. Here we have seen attempts to cope with the problem by using environmentalist arguments selectively, by redefining external factors as products of internal ones, and by establishing loops of cultural transmission that confound cause and effect. By methods such as these an uneasy equilibrium could be, at least temporarily, achieved. But the conceptual muddle that this equilibrium required had essentially no resemblance to anything that might reasonably be called science.

8
Three Case Studies in *a priori* Social Science

Perhaps the best way to see how all these varied threads were woven together to produce the fabric of Victorian social science is to examine the approach that poverty theorists took to specific issues concerning the conduct of poor mothers. Three issues aroused not only great interest but an emotional intensity which often led poverty experts to reveal their most fundamental assumptions about the character of slum mothers. These issues were domestic expenses and management, child neglect, and infant life insurance.

Uneconomic woman goes shopping: reckless improvidence in East London

One of the central preoccupations of the poverty and "physical deterioration" debates of the late nineteenth and early twentieth centuries in Britain was the harm done by the "ignorant" and "feckless" slum mother.[1] The slum mother was generally assumed to employ bad child-rearing practices, which we shall consider in our second case study, and to manage her household incompetently, thus making her family less comfortable than their income might otherwise have permitted.

Even relatively sympathetic observers shared this view. Rowntree, for example, argues that "ignorant extravagance," drink, and gambling lower a family's standard of living.[2] He lists as the causes of Secondary Poverty "Drink, betting, and gambling. Ignorant or careless housekeeping and other improvident expenditure," although he immediately adds the reservation that the last of these causes is "often induced by irregularity of income."[3] Rowntree was not sure that this is an independent cause of Secondary Poverty – although he was also unsure that it is not.

Helen Dendy Bosanquet returns to this theme often in her accounts of slum life. She somewhat unsystematically blames maternal mismanagement for many family problems. Sometimes she singles out the inability to budget:

> Besides her ignorance, the London housewife often has to contend with a hopeless incapacity to spend her money properly. It is not that she cannot make good bargains; she may be a first-rate hand at that, and choose and buy as skillfully as any one. But her money, when it all comes in on Saturday, is irresistible to her; she cannot remember that it has to last seven days, and spends as if Sunday were the one day in the week.[4]

Sometimes the problem cited is the inability to understand that good boots will last longer than bad ones and therefore are cheaper in the long run.[5] In other instances Bosanquet blames impulse buying. Items easily obtained on credit soon lose their appeal and are repossessed.[6] Common to all these failings, of course, is the lack of forethought.

In "The Burden of Small Debts," Bosanquet criticizes the slum mother's frequent use of pawnshops and credit, noting that her limited resources would go much farther if she paid cash and avoided interest. She is sacrificing the future for the present.[7] This failure to save she attributes, not to low income, but to lack of foresight and weak impulse control.[8] Bosanquet acknowledges that this behavior does not display the rationality of Economic Man. "The economic man borrows with an eye to future profit; *our* man borrows for present convenience, and shuts his eyes to future loss."[9]

East Londoners who marry young, Bosanquet asserts, display "a childish inability to foresee even the inevitable claims of the future."[10] The assumptions of weak impulse control and lack of foresight on the part of the less developed are key elements, of course, of Social Darwinism. We have seen how E.B. Tylor, the most prominent British anthropologist of his era, used these concepts to explain cannibalism among South Sea islanders. At least Helen Bosanquet's East London housewives, who recklessly spent all their money on Saturday, did not then eat their neighbors. They merely pawned their Sunday clothes.

However excellent the fit between the assumption of primitive improvidence and recapitulationist theory, the notion was widespread before the ascendancy of Social Darwinism. Writing in 1859, Samuel Smiles observed, "There are large numbers of persons among us who, though enjoying sufficient means of comfort and independence, are often found to be barely a day's march ahead of actual want when a time of pressure occurs; and hence a great cause of social helplessness and suffering."[11] The everyday, common sense view of the English Protestant already expected to find lack of thrift and foresight among the poor before the recapitulationist concepts of Social Darwinism had attained their ascendancy over Late Victorian social thought, thus rendering the Social Darwinist view more plausible to those who encountered it.

Economic Man, of course, is one social science concept the recklessly improvident East Ender does not fit; Economic Man is, by definition, rational. Recapitulationist theory presumed that primitive men (of whom the poor are a subset) are less rational than developed men, and that woman is less rational than man. Thus the women of East London could not understand that "good management is cheaper than bad, good feeding than bad..."[12]

Or could they? No matter how obvious it is that the notion of reckless improvidence can be elaborated from recapitulationist social theory and popular religious ideas, the notion could still be a valid interpretation of the observed behavior of the poor. Social theory is supposed to explain human behavior. The social scientist necessarily begins with some idea of what he is studying and why. Ideally, the researcher would elaborate a testable hypothesis from theory and carefully gather information to confirm or disprove the hypothesis. To evaluate the validity of a concept like "reckless improvidence" we must not only understand its origins but also determine whether it is the most plausible explanation of the facts. The "reckless improvidence" theory of domestic management fails this test, however. Focusing on choices rather than constraints, it ignores several important factors in the shopping decisions of East London housewives: low income, slum housing, and constraints of custom and decency.

Purchasing food and coal in small quantities is a case in point. The poor bought coal in small quantities for cooking and heating, in spite of the fact that larger quantities came at a considerable savings. Low-income families never had enough disposable income at any given time to purchase several weeks' worth of coal; even if they had somehow obtained enough money, their small flats did not allow any space to store it.[13] These issues were even more important in the purchase of food. As the Fabian women who studied poor London housewives discovered, "A kitchen with the copper in it is a bad place for keeping food; a kitchen infested with any kind of vermin is also a bad place to keep food; a kitchen which is plagued with flies is equally impossible. The women whose lives are passed in such kitchens may feel that, in spite of the extra expense and waste, daily buying of perishable food is a necessity."[14] The poor simply could not afford to risk having their food eaten by vermin or spoiled by damp and lack of refrigeration.[15] Spoilage was not the only danger of buying food in larger quantities; for the very poor, smaller purchases would actually save money, "because it would keep always-hungry families from eating up the next day's provisions."[16] Foresight, not its absence, dictated "uneconomical" smaller purchases.

Most Victorian and Edwardian poverty theorists never considered sound reasons for patronizing the local shops rather than more distant, cheaper ones: costs of transportation on a low budget, compounded by small children in tow. Chain stores offered cheaper prices, but only for cash, particularly for food and household goods.[17] Even for cash, moreover, buying at the local shops could be "a form of insurance" against future misfortune. Regular cash customers living nearby could hope for credit if they encountered a family emergency like unemployment.[18] This "unwritten rule" was certainly observed in the Salford grocery run by the parents of Robert Roberts. He recalls his mother's comment that "In the hardest times... it was often for me to decide who ate and who didn't."[19]

The use of what Paul Johnson calls "premeditated credit" for the purchase of expensive and seasonal items made a great deal of sense for low-income families and provides evidence of foresight. Schemes like "boot clubs" and tally purchases of coal and winter coats, hire purchase of expensive household items, and Christmas clubs all involved full or partial payment in advance, rather than actual credit.[20] They were not the most economical ways to purchase such goods, but they did insure that small amounts of money scraped together from the weekly budget would actually be applied toward these expenses, rather than absorbed into the food budget or squandered. This involved advance planning for future needs, not a thoughtless descent into debt. Indeed, as Roberts points out, "The very poor never fell into debt; nobody allowed them any credit."[21]

Typically, low-income housewives purchased food and household supplies at a local shop on "tick," the only real credit available to them. Accounts were settled up each Saturday, when workers were customarily paid. Local shopkeepers made individual decisions on whether to permit this privilege, based on the established reputation of each housewife. "A wife (never a husband) would apply humbly for tick on behalf of her family. Then, in our shop, my mother would make an anxious appraisal – economic and social – how many mouths had the woman to feed? Was the husband ailing?"[22] Considerations like health, reputation, and known drinking habits determined a maximum weekly line of credit.[23] Continued maintenance of credit required prompt settlement of the account every Saturday – a far likelier reason for heavy spending than chronic inability to remember that the money had to last a week. In the very poorest homes, where it was least likely that the privilege of tick would be granted, it is probable that little or no food remained in the house on payday. A trip to the shops, now possible, would be imperative. And of course it was on Saturdays that rent was customarily collected; this was also the day when collectors of premiums for insurance policies called, while money was still available to pay.[24]

Another reason for higher spending on Saturday was maintenance of the customary observances of Sunday; it is here that constraints of custom and decency come into play. Many observers have chronicled the importance of Sunday dinner to social respectability in Victorian and Edwardian Britain.[25] A large body of testimony from memoirs and interviews of working-class Londoners indicates that, while often criticized as extravagant, a proper Sunday dinner represented proof of social respectability and a much-anticipated treat in otherwise difficult lives.[26] Almost as essential to respectability were Sunday clothes; "Everywhere Sunday clothes stood as a powerful emblem of status."[27] This is very much in accord with the observation that the era regarded clothes as "a sort of visible character reference."[28] Veblen saw this phenomenon not as an oddity of working-class life but as a general ethos working its way downward from the top; in the view of his "leisure class," "no apparel can be considered elegant, or even decent, if it shows the effect of manual labour on the part of the wearer, in the way of soil or wear."[29] Precisely because they were unnecessary, Sunday clothes constituted a kind of conspicuous consumption – especially for the poor, who could less easily afford them. But then they clearly believed that they could afford loss of personal dignity and reputation even less. It is an axiom of political economy that "Whatever form of expenditure the consumer chooses, or whatever end he seeks in making his choice, has utility to him by virtue of his choice."[30] A decision to spend scarce resources on the maintenance of respectability is not necessarily an irrational choice.

Nor was pawning one's Sunday clothes every week. Although Bosanquet depicts the East London housewife as repeatedly surprised by the weekly pay cycle, less censorious observers portray a careful deployment of resources. Some households pawned the same articles, often Sunday clothes, every Monday and redeemed them, circumstances permitting, every Saturday evening: "Housewives after washday on Monday pledged what clean clothes could be spared until the weekend and returned with cash to buy food. Often they stood in the shop and thanked God that *they* were not as certain others who, having no clothes but what they stood in, had sunk low enough to pawn ashpans, hearth rugs or even the 'pots off the table'."[31] Sunday clothes offered those who could barely afford them a double boost in status; worn on Sunday to demonstrate respectability, they could be pawned on Monday instead of more basic household items.

Resort to the pawnshop did cost money, as Helen Bosanquet and others frequently pointed out. Cash, not credit, was the most economical way to manage. Critics of the poor interpreted the weekly pawning cycle as evidence of lack of foresight, a way of meeting easily foreseeable (but somehow unforeseen) emergencies. Hence Bosanquet's comment that reliance on the pawnshop "is a part of their principle of life, the subordination of future needs to present fancies."[32] They could just as easily have seen it as a deliberate mechanism for controlling cash flow.[33] The housewife was trying to husband her assets, since "In households without storage space, the pawning of best clothes was the only way to make sure they would be properly hung until next needed."[34] Few middle-class observers regarded clothing as an asset, so they recommended that the poor save their money for times of need, rather than use the pawnshop. C.S. Loch observed that the poor consider in their purchases the potential value of an item at the pawnshop, but failed to take into account one advantage of pawning over saving from the perspective of the poor, namely liquidity.[35] Precisely because the poor were seen as impetuous and reckless, the few savings institutions that would accept such small depositors deliberately required considerable advance notice for withdrawal of savings. Pawnshops, on the other hand, were open more hours of the week and offered immediate cash.[36]

Viewed from this perspective, taking into account not just choices but the constraints under which they were made, the shopping and credit decisions of our slum mothers do not appear particularly irrational; nor does it appear that they were made by childlike, primitive housewives oblivious to future need. As Maud Pember Reeves concluded, "It may be, not good management, but the only management under the circumstances."[37]

Spending money on extra food, rather than on Sunday clothes, would better secure the family's physical survival, and buying more costly special foods for Sunday dinner conflicted with optimal nutritional standards for a low-income family. Rowntree said as much when he indicated that to maintain "mere physical efficiency" a very low-income family must avoid "luxuries of any kind."[38] Yet the desire for social respectability – or for that matter, for luxurious treats – was hardly confined to the lower classes of Victorian society. (Unemployed workers in the 1930s were widely criticized for purchasing tea, jam, and white bread on the dole. Switching to plainer, more nourishing food would be more sensible, Orwell said, but "no ordinary human being is ever going to do such a thing."[39]) Insisting on the cheapest possible foods as the constituents of a subsistence diet ignores the fact that certain foods are customary in a given culture and therefore necessary to maintain a family's self-respect and social relationships, if not its "physical efficiency."[40]

East End housewives did not and could not make all of their purchasing decisions with a purely rational focus on efficiency and physical survival, to the exclusion of pleasure or psychic needs. No one does. But a careful examination of the available evidence does not support the idea that they were significantly more irrational or incapable of planning ahead than others. They appear to have done about as well as might be expected under difficult circumstances. If those circumstances are ignored, however, an observer already predisposed to see them as childish, ignorant, impulsive, and oblivious to the future can easily find ways to interpret their behavior as confirmation.

Rowntree, having postulated "ignorant extravagance" as part of the problem, experienced second thoughts about the notion: "The inquiry, it is true, has shown that the money available for the purchase of food is not always spent in the most economical way, but the fact remains that unless an unreasonably stringent diet be adopted, the means to purchase a sufficient supply of nourishing food are not possessed by the labourers and their families."[41]

Resting in the daytime: negligent slum mothers in the Slough of Despond

Samuel Smiles, ever prepared to offer the era's common sense view, emphasized the importance of good mothering in fashioning good people:

> Between childhood and manhood how incalculable is the mischief which ignorance in the home has the power to cause! Between the drawing of the first breath and the last, how vast is the moral suffering and disease occasioned by incompetent mothers and nurses!

Commit a child to the care of a worthless, ignorant woman, and no culture in the after-life will remedy the evil you have done.[42]

In his view, the high rate of child mortality could only be due to "ignorance of the natural laws, ignorance of the human constitution, and ignorance of the uses of pure air, pure water, and the art of preparing and administering wholesome food."[43] (Smiles offers no comment about the practical difficulties of obtaining such items in the areas where child mortality was highest.) He was hardly alone in this perspective. Similar concerns moved Harriet Martineau to write *Household Education*, a manual on the rational care of children providing guidance in matters of proper diet, proper dress, ventilation, and other issues of child-rearing.[44] Martineau was herself both unmarried and childless.

Jeremy Bentham, also childless, was aware of the higher rate of infant mortality among the poor but attributed it to malnutrition of both mother and child due to poverty; it was to alleviate this problem, rather than to correct maternal mistakes, that he recommended providing for destitute families in his proposed workhouses.[45] By the middle of the nineteenth century, however, the serious doubts about the competence of poor mothers expressed by Samuel Smiles had become quite general. This concern is a very strong theme in the writings of several of our poverty experts and in the testimony of numerous witnesses before the Edwardian Royal Commission.

Thus Helen Bosanquet, for example, blamed the high rate of infant mortality in Shoreditch on the infants' "pleasure-loving" mothers who take them "out at night in all weathers." Exposure to "sudden changes of temperature" caused them to die of bronchitis.[46] Likewise the Minority Report of the Edwardian Royal Commission, largely written by the Webbs, recommended that all mothers receiving public assistance also receive supervision and instruction in child care, to ensure that maternal ignorance will not result in the deaths of their infants and children. The "mothers are, in the great majority of cases, extraordinarily ignorant on these points..."[47] The same Report, ironically, had earlier commented on the "starvation out-relief" on which these families were subsisting, and recommended that the payments be increased.[48]

Not all observers were convinced that maternal ignorance was to blame for the malnutrition of the young. General William Booth of the Salvation Army was uncompromising: "The bitter poverty of the poor compels them to leave their children half fed."[49] Helen Bosanquet did not agree. "[C]hildren look sickly for many other reasons than lack of food; and where they really are insufficiently nourished, it is more often from the ignorance of the parents than their poverty."[50] And again: "Improper feeding is a far more potent cause of starvation among the children of the poor than insufficient feeding, and if the benevolent people who every winter flood the East with soup would instead devise some way of teaching the women simple cooking and the elementary laws of health they would soon see better results from their work."[51]

The Minority Report of the Edwardian Royal Commission complained that the existing authorities lack the means to "discover a large amount of the destitution that exists among children in the great towns," failing "even in the matter of actual inadequacy of food, so that the powers entrusted to the Boards of Guardians for the prosecution of cruel or neglectful parents are hardly ever put in force, and many thousands of children are, for lack of the necessaries of life, growing up stunted, debilitated and diseased."[52] This wording implies that starvation is due not to low income but to "cruel or neglectful" parenting. Elsewhere the Webbs argued for school meals to remedy the malnutrition of the poorer students, to which "inadequate income" contributes in many cases but for which "careless mothering" is often to blame.[53]

The ignorance and carelessness of poor mothers explains the "improper feeding" of their children. Helen Bosanquet, for example, relates with approval a female slum doctor's campaign to help poor children by educating their mothers:

> being a doctor she knew that a chief trouble was inappropriate food. She arranged, therefore, to go round to several of the "mothers' meetings" in our district, and gave the mothers simple, clear advice as to the proper way of feeding and treating babies and young children; in this way going straight to the root of one of the principal causes of mischief amongst the poor.[54]

Elsewhere Bosanquet blames parental selfishness for inappropriate feeding. The children are given an "unsuitable diet" because "their needs have to conform to the taste of the parents, and often with disastrous results."[55] In some instances, Bosanquet blames fecklessness, opposing soup kitchens and school meals on the grounds that they encourage maternal neglect of children. Relying on them, a mother "cheerfully turns them loose upon the world in the confidence that they will pick a meal up somewhere."[56] The poor mothers of the East End are impulsively "pleasure-loving," ignorant, selfish, and feckless. These are, of course, the canonical attributes of savages.

Concerns about inappropriate feeding sparked the campaigns to influence the child-rearing practices of poor mothers that Ellen Ross so evocatively labels the "oatmeal wars."[57] A variety of "experts" from the ranks of physicians, visiting nurses, COS visitors, and infant welfare clinics worked to promote "poverty foods like puddings, oatmeal, rice, and macaroni," meeting with little success.[58] One difficulty in persuading slum dwellers to serve their children oatmeal rather than the customary bread breakfast was custom. While oatmeal was without question cheaper and more nourishing than white bread, it was also unfamiliar. "Food-ways," as Jack Goody notes, are often "the most conservative aspects of culture."[59] He does not mention, although any experienced mother would, that in matters of food the conservatism of adults is as nothing to the conservatism of small children. In Britain it had long been true that oatmeal was a customary food only in Scotland and in "the upland zones of the north and west of England;" in the south and east, including London, it had the status of a foreign (Scottish) food.[60] Samuel Johnson, that quintessential Londoner, regarded oats as "suitable only for feeding horses."[61]

Unfamiliarity was only one reason for the unwillingness of slum mothers to adopt oatmeal; another, and perhaps greater, reason was the manifold difficulties of preparing oatmeal in the conditions of a slum kitchen. Investigators sent into Lambeth homes by the Fabian Women's Group learned why nutrition campaigners had failed convert "the hard-worked mothers of families" to their "gospel of porridge."[62] The long cooking time of oatmeal required not only much tending by busy mothers with small children to supervise and keep away from the stove or grate, but also an amount of fuel that made preparation expensive. The children found oatmeal distasteful without considerable milk and sugar, which the family budget would not permit. Oatmeal tended to burn in the thin, worn, and patched pots of a slum kitchen. The pots, moreover, often smelled of fish or onions and imparted an undesirable taste to oatmeal. Many slum children, therefore, refused to eat it. The household budget could ill afford food that undernourished children would not eat.[63]

The experts also criticized East London mothers for feeding their children so little milk, assuming that they were ignorant of its nutritional value. Milk, however nutritious, presented low-income families with many problems. In the early Victorian period, "Milk was a dangerous drink even when fresh" because of tuberculosis, and it was often adulterated.[64] By the late Victorian period these difficulties had lessened, but the freshness of milk was never certain. No slum kitchen could keep milk fresh, so milk had to be purchased in uneconomic small quantities and consumed promptly. The alternative, of course, was canned milk, which at least started out unspoiled and remained fresh until opened. (Once opened, of course, unused canned milk required proper storage as well.) By the 1860s canned condensed milk had become a common item in the British diet, thanks to improvements in processing and distribution.[65] Canned milk, usually sweetened skim, was generally used in tea and was not a suitable food for infants.[66] But fresh milk, which was more nutritious (if impossible to keep fresh without refrigeration of any kind), was also considerably more expensive. The Fabian Women's study estimated the cost of a daily quart of fresh milk for a young child at just over 2 shillings per week, out of a total family food budget of 8 to 9 shillings. Their conclusion: "The reason why infants do not get milk is the reason why they do not get good housing or comfortable clothing – it is too expensive."[67]

The poverty experts did not, for the most part, agree. Jane Lewis finds that most of the witnesses before the Inter-departmental Committee on Physical Deterioration of 1904 attributed the inadequate use of milk and the use of canned, rather than fresh, milk to maternal ignorance. On those rare occasions "when a witness indicated that poverty rather than ignorance might be the reason for the use of canned milk, for example, the point was never pursued."[68] Beatrice Webb apparently accepted expert witness testimony before the Edwardian Royal Commission that maternal ignorance was the major cause of the inadequate diets of poor children. The Minority Report lauded the efforts of some local Health Authorities to provide subsidized supplies of fresh milk to poor families with infants and small children:

> the special interest of the "milk dispensary" to the sanitarian is the personal supervision which it enables the Medical Officer of Health to exercise over these ailing babies. At Finsbury the supply of the milk is made conditional on the babies being brought regularly for inspection, accurate weighing, and hygienic advice. Those who cannot be brought are visited in their homes.[69]

The chief function of the milk dispensary is to dispense, not milk, but supervision:

> Here, too, as with the advice given to the mothers by the Health Visitors, the most prominent features of the work are the education of the persons aided, and the stimulus to their sense of responsibility.

When the baby has to be regularly brought to be inspected and weighed, the mother's interest in its physical condition is not allowed to slacken; there is praise and approval if the baby goes on well; there is blame and warning if it sickens. The connection between irregular hours, dirt, carelessness about the food and other forms of neglect, and the ups and downs of the baby's physical development are brought home to the most ignorant and apathetic of mothers.[70]

Poor mothers, the experts agreed, have little interest in the lives of their babies. Despite the general sentimentality of Victorians on the subject of a mother's love, this view does not appear to have been challenged by the Commissioners. They postulate mothers whose "sense of responsibility" must be "stimulated" by professional experts and who will respond to praise or blame from these experts by providing better care. These mothers are themselves children, to be shaped by responsible authorities. The recapitulationist assumptions of the experts and Commissioners are as evident to us as they were invisible to them.

Although the Majority Report admits that poor law benefits for clothing and feeding children are inadequate, it emphasizes the importance of supervising outrelief families. Money is not the sole, or even principal, solution. If authorities doubt "satisfactory conditions in the home can be assured," then "the children should be maintained in a Poor Law institution or an industrial school."[71] It is in this light that we can best interpret the eagerness of Helen Bosanquet, principal author of the Majority Report, to separate the unfortunate Mrs B. from her children.[72]

Since both Reports conceded the inadequacy of income in many homes to purchase sufficient nourishing food, why did they also both emphasize neglect and supervision? For experts and Commissioners, "inappropriate feeding" was but one of a whole set of related maternal defects among the poor – ignorance, irresponsibility, lack of foresight, and laziness. They were concerned that public provision for children might undermine the fragile sense of maternal responsibility. When Octavia Hill opposed provision of school meals for poor children, she complained that "women were standing gossiping or quarreling, dirty and draggled, while we are cooking at school for their children the dinner they should be preparing in the tidy house."[73] Some members of the COS, like Helen Bosanquet, were occasionally more inclined to see school meals as encouraging paternal, rather than maternal, irresponsibility. Octavia Hill and C.S. Loch, however, saw maternal irresponsibility as likelier to be undermined.[74]

Uncoordinated and unsupervised school feeding, the Minority Report suggests, is undermining parental responsibility.[75] Its conclusions on infancy and motherhood are all concerned with advice and supervision for mothers and enforcement of maternal responsibility.[76] (Later, in their history of the English poor laws, the Webbs did not mention parental responsibility as a potential casualty of school meals but did urge them as an antidote to "careless mothering" which, along with ignorance, often results in child malnutrition.)[77] The Report attributes the low survival rate of illegitimate babies upon leaving the Poor Law hospitals to the undermining of the mother's sense of personal responsibility by public provision of maternity services.[78] Their proposed remedy is not the elimination of medical services to the poor, but supervision of mothers after release.[79]

East Londoners themselves do not appear to have worried much about the responsibility of poor mothers. Memoirs and oral histories show that the adults raised by slum mothers were grateful for their mothers' labors and sacrifices in such difficult circumstances.[80] Young and Willmott found Bethnal Greeners of the 1950s to be generally devoted to their mothers. One of their informants, planning a special family party for her mother's eightieth birthday, commented, "My Dad died when I was 14. Mum was a brick. Even if we never had shoes on our feet, we always had good grub... Since we've had a family of our own, we realise how Mum's worked for us in the past." (The mother in question, born in 1876, was raising her children in the Bethnal Green of the Late Victorian/Edwardian era.)[81] Marie Lloyd, the most popular music hall performer of her era and herself a child of the Hoxton slums, generously provided "stout winter boots" and other items to the children of her home district, apparently unconcerned about undermining parental responsibility for their welfare.[82] To the experts and officials of the time, it seemed otherwise. Roberts catalogues the techniques used by Manchester school authorities, including deliberate public humiliation of children and threatened disenfranchisement of their fathers, to dissuade families from taking advantage of school meals.[83] The primary concerns of the authorities were budgetary constraints and parental responsibility, not child nutritional standards.

Poverty experts were concerned not only about feeding practices but also about the general level of care afforded by low-income mothers. In the files of the Massachusetts Society for the Prevention of Cruelty to Children during the late nineteenth and early twentieth centuries, Linda Gordon finds, single mothers and the very poor were much over-represented among "neglectful parents." She attributes this to the lack of privacy in overcrowded slums, misunderstanding of immigrant culture, and the fact that "poverty accounted for a considerable proportion of what maltreatment of children was."[84] MSPCC workers had been trained to watch for dirty clothing, lice, malnutrition, and overcrowding – all to be found in abundance in the slums. These were assumed to be the result of poor childcare practices rather than of bad housing or poverty.[85] What was true in Boston was also true in London. A sympathetic slum doctor, Edward Berdoe, defended the mothers of his district against the accusation that they neglect their children, while conceding that they are often "woefully ignorant, horribly dirty and indolent…"[86]

Other observers were even less charitable. Lewis found abundant evidence that most social policy makers believed working-class and poor mothers did not care much about their children.[87] The Minority Report of the Royal Commission, in advocating supervision of poor mothers by the Local Health Authority, saw such supervision as having a "humanising and educational character." "The poverty-stricken mother, tempted to regard the newly-born infant only as an additional burden, finds herself reminded of the importance of the child's life, finds its welfare a matter of interest to the visitor, and finds herself gradually acquiring a higher standard of child-rearing."[88]

This brief passage compresses strong recapitulationist and religious feeling. The childlike and primitive poor mother needs a "humanising" influence, an adult middle-class authority, to protect her from temptation and to remind her of the importance of her own child. With this guidance, she can rise to "a higher standard" of childcare. The passage does not explain why this mother feels so little attachment to her own child, nor does it explain how the home health visitors – themselves generally unmarried and childless – have acquired such superior child-rearing knowledge.[89] The assumption was a common one. Young and Willmott found some remaining tension between the "expert knowledge" of welfare service clinics and the advice of grandmothers in the Bethnal Green of the 1950s. Clinic workers asserted expertise superior to that of the young mother's Mum, yet from the family's point of view "The daughter's very existence demonstrates that she knows what she is talking about."[90]

The Minority might have taken a different view. Its Report acknowledges that the "less eligibility" principle of the Victorian Poor Law is useless, since "the condition of the lowest grade of independent labourers is unfortunately one of such inadequacy of food and clothing and such absence of other necessities of life that it has been found, in practice, impossible to make the conditions of Poor Law relief 'less eligible'."[91] In view of this, and of the observed fact that infant survival rates and the heights of London school children were directly correlated with family income, why invoke negligent mothering?[92] Perhaps because Victorian poverty experts believed they saw evidence of this negligence everywhere.

English Puritan tradition attributed idleness and poverty to ignorance and sin. Hence the guilt of Bunyan's Christian, who had so far "indulged the flesh" as to "sleep in the day time!"[93] Malthus judged "the acknowledged indolence of man" too strong to be overcome by anything other than the threat of starvation.[94] By the late Victorian era, while a general human disposition to idleness was still acknowledged, the idleness of the poor had become a subject of greater interest. Veblen, of course, dissented: the rich are a bad influence on others because "the characteristic feature of leisure-class life is a conspicuous exemption from all useful employment."[95] Helen Bosanquet voiced the view more common among poverty experts when she claimed that many applicants for public relief "are suffering from sheer laziness."[96] Beatrice Webb shared this concern. She worried that health insurance for workers would encourage malingering.[97] Charles Booth even considered laziness a plausible cause of prostitution; the prostitute "merely seeks her living in the easiest way open to her."[98] More recent researchers like Susan Kent and Judith Walkowitz have paid considerably more attention to the limited opportunities "open" to the capital's prostitutes, stressing constraints rather than laziness in their interpretations.[99]

Octavia Hill, a champion of sanitary reform, endeavored to rouse her tenants and people like them "from the lethargy and indolent habits into which they have fallen."[100] She deduced these defects from the condition of the dwellings of the poor, acknowledging, however, the deficiencies of the buildings: "The people's homes are bad, partly because they are badly built and arranged; they are tenfold worse because the tenants' habits and lives are what they are."[101] Bad as tenement conditions might be, it is the behavior of the occupants that makes them slums. Hill insisted that if slum-dwellers were moved to "healthy and commodious homes" without the training required to "make them fit" for decent housing, they would merely "pollute and destroy them."[102] Left to their own devices, tenants were inclined to idleness and squalor, rather than to industry and order.

Critics of the poor particularly disliked gossip. "Pauper women are all gossips," testified a witness before the Royal Commission of 1832; "the men all go to the ale-house..."[103] As we have seen, Octavia Hill derided mothers who gossip while others prepare school meals for their children. Helen Bosanquet inclined to the same view. Describing the squalor of slum life, she noted that a working mother claims to have "'no time' to keep home and children clean." "More likely she spends long hours gossiping with like-minded neighbors – shrill, futile gossip, which serves to pass the time as well as the afternoon calls of their wealthier sisters."[104] Bosanquet, here as elsewhere, appears equally scornful of women above and below her. Her full attention, however, is devoted to the failings of the poor rather than of the rich. Less censorious observers have found value in neighborhood gossip. Ellen Ross, chronicler of East London motherhood, sees gossip as a lifeline of information and help for low-income women. Roberts recalls it as playing "a vital role in a milieu where many, through lack of education, relied entirely on the spoken word."[105] Such utility was not apparent to contemporary poverty experts, who viewed it as a waste of time.

The filth of the slum environment was evident to all observers; most blamed it on the residents. And of course, by custom, cleaning was primarily a woman's responsibility. The Public Health Movement associated dirt with disease, cleanliness with morality, and disease with immorality. We see all of these associations in commentary about the dirtiness of slum residents. General William Booth celebrated the work of the Salvation Army's "Slum Sisters" among the poor: "To form an idea of the immense amount of good, temporal and spiritual, which the Slum Sister is doing: you need to follow them into the kennels where they live, preaching the Gospel with the mop and the scrubbing brush, and driving out the devil with soap and water."[106] Octavia Hill, too, sought to lead her tenants to spiritual growth through sanitation. Training girls to scrub the hallways and learn "habits of cleanliness," she aspired "where God gives me authority" to lead them "to arise and cast out the sin..."[107] In her struggle to civilize the denizens of a new court of houses that came under her management in 1869, Hill emphasized their personal slovenliness, although the buildings lacked running water.[108] Hill always insisted that without proper training, improvements in housing were useless.[109] She could logically have asserted precisely the converse.

Slum mothers had to do a great deal of heavy manual labor in coping with tasks like laundry and cleaning without benefit, in most cases, of convenient running water. It is probably difficult for most modern housekeepers to imagine quite how much work was involved. Ross provides estimates from knowledgeable contemporary sources:

> A speaker at a British Nurses' Association meeting in 1891 calculated that a woman living in a third-story flat who carried water and slops up and down from a ground-floor tap was doing "the equivalent

of a day labourer's work." A Manchester City Council survey in 1918 concluded that it took close to ten hours per week (much of it very heavy labor indeed) to do the laundry of a family of just five people.[110]

The conjunction of illness, dirt, and maternal care brought all of the concerns of the Public Health Movement into sharp relief. Helen Bosanquet was sure that the high infant death rate in the poorer parts of London was caused by bad mothering – inappropriate feeding and taking babies outdoors in all weather. Had she bothered to ask public health officials, she would have learned that the principal cause of infant mortality in Late Victorian Britain, as in the Third World today, was infant diarrhea. Unsatisfactory sanitation, then as now, was to blame.[111] The Chief Medical Officer to the Local Government Board pointed to "bad sanitary arrangements," especially ashpits and midden privies, as sources of infection. By 1900 such arrangements were most common, of course, in slum neighborhoods.[112] In rural areas, where they were also found, they were considerably less dangerous due to low population density. Only after 1909, as water closets replaced privies, did urban infant mortality begin to fall significantly.[113] Edwardian poverty experts, however, had little doubt that maternal negligence was primarily to blame.[114]

Poverty experts also blamed mothers for the prevalent diseases of malnutrition. As we have seen, the experts assumed that "inappropriate feeding," rather than starvation, was at fault. Rickets was especially common in slum children. The City of Westminster Health Society found in 1912–1913 that 19 per cent of the infants and nearly 25 per cent of the children aged one to two attending their clinic in Soho were affected.[115] The cause of rickets was not well understood; medical opinion was divided as to whether infection or nutritional deficiency induced the bony deformities.[116] We now know that rickets is the result of a deficiency of Vitamin D. The best sources of Vitamin D then available in the British diet were eggs and liver, both in short supply in the diets of poor London children. The other source – sunlight – was also limited in this smoggy northern city.

Household accidents also caused childhood death and disability. Open fires in grates, pots of boiling water, steep dark staircases, and unscreened windows tempted and threatened small children in slum housing, straining the resources of their overworked mothers and distracted older siblings.[117] Negligent parenting, however, was the preferred explanation of disabilities due to rickets and accidents. Hence

Helen Bosanquet's complaint that "apart from the fact that there is hardly a child in East London which gets a fair start into life without its digestive organs being impaired, there are great numbers of them who are hopelessly crippled for life by sheer neglect."[118] Adding insult to injury, Bosanquet adds that East End mothers do not mind their children being crippled, because they are attracted to the shiny new surgical appliances on offer from the Poor Law hospital. "Steel and leather are but poor substitutes for bone and muscle, but their very ingenuity recommends them, and gives their owner – at least while they are new – a sense of pride which they would never have felt in an ordinary human limb. And so the pathetic spectacle goes on of mothers ruining their children's lives through almost brutal ignorance and care-lessness, while our highest science and skill is taxed to apply inadequate remedies."[119] (Among other things, this passage brings instantly to mind the image of childlike savages transfixed by the sight of shiny trinkets.) Destitute families given restorative food for invalids, Bernard Bosanquet asserted, must be supervised to make sure that the food actually reaches its intended recipient.[120] Dr Edward Berdoe, who actu-ally attended the sickbed of many a child in East London, argued force-fully that their mothers would do without in order to provide proper nourishment for them, making great sacrifices and nursing them devotedly.[121]

Helen Bosanquet was also quick to diagnose maternal malpractice as the root of the character failings she found in children who had survived a slum childhood without apparent physical disability. Slum mothers, in her view, displayed "an entire absence of all method, patience, and discipline, combined with alternations of excessive harsh-ness and indulgence," which inevitably produced selfish and unprincipled adults.[122] Young children of the slums were "permitted to indulge every freakish fancy which comes into their heads," leading inevitably to an undisciplined character.[123] In the cramped quarters of slum housing, over-worked mothers are unlikely to have given young children free rein. The evidence suggests that slum toddlers were subject to a great deal of restraint, lest their high spirits endanger them or the household.[124] Bosan-quet's view probably derives not from her observation of slum life but from her assumptions about the character failings of the poor. Like the lunatic only children Samuel Smiles described, her East Enders must have had early experiences of a certain kind to account for their presumed character failings. Therefore, they have had them.

In their review of an ethnographic study of child mortality in a Brazilian shanty-town, Lassalle and O'Dougherty remark that its author furthers the case for maternal negligence as decisive by carefully ignoring all other contributing factors, thus leaving mothers as "the sole agents endangering the family's survival."[125] In the same way, Late Victorian and Edwardian social science focused relentlessly on the alleged failings of slum mothers, ignoring or minimizing constraints of income, housing, and sanitation on the lives of their children. Steeped in a tradition that called the character of the poor mother into question, poverty experts blamed mothers entirely or in part for most of their children's problems. Living in a culture that regarded prosperity as the likely consequence of virtue and industry, they expected vice and laziness in the poor. In the tradition of the Public Health Movement, they regarded illness as possibly the wages of sin, with dirt its inevitable companion. The slums, in their view, had ample dirt and illness and, therefore, sin. Versed in recapitulationist social science, they interpreted the customary behavior of the poor as childish, primitive, and ignorant. Each assumption reinforced the others, lending such plausibility to their interpretations that no justification seemed necessary. This understanding may prepare the reader for the third of our case studies, the furor over infant life insurance.

Economic woman liquidates an asset: the infant life insurance scares

Certain that poor mothers were negligent and cared little for their children, medical practitioners and poverty experts were concerned about the practice of insuring the lives of infants. Could high infant mortality among the poor mean that they were killing their children to collect on their insurance? Parliament stepped in, forbidding Friendly Societies to insure the lives of children under six (in 1846) and limiting the amount of insurance they could sell on children under the age of ten (in 1850).[126] Cycles of relaxed and tightened restrictions reflected renewed concerns about the practice. "Doctors, coroners and judges concurred that infant life insurance put temptation in the path of the poor."[127] The concept of temptation, as we have seen, carries with it religious undertones. Its use, therefore, often indicates implicit motivational modeling that today's social science would question.

Most of the lower working class and the poor, of course, were not members of Friendly Societies. They tended to purchase this coverage from the newer Industrial Assurance Companies, who typically sent agents around every Saturday to collect small premiums.[128] The practice continued to receive periodic scrutiny and restriction as new alarms were raised. A *Lancet* editorial of 1861 chronicles the history of infant-icide, asserting that "this atrocity is far from being rare in Great Britain."[129] After enumerating the dead infants found in London from 1856 to 1861 (about 300), the author reports a conversation with the clerk of the Manchester Union. Parents had allowed their baby to starve, he asserted, so they could collect insurance money from ten different burial clubs. Six previous siblings had preceded it to an early grave. A coroner's jury had acquitted the parents of murder, much to the clerk's disgust. He observed that the family need only have spent a tiny portion of the insurance money on the funeral, pocketing the rest. Assuming without evidence that this horrifying couple has actually murdered seven children, the editorialist proceeds to the sweeping conclusion that "Instances of this kind are innumerable."[130]

Three hundred infants found dead represent tragedy but not the crime under discussion, since abandoning a dead or dying infant pre-cludes collecting on its insurance. There is, of course, a thematic rele-vance, however: the poor discard their children. Like Helen Bosanquet, whose conversation with one coroner led her to assert widespread fatality from inappropriate feeding, the *Lancet*'s author makes a flying leap from anecdote to generalization.

The *Lancet* revisited this subject two weeks later. "Premiums for Infant-icide" makes further allegations: "The legislative restrictions which fol-lowed the public scandal caused by many murders obviously due to the excited cupidity of parents who had entered their children in a number of burial clubs, have not been sufficient to check the evil. It exists now in a very palpable and horrible degree."[131] From this sensational claim the author then retreats slightly. "There is no charge of direct and indi-vidual infanticide substantiated by this statement; but it would appear that from the moment the death of a child is systematically contem-plated and provided for it is likely to be neglected or less anxiously watched, and its chances of life are diminished." What is to be done? "There is only one apparent remedy for this large and perpetually active cause of infantile mortality: it is the abolition of burial clubs."[132] Although the author is unsure whether murder or negligence is the problem, he is certain that infant life insurance kills.

He was not alone. In a paper read to the National Association for the Promotion of Social Science in 1864, Dr J.I. Ikin discussed high infant mortality in the larger towns and cities. As to the role of "death clubs" he notes that "the evidence is not so strong;" however, "From my own experience at the Women and Children's Hospital, I have no hesitation in stating that the system of insuring children's lives is much abused, and great carelessness, if not positive crime, is committed."[133] Whatever the evidence, he concludes, insuring infant lives should be made illegal.

General William Booth, generally sympathetic to the poor, also believed them capable of killing their children for money. He, too, required very little evidence to convince him that many did so. "When an English judge tells us, as Mr. Justice Wills did the other day, that there were any number of parents who would kill their children for a few pounds' insurance money, we can form some idea of the horrors of the existence into which many of the children of this highly favoured land are ushered at their birth."[134] General Booth, as was his custom, saw this as an indictment of society rather than of the poor. Yet he did not doubt either that the phenomenon existed or that the deaths were deliberately caused.

The power of this belief reached into the Minority Report of the Edwardian Royal Commission. Complaining that mothers who receive public assistance are not supervised to prevent inappropriate feeding and other forms of maternal malfeasance, the Minority laments: "they may even insure their little ones with the Industrial Insurance Companies, and so use some of the Guardians' Outdoor Relief money thus hideously to speculate in death..."[135] The choice of the word "speculate" implies that neglect, not murder, will occur. It also implies, logically, that it is possible to turn a profit on the child's death.

Dr Edward Berdoe's extensive practice in East London made him familiar with slum families. He was also one of the few public defenders of the poor. In 1891, he indignantly denied that infanticide for insurance money was common. "The implications on working people which the proposal to limit the insurance of their children's lives suggests are certainly not justified by the facts."[136] Berdoe was particularly indignant that this suspicion caused coroners to question bereaved parents accusingly. "It is very hard, indeed, to see how, in nine hundred and ninety-nine cases out of a thousand, a family could make any profit whatever from the insurance money on a dead child."[137] Puzzled by the frequent accusations of infanticide for profit, Berdoe concluded that they must result from the common belief that poor mothers do not care about their children. In Berdoe's experience, slum mothers nurse their sick children devotedly and will sacrifice anything on their behalf: "The member of the family who, if anyone, has to be stinted, is the mother. I have very rarely indeed known a sick child to want for anything within her means, even if she have to go without necessaries for herself." Far from speculating in infant death, "She is as regular in calling for the medicine, as minute in her attention to the different

symptoms as they arise, and as emphatic in making the doctor understand and duly appreciate them, as though she were pecuniarily interested in saving her child's life, instead of being, as is charged, anxious
to finger the gold promised by the death-club."[138]

Berdoe's brief in defense of poor mothers is particularly compelling
because he is by no means uncritical of the poor in general or of poor
mothers in particular. "I could not give the fathers by any means so
good a character in this respect as I am proud to give the mothers," he
quickly adds. Berdoe here appears to accuse "the beery and self-indulgent
pauper male parent" merely of being "careless enough of his family,"
not of murdering them.[139] Over the course of the article he discusses
the "shiftlessness" and ignorance of slum mothers, particularly of the
young ones. But he will not see them accused of not caring for their
children, much less of murdering them.

Berdoe's defense of the slum mother raises the same issues as the contention of witnesses before the 1832 Royal Commission that unprincipled
pauper women were producing bastards (or extra children) for profit.
Is this economic model an accurate picture of the motivation of the
actors? And, for that matter, was it even possible to make a profit? Nearly
two decades later, however, we still find the Minority Report of the
Edwardian Royal Commission concerned about "speculation" in infant
death. Similar objections, it may be recalled, were raised in Parliament
in the 1830s about the economic model of bastardy. Then, too, they
were largely ignored.

We have already seen just how fragile the bond between poor mothers
and their children was assumed to be. The very existence of foundling
hospitals, Samuel Smiles felt, encouraged the poor to abandon their
children and avoid the expense of raising them.[140] The COS strongly
concurred – hence their opposition to Dr Barnardo's Homes.[141]
Interestingly enough, the archives of workhouses and industrial schools
show that children surrendered to the authorities during family crises
were often retrieved by their families once those crises had passed.[142]
This practice would make no sense, of course, had their parents merely
wanted to rid themselves of the expense and trouble of caring for
them.

If Dr Berdoe was correct that the insurance was used for burial expenses,
rather than for profit, then why did families living so close to the margin
set aside money out of tight budgets to pay for it? Rowntree was quite
explicit in naming both "sick clubs" and "funeral clubs" among the
expenditures that could not be afforded in the budgets of many York
laborers if they wished to avoid Secondary Poverty and maintain "mere

physical efficiency."[143] Maud Pember Reeves would certainly have agreed. The food budget was the only elastic item in the budget of very poor families, so the money for burial insurance would have been better spent on raising the nutritional standards of the children, thus improving their health.[144] While she regretted the practice, she did not criticize the families. She knew why they made this choice – to avoid the horrors of a pauper burial.

> If they decide not to insure, and they lose a child, the question resolves itself into one of borrowing the sum necessary to pay the funeral expenses, or of undergoing the disgrace of a pauper funeral. The pauper funeral carries with it the pauperization of the father of the child – a humiliation which adds disgrace to the natural grief of the parents. More than that, they declare that the pauper funeral is wanting in dignity and in respect to their dead.[145]

It is not difficult to understand why families fought so hard to avoid burial on the parish, which involved no ceremony and interment in a common grave.[146] Families who accepted a pauper funeral were penalized by disenfranchisement and by social disgrace, "a stigma not only on the dead, but on those living who could not pay for a more becoming interment."[147] Indeed, as Dr Berdoe pointed out, "the taint [of pauperism] clings to the third and fourth generation."[148] To prevent this, uninsured families were known to sell off all of their belongings and to cut back expenditure on food, thus raising the chance that further funerals would follow.[149] The supreme irony here is that the Victorian poor law was intentionally stigmatizing. The workhouse test "was meant to be cruel – not in terms of food, or physical conditions, or arduous labor, but conceptually, the very idea of it being shameful and disgraceful."[150] Pauper burials were what they were in order to discourage the poor from using them, yet the experts considered the motives of parents who turned to insurance in order to avoid burial on the parish suspect.

Another irony is the inability of middle-class observers to recognize lower-class thrift when they saw it. The same critics who frequently remarked on the failure of the poor to save for old age assumed evil motives for their purchase of burial insurance for their children.[151] Dr Berdoe understood the function of the insurance and recognized the failure of others to see it for what it was. "It is most unfortunate that this prejudice against infant life assurance has arisen. The provident habits of the working classes ought to be encouraged, and any legislation tending to deter them from such habits should be founded on very sure ground."[152] Even Bentham, whose proposals gave rise to the workhouse test, was willing to allow burial expenses to the working poor outside the house, along with medical and obstetrical aid, when they were necessary.[153] The framers and enforcers of the Victorian poor law, however, saw the matter differently, insisting on full pauper status even for poor law medical assistance until 1885 and for poor law burials throughout our period.

As sociologist Erving Goffman observes, "By definition ... we believe the person with a stigma is not quite human."[154] Veblen argued that property confers status and its lack damages status, both in society's eyes and in the individual's. "Only individuals with an aberrant temperament can in the long run retain their self-esteem in the face of the disesteem of their fellows."[155] Small wonder, then, that poor families would go to great lengths to avoid a deliberately stigmatizing poor law burial. Parents felt that "a decent funeral was the only thing left to offer the dead child."[156] For this reason, as well as to avoid social disgrace, families would even go into debt. In the context of Victorian society, minimal private funerals were nearly as traumatic as poor law burial. The Parliamentary Act of 1870 set limits on child death benefits so low that even insured low-income families had to borrow and pawn to pay for a decent funeral.[157] Of course the general Victorian taste for ostentatious funerals was well known to Veblen and analyzed under the heading of "conspicuous consumption," although he noted society's "tabu on luxuries" for the poor.[158] Maud Pember Reeves carefully calculated the cost of a minimal private funeral for a young child at more than the weekly income of most East End families. This made insurance essential. The policies were written, not for a family, but for each child separately. Given the tight food budgets of her study population, this money "as far as the welfare of the children themselves go, might as well be thrown into the sea."[159] The benefit levels set by law to prevent infanticide were so small that more money had to be found somehow to pay for a decent funeral. While most of the premium money was wasted, "The small proportion which does come to them is swallowed up in a burial, and no one but the undertaker is the better for it.[160]

One explanation for the persistent belief in "speculation in death" may be the observed "fatalism" of poor mothers who had, as many did, lost several children. Doctors and coroners often remarked on it. Since no concept of clinical depression existed in the nineteenth century, obvious symptoms of depression might be interpreted as indifference.

Ellen Ross found in her study of East London memoirs that "Illness and depression were strikingly common in women whose children had died, though it is impossible to separate the grief from the exhaustion and semistarvation of the weeks of the child's illness or from injuries of pregnancy and childbirth as precipitating causes."[161] A bereaved mother who is silent and withdrawn, unable to get out of bed or focus on her daily tasks, would today be diagnosed as clinically depressed and in need of medical care. The Victorian poverty experts, however, would likely have seen her as apathetic, lazy, and indifferent to her remaining children. And a coroner concerned about infant life insurance might well see her as unemotional at the death of her child, perhaps even as the cause of it.

Reflections on the three case studies

The Ignoble Savage, plaything of her appetites and incapable of planning, lacks the rationality of the model of Economic Man. That is why she is such an inept shopper. While late Victorian social scientists usually portrayed the slum mother as Ignoble Savage, they could also, like the members of the 1832 Poor Law Commission, imagine her as Economic Woman – an unemotional calculator who sees her baby as a financial asset. The experts, with few exceptions, used whichever model portrayed the slum mother in a worse light. There is no indication that they were aware of any inconsistency in this regard.

What did remain consistent was the assumption of the moral deficiencies, even depravity, of the poor. Whether she is seen as selling herself on the street to avoid work, wasting money on Sunday dinner, idly gossiping while her children go dirty and unfed, or smothering her baby to collect the insurance, the slum mother is always assumed to act from unworthy motives. She is bad; therefore she does bad things. These social researchers, like the South Seas missionaries who provided field observations for Victorian anthropology, had ventured into hostile territory to find proof of natural depravity, and find it they did.

9
Unanswered Questions, Unasked Questions, and an Experimental Counter-Hypothesis

> The investigator must have in his mind, at any rate in all but the concluding stages of his work, not one hypothesis but many mutually inconsistent hypotheses. To start with a single hypothesis involves bias, which will hamper, if not prevent, the attainment of the very object of investigation, which is to discover new truth. For this reason, the investigator must specially beware of every kind of orthodoxy. The customary categories, in which the ordinary citizen is imprisoned, are exactly those from which the investigator must be perpetually trying to escape.
>
> Sidney and Beatrice Webb, *Methods of Social Study*

We have seen how the strong preconceptions of nineteenth-century poverty researchers shaped their work on the causes of, and appropriate remedies for, "pauperism." Since these researchers tended not to examine their assumptions, they never asked a number of important questions about the poor – questions whose answers would greatly facilitate our understanding of nineteenth-century poverty.

Was heavy drinking really significantly more common among the poor, or was it merely more public?

"To the upper-class visitor or spectator," Abrams has observed, "drink *was* the most visible thing wrong with the poor."[1] The problem was visible, of course, because the poor did most of their drinking in pubs, where they could be observed. Himmelfarb asserts that the role of drink in the problems of the poor was "axiomatic" among Victorians, noting that Charles Booth did not fully agree; he attributed the misery of 14 per cent of "the very poor" and of 13 per cent of "the poor" to a combination of "drink and thriftlessness."[2] Booth recognized the importance of the pub as a social institution in poor neighborhoods. Roberts, an insider, volunteers the opinion that in the Salford slums of his boyhood "Drunkenness was, of course, the major social problem."[3] He appears to feel, however, that drink was the result of poverty, not its cause. "On account of it one saw many a decent family drift down through poverty to total want." Yet, in his view, the poor drank in order to dull the mortal fear that was "the *leitmotif* of their lives."[4]

The poor probably did drink more on average than did the members of higher strata of society, yet we lack hard evidence. Poor drunks were probably likelier than comfortable or wealthy ones to become destitute, to be arrested, or to have their children removed from their homes. The affluent drank less visibly, in clubs and private homes. Without reliable data on the alcohol consumption of all social classes, we cannot be confident that the poor drank more than others.

Did the commitment of the poor to the work ethic really differ from that of members of other social classes?

Our poverty researchers and Poor Law Commissioners believed that it did. Again, however, they simply assumed that the difference existed. George Lansbury strenuously denied this premise, insisting that the poor wanted work, not doles.[5] One of his objections to the work of the Royal Commission on which he served was its excessive attention to the individual failings of the unemployed. These defects, in his view, explained not how many would be unemployed but merely who would be laid off first.[6] Beatrice Webb and William Beveridge raised this point in cross-examination of witnesses before the Royal Commission regarding unemployment.[7] Yet in the Minority Report this perspective is not emphasized, while in the Majority Report it is completely absent.

We have no way to test the commitment of the Victorian poor – or for that matter of any Victorian – to the work ethic. The poverty studies of our own time, however, may if used carefully provide some clues. Contemporary American poverty surveys, invariably based on market models, always include questions about incentives to work.[8] They do not, however, question the *appropriateness* of market models or examine the willingness to work of people who are not poor. In this they follow the established practice of Victorian social science. Comparing American poverty research to European, Korpi emphasizes this point. Regardless of levels of overall unemployment, American and British research focuses narrowly on the work motivation of the poor.[9] What little research exists on the work motivation of all classes, Korpi argues, suggests that the attitude of the poor is no different from anyone else's.[10] Pettigrew, in his survey of social psychological studies on the poor, cites Goodwin's unpublished report for the Manpower Administration of the U.S. Department of Labor: Goodwin found that "the work orientations of both men and women receiving welfare do not differ from those of the non-poor."[11]

Even if a weaker work ethic among the poor could be demonstrated, moreover, social psychology offers an alternative explanation – "learned helplessness." The phenomenon, as Pettigrew notes, has been established experimentally in fish, rats, and humans. In poverty it would operate like this: having learned that "they cannot control most of the highly adverse events in their lives," the poor might then "generalize this lack of control to situations that they could actually influence." Motivational symptoms in the form of "lessened response initiation" – in other words less strenuous efforts to escape from poverty – would result.[12]

None of this demonstrates that the nineteenth-century British poor did not have a weaker commitment to the work ethic than their better-off contemporaries. It does suggest, however, that some caution should be exercised in assuming that they did, much less that this weak commitment caused their poverty. Improved employment prospects in the first year after World War I saw the rates of incarceration for vagrancy, begging, and "sleeping out" plummet in comparison with their levels in 1908.[13] Many of the "work-shy," it would appear, were willing to work given a chance to do so. Finally, as with drink, we must concede that we know at least as little about the work motivation of the better off as we do about the work motivation of the poor.

Did poor mothers actually take less care with their children than better-off mothers did?

Most of our poverty researchers would say yes. Not all of their contemporaries, however, would have agreed. Dr Edward Berdoe insisted that the slum mothers in his practice were as caring as any.[14] Maud Pember Reeves found the slum children in her study to be "on the whole, well brought up as regards manners and cleanliness and behavior," and believed that "All of them were kindly and patiently treated by their mothers."[15] Roberts recalled a lack of kind and patient treatment in the hard-pressed mothers of the slum children with whom he grew up, yet "Despite poverty and appalling surroundings parents brought up their children to be decent, kindly and honourable and often lived long enough to see them occupy a higher place socially than they had ever known themselves: the greatest satisfaction of all."[16]

Even the Webbs, who so insisted on the supervision of poor mothers, also conceded this point: "The working-class woman is as devoted to her children as any other mother."[17] They added, however, with their customary ambivalence, that the conditions of slum housing would "almost inevitably" cause standards of care to decline.

There were truly horrifying parents in the slums of London. They can be found not only in the annals of the COS but in the police and hospital records which Ellen Ross has so effectively mined for information on mothering in "outcast London." It is likely, however, that bad parents among the poor were much likelier to come to the attention of the authorities than the bad parents of other social classes.[18] Once again we are faced with a lack of reliable information on the non-poor population that makes comparison difficult, if not impossible.

Poor mothers had to cope with the drudgery of hauling water up and down the stairs for laundry and cleaning. On average, moreover, they had larger families. It does seem probable that they had less time to spare for the emotional needs of each child. On the other hand, they cared for their children themselves and did not entrust the task to servants or boarding schools. We do not have sufficient evidence to warrant an assumption that poor mothers were less careful than others with their children.

An experimental counter-hypothesis

Edward T. Devine, General Secretary of the COS of the City of New York, opens his report on the causes of poverty with a discussion of the universal assumption of the moral defects of the poor:

> I have come to believe, nevertheless, after some years of careful, candid, and open-minded consideration of the subject, that this entire view of poverty is one which rests upon an unproved and unfounded assumption.[19]

Devine did not doubt that large numbers of morally defective people could be found among the poor – but were these defects the cause of their poverty?

> [T]he burden of proof is upon those who allege, and no charitable society is justified, no public relief agency is justified, in basing its

policies upon the assumption that because these men before us are afflicted in mind or body, therefore either they or their parents have sinned.[20]

Among the many undemonstrated assumptions about the causes of poverty, the most fundamental is that the personal defects of the poor cause their poverty. Embracing the open-mindedness that the Webbs, whether they maintained it or not, argued must underlie social research, let us consider another hypothesis "mutually inconsistent" with the one that they – and the majority of their colleagues – favored: Immoral behavior causes poverty only among people who are economically vulnerable in the first place. For most of the poor, immoral behavior is either a secondary cause of poverty, a result of poverty, or not involved.

A poverty researcher making this assumption would look at different factors from the ones the Victorians chose, emphasizing for example the structure of the unskilled labor market rather than laziness, or the health hazards of slum housing rather than maternal ignorance. This assumption would also suggest different policies, such as supplemental food and better housing, rather than supervision, to lower infant mortality.

Contra-factual arguments are always problematic. One can rarely know why something did not happen. Examining the objections to our counter-hypothesis might, however, help us to understand the overwhelming loyalty of Victorian researchers to the personal defects theory of poverty. Our counter-hypothesis was just as conceivable in the nineteenth century as it is today, yet it was never tested and seldom even considered in the poverty research of the Victorian and Edwardian eras. Although other reasons might well be imagined, four possible explanations will be considered here:

Possibility One: Because it is simply wrong. (Let us call this one the Crank Theory)

Possibility Two: Because it is a novel idea that had not occurred to most people. (Inertia Theory)

Possibility Three: Because this idea was systematically excluded from consideration by powerful players with a vested interest in the existing system. (Conspiracy Theory)

Possibility Four: Because this idea was in conflict with important and highly valued concepts like divine providence and economic fairness. (Comforting Ideas Theory)

Possibility One: the Crank Theory

The case for the personal defects theory is, as Scottish justice would have it, "Not Proven." Outside the cultural perspective of the English-speaking world, this theory has never been dominant. Chinese tradition, for example, holds that widespread poverty is the fault of bad government, not of the poor. [21] If the government fails in its responsibility to provide for the people's livelihood, then people will behave badly because they are poor:

> Only the true scholar is capable of maintaining, without certain means of livelihood, a steadfast heart. As for the multitude, if they have no certain means of livelihood, they surely cannot maintain a steadfast heart. Without a steadfast heart, they are likely to abandon themselves to any and all manner of depravity. If you wait til they have lapsed into crime and then mete out punishment, it is like placing traps for the people.[22]

The experience of other societies refutes many Anglo-American poverty theories. Sweden, Austria, and Germany, for example, offer more generous benefits to unwed mothers and also have lower rates of adolescent pregnancy than the United States and Britain.[23] In his discussion of the allowance system under the Old Poor Law, Marshall points out that "thus far the evidence for the effect of allowances and subsidies on population is largely negative."[24] Child allowance in Canada, research indicates, does not diminish parental responsibility, increase the number of large families, or encourage misuse of the money.[25] Ethnographic studies of India and other developing countries suggest that high fertility may be a rational strategy for coping with high infant and child mortality, rather than a sign of inability to exercise self-control or plan ahead.[26] Even the Bible, as we have seen, offers more passages vouching for the moral superiority of the poor than for their depravity.

None of this, of course, proves Shaw's contention that "the difference between a lady and a flower girl is not how she behaves, but how she's treated."[27] On the other hand, the counter-hypothesis is certainly worth exploring.

Possibility Two: the Inertia Theory

Since the assumption of moral defects in the poor has survived for so long in the face of considerable evidence against it, the role of inertia seems compelling. Making a case for open-minded social investigation, the Webbs reminded their readers: "most people, without being aware of it, would much rather retain their own conclusions than learn anything contrary to them."[28]

Habits of mind are hard to change. In a national American survey of popular attitudes on the causes of poverty conducted in 1975, most respondents chose what most Victorians would undoubtedly have chosen: lack of thrift, lack of effort, loose morals, and drunkenness.[29] To receive help from charitable food banks, the poor must often put up with patronizing advice given to them on the assumption that they are "bad shoppers, poor cooks, ignorant dietitians, and thoughtless eaters."[30] This recalls, of course, our "Uneconomic Woman" of East London, reinforcing the observation that "history can be a potent force even when mythical or untrue."[31] We have seen how Charles Murray still found analysis of reproduction among the poor based on the model of Economic Couple compelling in 1984, as did many of his readers. Long-held preconceptions are in a sense "the vested interests of the intellectual world" and thus unlikely to be easily abandoned.[32] Hence the tendency of intellectuals, not merely of Beatrice Webb's "ordinary citizens," to be imprisoned in customary categories. Moral and philosophical campaigns based on a given set of assumptions, Harrison suggests, develop a "vested interest" in maintaining those assumptions, at the risk of losing their missions.[33]

Cultural inertia undoubtedly played a significant role in blocking consideration of alternatives to the personal defects theory of poverty, yet it fails as a full explanation. A strong objection, of course, lies in the fact that the personal defects theory of poverty itself represents a change from the older Christian tradition of almsgiving and sympathy for the poor. The classic Protestant view of poverty, as we have seen, constituted a reversal of earlier views and was never fully accepted by parts of the population. Anglicans who did not embrace the evangelical wing of their church were more inclined to traditional benevolence. Richard Oastler, for one, opposed the New Poor Law because, as he said, he believed in Christian charity but not in political economy.[34] The very emergence of the harsher Nonconformist and evangelical views of poverty demonstrates that change is possible.

The nineteenth century's rapid progress in science, technology, commerce, and finance would have been impossible without new ways of thinking. A cultural inertia, which permits the invention of steamships, mechanized wool spinning, and department stores but not a reexamination of views on poverty, requires further explanation.

Possibility Three: the Conspiracy Theory

In approaching our conspiracy theory, it is useful to bear in mind that attempts to emphasize traditional morality in social policy often further the ends of conservative groups with a vested interest in maintaining the *status quo*. [35] This does not necessarily mean that the moral beliefs are promoted for the purpose of reinforcing the position of dominant groups – merely that they can be useful for that purpose. An argument that members of dominant groups had an interest in upholding the personal defects theory of poverty does not logically require the assumption that they had cynically invented the theory, or even that they did not themselves believe it.

A glance at the sponsors of the COS would make the heart of anyone attempting to validate our conspiracy theory beat faster. The Queen was a patron. The Earl of Derby presided over its first meeting, attended by the Bishop of London (president), Lord Lichfield, the Marquess of Westminster, Lord George Hamilton, W.E. Gladstone, Sir Charles Trevelyan, Major-General Cavanagh, and many other pillars of the establishment.[36] While we have no reason to doubt their sincere desire to benefit the poor, none of them advocated radical social change.

Opponents of the New Poor Law criticized it at the time as a piece of legislation that favored the rich over the poor. (We need only recall Cobbett's comments on the preferential treatment of aristocratic bastards.) Critics blamed Malthus, who had not only argued for the elimination of family allowances but upheld the economic value of luxurious expenditure.[37] Nassau Senior, who disagreed with his friend Malthus on this point, argued that no "perfectly unbiassed" observer would defend the general utility of luxurious expenditure but that this view is "favorable to the interests, or to the supposed interests, of the most influential members of every community" and therefore taken seriously.[38] Checkland, answering his own question about whether the propertied classes and the Commissioners were "using a system of ideas deriving from their own interests, but projected as neutral social science," notes that the New Poor Law, passed by a legislature in which working men had no role, provided for unemployed laborers at a bare subsistence level to save money for the rate-payers.[39]

The limited franchise in the early nineteenth century meant, inevitably, that the New Poor Law was framed and enacted by members of the groups least likely to fall under its provisions except as taxpayers. Even as late as 1865 about a third of all Members of Parliament were "aristocrats in the most restricted sense of the word."[40] As taxpayers, of course, the groups whose members sat in Parliament had a strong interest in keeping expenses down. When Parliament debated adoption of the 1832 Commission's recommendations, Lees notes, facts were scarce. "The major signal contemporaries had about the extent of poverty came from the cost of the poor laws."[41] Poor relief was a major expenditure in many parishes, weighing heavily on the local rates. Strong national traditions of voluntary charitable benevolence and dislike of taxes combined to recommend a retrenchment in poor law expenditure.

A strong interest in keeping poor law rates – and thereby the local taxes – down persisted throughout the life of the New Poor Law, sometimes warring with the theory behind the system. The reason why the system of outdoor relief was never completely abolished, Rose argues, was its relative cheapness. Small cash payments that kept the poor in their own homes were far less expensive than undertaking the entire support of an applicant in the workhouse.[42] In the original Parliamentary debate on the New Poor Law, members who took the intended abolition of out-relief seriously argued that the only purpose of the workhouses was to serve as "prisons for the purpose of terrifying applicants from seeking for relief."[43] Roberts catalogues the many ways in which the school authorities in Edwardian Salford attempted to keep the expense of rate-supported school dinners low by dissuading children from accepting them and by making them as unappetizing as possible.[44]

Proponents of the New Poor Law blamed allegedly generous relief for an allegedly work-shy laboring class. The case can easily be made, therefore, that the purpose of stingy relief, whatever its theoretical justification, was to enforce work discipline and depress wages. This is the "social control" thesis. Piven and Cloward have formulated its classic statement, arguing that to keep people at very low wages, "they must be coerced into staying at their jobs by the spectacle of degraded paupers."[45] Roberts recalls that "Even late in the nineteenth century able-bodied men from some Northern poorhouses worked in public with a large P stamped on the seat of their trousers,"[46] tangibly providing the kind of spectacle Piven and Cloward have in mind.

The Quarterly Review opposed adoption of the New Poor Law precisely because it would probably reduce wages.[47] The only way to avoid this, in the editor's opinion, would be to set relief rates at about the level of local wages. "No radical," notes Himmelfarb, "put the case for the old law and against the new more persuasively than this high-Tory journal."[48] The argument did not persuade a majority of Members of Parliament, however. The New Poor Law did not give full play to market forces in setting wage rates since, despite the recommendation of the Commissioners, the Act of Settlement was not repealed.[49] But the new system left little reason for unemployed workmen not to migrate in search of jobs rather than trust themselves to the meager benevolence of their local parish Guardians.

Low levels of relief, especially if available only under deliberately harsh and stigmatizing conditions, can also be useful in avoiding pressure to improve working conditions, raise wages, or permit unionization.[50] In the Salford of Roberts's boyhood, "Most people in the undermass... toiled on through mortal fear of getting the sack."[51] In his view, moreover, the workhouse and the prison "played a major role in keeping the poor profoundly deferential before any kind of authority."[52] Whether or not the purpose of the poor law was the maintenance of the existing social and economic hierarchies, there can be little doubt that it did help to maintain them.

Welfare programs stressing the faults of individuals, it has been argued, are politically popular because "they do not require income redistribution or the sharing of power or other resources."[53] "[I]f the justification given for welfare restrictions is usually moral, the functions these restrictions serve are typically economic."[54] The economic elite might prefer stringent welfare requirements to the alternatives – more generous (and thus more expensive) welfare payments or "reforms in economic policy that would lead to full employment at decent wages" but would eliminate some of the advantages of the wealthy.[55] Hobson, writing in 1896, was of much the same opinion, defining charity as "a feeble sort of conscience money, an irregular and inadequate return of fragments of unearned income to those who have earned it."[56] Or, as Shaw has Alfred P. Doolittle say, "What is middle class morality? Just an excuse for never giving me anything."[57]

We have considered the inadequacy of inertia as a complete explanation for the long tenure of the personal defects theory of poverty. There were interested parties who had an economic stake in the invention of steamships, mechanized wool spinning, and department stores. They did not, however, have anything to gain from a reconsideration of received wisdom on poverty. In fact, the propertied had an economic stake in maintaining work discipline, low wages, and low taxes. It would be difficult, if not impossible, to argue that this had no effect on the continued dominance of "the principles of 1834," since it would require arguing that the powerful and influential are, in fact, not powerful and influential.

One obvious problem with our Conspiracy Theory, however, is the fact that opinions critical of the personal defects theory did in fact make their way into Parliamentary debate and into print. We have encountered a number of them over the course of this study. Dissenting perspectives were both published and heard, at least on occasion; clearly the "ruling elite" was not united in its views. Various religious opinions disagreed with the Nonconformist and evangelical views of poverty. The COS never won a decisive victory over the charitable societies granting "indiscriminate" relief, despite its vehement disapproval. Unlike the COS, the Salvation Army is alive and well – and still feeding today's derelicts.

If, moreover, the purpose of the New Poor Law was to avoid pressure to improve working conditions, raise wages, or permit unionization, then in the long run it failed in all of these aims. During its span both working conditions and wages improved dramatically. By the time of the Edwardian Royal Commission, organized labor was already an important force. Logically, of course, we cannot equate lack of success with lack of intention, however.

Another objection to the Conspiracy Theory is the fact that not everyone who shared the COS viewpoint had much of an economic stake in it. The trades unions, always active in the cause of wages and job security, showed little interest in reform of the poor law. Francis Place was one of many trades unionists active in the temperance movement; generally from Nonconformist (especially Wesleyan) backgrounds, they firmly believed that much poverty was self-inflicted through drink.[58] The Salford of Roberts's boyhood was a society in which social respectability mattered very much even to the poor. The death of a family member in the workhouse was a serious blow to social standing.[59] A system that depended on stigmatizing relief recipients could not have operated successfully if recipients and their neighbors had refused to feel stigmatized.

Although the COS was supported by the rich and powerful, it was also sustained by many of far more modest means. Charles Booth, by no means the most judgmental of our poverty theorists, was probably one of the wealthiest. Octavia Hill, arguably the harshest critic of the poor among our experts, was probably the least affluent. She had been left in her teens, with her mother and sisters, to support herself. Although gifts from admirers gave her a modest income later in life, she was never wealthy. Her colleague Helen Bosanquet, also left without paternal support, first joined the COS as a paid employee. Her views on poverty were well formed long before her marriage to a comfortably well-off, but by no means wealthy, widower. George Lansbury, of all our Commissioners, was the least impressed by the personal defects theory; he was also from a working-class background. This probably mattered, but few of his colleagues came from truly elite backgrounds. Did social class distinguish him from the others? Was it his evangelical, rather than Unitarian, home? Was it his lack of participation in the institutions and traditions of poverty research? Was it some kind of private difference? The answer may lie in a combination of some or all of these. Neither class nor wealth alone provides a full explanation.

Possibility Four: the Comforting Ideas Theory

Edward Devine, General Secretary of the COS of the City of New York, introduces us to our fourth possibility. As the Majority and Minority Reports of the Edwardian Royal Commission were published, Devine expressed serious doubts about the personal defects theory despite its broad acceptance:

> There is comfort for those who are not miserable in the theory that misery is but the natural working out of human character, that it is due to natural depravity, to deliberate wrong-doing and a conscious choice of evil ways, in the theory that suffering is proof of sin; and because of this satisfaction this view becomes the conventional, orthodox view.[60]

Sixty years later, a social psychologist conducted a series of laboratory experiments he interpreted as demonstrating that "We want to believe in a world where people get what they deserve or, rather, deserve what they get."[61] Because most people need to believe they live in such a world, he concluded, they will adjust their perceptions in order to protect their belief in the fairness of life.[62]

Lerner's idea is interesting. It agrees not only with Edward Devine's reflections on poverty, but also with Goffman's remarks on stigma. Goffman's concern is the process of "elaboration on the original difference," as a society justifies ostracism and explains the inferiority of the stigmatized group.[63] Goffman never addresses poverty or "pauperism" as a basis for stigma. His examples are criminality, mental illness, deformities and disabilities, homosexuality, and race. He describes the process by which "We tend to impute a wide range of imperfections on the basis of the original one."[64] This idea serves just as usefully to analyze the social science of poverty under a deliberately stigmatizing poor law.

Malthus, as he describes the thoughts of a man who has married too young and fathered too many children, unselfconsciously sketches the process by which the personal defects view of poverty deflects attention from the fairness of God and of the economic system:

> He of course finds himself miserably distressed. He accuses the insufficiency of the price of labour to maintain a family. He accuses his parish for their tardy and sparing fulfillment of their obligation to assist him. He accuses the avarice of the rich, who suffer him to want what they can so well spare. He accuses the partial and unjust institutions of society, which have awarded him an inadequate share of the produce of the earth. He accuses perhaps the dispensations of Providence... The last person he would think of accusing is himself, on whom, in fact, the whole of the blame lies...[65]

We have seen how, through the doctrine of general providence, many Nonconformists were able to reassure themselves on questions of theodicy. God, who does not intervene directly, is blameless in human suffering. He has set up the laws of nature and society to ensure that the well behaved will prosper. Harriet Martineau's popular books, *Poor Laws and Paupers Illustrated* and *Illustrations of Political Economy*, reassured her middle-class readers that religious faith and capitalism were compatible; market forces would eventually make all segments of society more prosperous.[66] Martineau, like so many of our poverty theorists, was a Unitarian. R.K. Webb provides a full and compelling analysis of the importance of this solution to problems of theodicy in the lives of Unitarians, concluding that "The final result of this solution to the problem is of course highly comforting... the misery and evil which we see about us have been explained away as part of a larger scheme."[67]

This comfort sustained Charles Booth through his loss of religious faith; driven to agnosticism "due to an inability to accept that a good God would permit the destitution and misery he saw around him," Booth was nonetheless able to retain the "steadfastness of his faith in competitive individualism..."[68] After removing imperfections like the widespread poverty of the elderly and the demoralizing presence of Class B, Booth was satisfied to allow the free play of the market to settle the fortunes of the rest, tempered where necessary by private philanthropy.[69]

George Lansbury had far less faith in the fairness of the economic system. Unlike Booth, however, Lansbury was an evangelical of strong faith who proclaimed that he opposed the First World War "because I was an international Socialist and a Christian."[70] Rejecting faith in the fairness of capitalism but not in the fairness of God, Lansbury came enthusiastically to embrace our experimental counter-hypothesis:

> My conviction grows stronger as the years pass that everything we do on palliative lines leaves some evil behind it, and that there is no remedy for poverty and destitution except the total and complete abolition of the causes which produce these evils, and that in the main, though there are many individual exceptions, these evils are social and not personal; that drunkenness and other crimes of that sort are incidental, and not of themselves the primary causes which bring about the destitution most people deplore.[71]

George Lansbury was a socialist. The logic of his position requires that the person who holds it work for the abolition of the existing system – an uncomfortable prospect for a citizen not eager to take on the world. Yet traveling through life without a reassuring belief that life is, on the whole, fair is a difficult – even frightening – thing to do. A majority of Lansbury's countrymen preferred to believe, along with Samuel Smiles, that in their economic system "All may not rise equally, yet each, on the whole, very much according to his deserts."[72]

"We believe certain things," perhaps, "because they ought to be true."[73] Although the personal defects theory of poverty was useful in defending the Victorian and Edwardian *status quo*, this does not fully explain its long persistence. Its usefulness reinforced normal cultural inertia and encouraged some powerful elements in the society to maintain their belief in the received wisdom about poverty. Most Victorians and Edwardians were neither wealthy nor destitute. Like Edwin Chadwick, they chose to believe that "unavoidable and blameless poverty" is rare.[74] Charles Booth continued to function without faith in a just God, because he believed in a just economic system. George Lansbury lacked faith in that economic system but believed in a just God who would sustain him in his lifelong struggle against the system – something very few of his contemporaries would have found appealing. To abandon both faiths would be to surrender any hope of justice in this world or the next. Few Britons were willing to contemplate a life without such hope. How much easier it was to believe what ought to be true.

Why was nineteenth-century social science so unwilling to consider alternatives to the personal defects theory? Both cultural inertia and the usefulness of the notion in defending the *status quo* played their roles, but they do not fully explain the matter. The missing piece of the puzzle seems to be "comforting ideas." The idea of widespread poverty with no particular connection to personal defects conflicted with other ideas, divine providence and economic fairness, that people wanted and needed. For most of them, the personal and cultural costs of discarding these comforting ideas would simply have been too great to contemplate.

10
Why Critique the Victorian Social Science of Poverty?

> History is a dangerous discipline because it surrounds self-deception with dulcet odours of antiquity, and anything which has stood there a long time has claims to respect. Young people, and not so young, learn historical attitudes; probably historical attitudes are more important in framing their outlook than historical evidence; and if the historical evidence is wrong, the attitude is imbibed and is still important.
>
> Owen Chadwick, *The Secularization of the European Mind*

The time has come to summarize what we know about Victorian poverty theory and to consider why it has dominated poverty research, and poverty policy, in the twentieth century.

Victorian and Edwardian social science of poverty: a summary view

Over the course of the nineteenth century poverty experts in the emerging social sciences built up a considerable body of work on the causes of, and best remedies for, "pauperism." We have seen how the Protestant view of poverty shaped their thinking, establishing the presupposition that there is something morally wrong with the poor, that a pauper's lack of worldly success is a reflection of laziness and inadequate self-restraint. We have also seen how these religious ideas continued to influence the work of apparently secular theorists, even those who no longer maintained any personal religious belief. Thus the doctrine of general providence prepared many people to expect that the laws of God and of nature are one and the same, an expectation that often outlived a strong belief that it was God who had set the laws of nature in motion in the first place. Unitarians, in particular, looked for a rational and scientific basis for social policy that rejected a role for revelation but still demanded precisely the same virtues from the poor that the Calvinist God had required, assuming their absence in a destitute person. The over-representation of Unitarians and former Unitarians among our poverty theorists was by no means coincidental.

We have also seen how the concept of temptation often served to block any consideration of what the true motivation for a pauper's actions might have been. The assumption that force of character can transcend mere physical hardship promoted a tendency not to take poverty very seriously as a disabling set of circumstances. The mind is the man.

These habits of thought were powerfully reinforced by Malthusian population theory and by political economy, both quite compatible with the Protestant view of poverty. Each added its own dimension to the development of poverty theory. After Malthus, it has always been presumed that there is a connection between public assistance and the reproductive decisions of the poor. Yet there has always been confusion (often unnoticed) over how public assistance affects these decisions. Do the poor have babies to get relief money? Or do the poor simply do what comes naturally, unwisely raising families they cannot afford to feed because society will take up the slack? Analysis based on political economy, as we have seen, has always tended to support the former model. Seeing the poor as "Economic Men" who make rational decisions for profit, such analysis ignores any constraints on their choices and all non-economic factors that might influence them. Analysts who emphasize the dishonesty of the poor, rather than their alleged sexual depravity, have also preferred the first model. Following the view usually taken by Malthus, analysts who emphasize the poor's lack of sexual self-control or their lack of planning and foresight have tended to embrace the second model. Many critics of the poor, oblivious to inconsistency, have swung back and forth between these positions as needed. These streams of thought emptied into the testimony before the Royal Commission of 1832 and its resulting report, the basis of the New Poor Law.

As the century wore on, social science began to find more sophisticated approaches to social problems. From the beginning, poverty and "pauperism" were such central concerns that the history of social science in Britain and the history of British poverty theory are nearly identical. Each of the schools of social science developed during the nineteenth century involved key figures in one or both of the two Royal Commissions that bracket the Victorian poor law. Each of these schools left its mark on poverty experts and thus on the policies they recommended.

The public health movement demonstrated that health issues had a major impact on the lives of the poor and their children. Its leading figures, nonetheless, tended to blame the poor for their own problems. The public health movement bequeathed to poverty theory a preoccupation with dirt, a suspicion that the health problems of the poor were the result of their own (or of their mothers') immorality, a notion that the destitute are a source of contagion, and a desire to "treat" the poor for their own sake and the sake of society.

The statistical movement's passion for collecting "facts" about the economy and society contributed a desire to accumulate information, but little in the way of wisdom on how to use it. Its legacy was a strong sense that statistics matter but not of how to judge what they mean, or of how to avoid having the question asked predetermine the answer received.

The social science movement's attempt to develop ameliorative public policy from sound information laid the basis for poor law policy made by experts. It also left a legacy of confusion about cause and effect, environmentalism versus moralizing, and the proper use of theory. Governed by *a priori* reasoning, and using numbers only to "prove" what they already assumed to be true, researchers in this tradition drifted into conceptual muddles when confronting unwelcome but undeniable evidence.

The COS turned this muddle into an institution by developing the practice of social casework. Originally employed as a tool to "treat" the poor and overcome their assumed personal defects, casework was carried over into the twentieth century as a method for providing "collectivist" help for, and supervision of, the poor. The poor, in other words, were still assumed to be defective – victims perhaps, not of their own immorality but of their own pathology, their own incompetence. Or perhaps of their own immorality, after all.

The recapitulationist assumptions of Social Darwinism powerfully reinforced these trends, defining the poor as children, as primitives, as savages. Each school of thought we have considered reinforced the others. Each made the others more plausible. If the elect are frugal, hardworking, sober, provident, self-restrained, and successful, then the poor must be wasteful, lazy, drunken, careless of the future, and impulsive. If the laws of God and the laws of nature (including economic laws) are one and the same, then the lack of these virtues would result in poverty and misery just as surely as in damnation. While we cannot directly observe damnation, poverty is visible all around us. The more evolved and civilized races and people are frugal, hardworking, sober, provident, self-restrained, and successful, so "savages," including the members of the "residuum" inhabiting such places as London's East End, must be the opposite. The remarkable consistency of these desirable and undesirable traits might suggest that each list is derived from its predecessors without regard to empirical findings. To the Victorians, however, while this consistency was also apparent, it constituted reassurance that the views of their poverty theorists were correct. Each point of view reinforced the others, shaping a coherent world-view and discouraging skepticism. And, as the Webbs observed, we see more or less what we expect to see.

Thus Late Victorian and Edwardian social scientists did what they needed to do to preserve their world-view. They considered their work "scientific" because they gathered facts and used concepts borrowed from the natural sciences. On the basis of these concepts, however, they routinely engaged in *a priori* reasoning without testable hypotheses, moved uncritically from anecdotes of unproven significance to unsupported generalizations, and used ideal types as if they were evidence. They ignored the possibility that their survey design decisions were predetermining the outcome of their investigations, made little or no effort to guard against bias, and protected themselves from unwanted perspectives by redefining external factors as products of internal factors. Like the political economists whose narrow view social science intended to replace, they focused on choices and ignored the constraints under which those choices were made. This generally allowed them to find what they expected to find. A growing body of unwelcome evidence about economic and social problems outside the control of the poor did, over time, force even the most determined moralists to acknowledge environmental factors. By constructing elaborate causal loops that confounded cause and effect into a self-perpetuating cycle of pathology, however, they were able to avoid facing the full implications of this evidence. Drinking causes malnutrition, which causes drinking, which causes malnutrition.

The approach of poverty experts to slum mothers shows how these factors fit together to dictate which factors were studied and how behavior was interpreted. In their role as household purchasing agents, these mothers were uniformly depicted as "recklessly improvident" primitives who could not plan ahead or understand economies of scale. Our poverty experts ignored the constraints of low income, of slum housing, and of custom on the purchasing decisions of slum mothers, assuming that they bought provisions in small quantities out of ignorance, rather than lack of money or suitable storage facilities, that they were surprised every week by the ebb and flow of cash on a weekly pay cycle. Further investigation of their behavior would have been possible; the Fabian Women's Group did look further into the domestic economy of slum households. To our poverty experts, however, no further investigation seemed necessary. Their theoretical presuppositions had already told them everything they needed to know: bad management, rather than low income, dictated the low standard of living of the poor.

The ignorance, laziness, and negligence of slum mothers, poverty experts believed, caused the high rates of infant and child mortality in slum families. They assumed, as the public health movement had assumed, that the high correlation of dirt and disease implied some kind of causality, whether or not the exact mechanism could be determined. Ignoring epidemiological evidence that unsatisfactory sanitary arrangements caused widespread infant death from diarrhea, as they do in the less developed nations today, our poverty experts blamed infant deaths on "inappropriate feeding" and neglectful care. The difficulties of obtaining and storing fresh milk on a low income, the difficulties of cooking in a slum kitchen, the near hopelessness of maintaining cleanliness in a third-floor or basement flat with abundant vermin and no running water – none of these considerations intruded on the experts' narrative of maternal ignorance, neglect, and carelessness. Hence the COS preference for removing children from destitute homes to institutions and the insistence of both the Majority and Minority reports of the Edwardian Royal Commission on the importance of supervising slum mothers. In arguing that the primary value of milk depots is not the provision of fresh milk to slum children but the supervision of their mothers, Beatrice Webb demonstrated that she had not discarded personal defects in favor of an environmental approach. Poverty causes bad mothering, which causes poverty, which causes bad mothering. It could be argued that Helen Bosanquet emphasized the bad mothering more, while the Webbs emphasized the poverty more. Either way, we end up in the same loop. How much does it matter which came first, the chicken or the egg?

The controversy over infant life insurance demonstrates the extremity to which this kind of analysis could be taken. Slum families purchased this insurance, contemporaries like Dr Edward Berdoe pointed out, as a preparation for the all-too-likely possibility they would have to bury one or more of their children. The insurance money, in virtually all cases less than the cost of a minimal funeral, was a guard against the horrors of a poor law burial. The premiums were paid out of the family food budget, the only area of elasticity in very low-income homes, and thus made likelier the very contingency against which they were undertaken. Yet, as we have seen, the widespread assumption of maternal negligence and moral failings among the poor led many poverty experts to believe that children thus insured were often murdered, or at least cared for less diligently, with an eye to their financial value. The experts do not appear to have wondered how a slum mother unable to manage her money through the weekly pay cycle could plan to use her baby as a financial asset.

It would be difficult to deny that cultural inertia and the economic interests of powerful groups within British society helped to maintain the ascendancy of the personal defects theory of poverty among policy makers. We have considered the evidence for such an effect and the reasons why these factors do not fully explain the stubborn persistence of moralizing in the face of mounting evidence for environmental factors. Although some observers have understandably interpreted this apparent willful blindness to reality as deliberate deception in the interests of social control, it seems likelier that our Edwardian poverty theorists really saw confirmation all around them for the correctness of their views. The traditions of the religion in which they had been raised and of the social sciences in which they had been trained worked very well together, each reinforcing the plausibility of the others. Why ask different questions, when you feel that you already know the answers? In the end, the experts considered the personal defects theory of poverty just as compelling in 1909 as they had in 1834. This is the unifying idea that links the report of the 1832 Royal Commission to the two reports of the 1905 Royal Commission. Seventy-three years of social science between them account both for the differences in detail and for the sameness in spirit.

Why critique Victorian social science?

Is it really fair to critique Victorian and Edwardian social scientists for failure to meet later standards of "value free" methodology? A strong case could be made that criticizing Edwin Chadwick or Helen Bosanquet for not using today's research protocols is very much like criticizing Napoleon for not using tanks. In the development of any disciplinary tradition it is necessary to work out the conventions that researchers must follow in order to insure the validity of their work and its usefulness to other scholars. The theorists whose work on poverty we have examined here were among the pioneers of social science. They did not have the advantage of established procedures and were forced, in many instances, to find out the hard way what works and what does not. Charles Booth, in particular, is noteworthy for his willingness to imagine difficulties and his genuine inventiveness in trying to guard against bias and error. His personal contributions to the advancement of survey technique have probably never been given the full recognition they deserve.

Booth's devotion to finding useful data about the lives of his poorer countrymen, of course, also merits respect. Like Rowntree, he expended not only years of effort but considerable amounts of his own money in the pursuit of information that could be used to understand, and thus to improve, the lot of the poor. All of our principal theorists devoted their lives to matters of social improvement – some of them exclusively to the lives of the poor – rather than to individual goals. Gertrude Himmelfarb, among others, has rightly called attention to the tremendous force of civic and social activism that characterized the Late Victorian age and drove its great debates about progress and reform. Any fair-minded assessment of the work of our poverty theorists must, in justice, take this altruistic passion into account.

This is not to say, however, that we are obliged to accept all of our poverty experts at their own valuation. After all, not all of their contemporaries did. We have seen the judgment of John Hobson, also among the founders of British sociology, on the narrowness of the COS approach. We have also seen, in George Lansbury's unflattering account of the work of the COS in East London, that the Edwardian poor did not necessarily endorse the selflessness of the Edwardian social worker, paid or unpaid. Close reading of some of this literature – particularly of the writings of Octavia Hill and Helen Bosanquet – reveals some rather disturbing notes of self-righteousness and even, in some instances, of intense malice. While admirers see these volunteer social activists as devoting their lives to trying to improve the lot of the unfortunate, their detractors are likelier to share the view of George Lansbury, who saw them as devoting their lives to bullying the powerless and kicking people when they were down – in other words, of cruelly blaming the victim. Now as then, their motivation rests in the eye of the beholder.

It makes no sense to expect nineteenth-century social scientists to adhere to conventions not yet invented. Nor is there any point in criticizing Victorian and Edwardian people for thinking like people who lived in their time, place, and culture – although, as we have seen, not all of their contemporaries approached poverty precisely as they did. Why, then, critique the approach of Victorian and Edwardian social science to research on poverty? Because twentieth-century poverty research shows unmistakable signs of its ancestry. Despite the development of modern research protocols and statistical methods, many poverty theorists have continued to make the same assumptions and pursue the same questions as their predecessors. They have even, in many cases, employed the same styles of argument. Oblivious to the possibility of error, they have confidently marched forward toward familiar conclusions, casting about on the way for bits of information they can cram into the familiar molds. Some of the "modern" social science of poverty is conducted in a "modern" way, particularly in the field of sociology.[1] But the poverty theorists whose work has informed public policy in the twentieth century have continued along the well-established path, and public opinion has followed.

We cannot fairly criticize Victorian and Edwardian poverty experts for thinking like Victorians and Edwardians. But when we find late-twentieth-century poverty experts thinking like Victorians and Edwardians, it is certainly appropriate to ask why.

The vigorous afterlife of Victorian social science

In 1883, near the end of his short life, economic historian and COS member Arnold Toynbee was invited to give a series of lectures to London working men. Breaking at one point from his prepared text, Toynbee suddenly declared:

> We – the middle classes, I mean, not merely the very rich – we have neglected you; instead of justice we have offered you charity, and instead of sympathy, we have offered you hard and unreal advice; but I think we are changing.[2]

Throughout the nineteenth century and beyond, the destitute mothers subject to poverty research and to the Victorian poor law continued to receive far more "hard and unreal advice" than sympathy or help from the poverty experts whose views we have considered here. The tradition these experts established has been too dominant to permit much in the way of change, contrary to Toynbee's perception. We have considered several possible reasons why this might be so, and there is no inherent reason why they would be less compelling today than they were during the life of the Victorian poor law.

We can now see precisely what was meant by the Prologue's claim that Charles Murray, in *Losing Ground*, was engaging in Victorian social science. Murray assumed, without proof, that work will always be avoided if it can be, postulated motivation based on the idea of temptation, emphasized choices while ignoring the constraints under which they were made, ignored the limitations of Economic Man as a behavioral model, used an ideal type as if it were evidence, cherry-picked his statistics to "prove" what he already meant to find, and avoided mentioning structural changes in the labor market that might indicate problems, not with poor people, but with the national economy.[3] And why did he do this? For precisely the same reasons as our poverty experts of the Victorian and Edwardian eras: in order to continue to believe what ought to be true. As Murray himself tells us, "I attach considerable value to the principle that people get what they deserve."[4] In this he is, precisely as he claims to be, "a fairly typical citizen."[5] Would his book have been so influential otherwise? Nor was Murray's pursuit of Victorian social science in a twentieth-century world unique.

Consider, for example, the influential work of Edward Banfield, who in the early 1970s offered an unselfconscious revisitation of the recapitulationist themes familiar to any student of Late Victorian poverty research. In Banfield's view, the principal failing of the poor is their lack of a "psychological orientation toward the future."[6] Banfield explains that "Improvidence and irresponsibility are direct consequences of this failure to take the future into account," cheerfully conflating cause with effect by noting that "the lower-class person" lacks "ability or willingness to provide for the future..."[7] – an undoubtedly unconscious echo of C.S. Loch.[8] Banfield furthers his argument by the familiar device of focusing narrowly on choices, rather than on constraints, as when he claims that "the lower-class individual" shows his carelessness when he "seeks medical treatment only when practically forced to do so: symptoms that do not incapacitate are often ignored."[9] As Banfield's account proceeds, more classic traits of the savage emerge: "Impulse governs his behavior, either because he cannot discipline himself to sacrifice a present for a future satisfaction or because he has no sense of the future. He is therefore radically improvident..."[10] Needless to say, the savage mother "is likely to have a succession of mates" and "is characteristically impulsive: once children have passed babyhood they are likely to be neglected or abused, and at best they never know what to expect next."[11] Unlike Helen Bosanquet, Banfield knows and freely admits that he is using an ideal type; exactly like Helen Bosanquet, he then proceeds to use this recapitulationist stereotype as if it were evidence.[12] As Owen Chadwick would say, it has stood there a long time and therefore has claims to respect. There is every reason to believe, however, that the historical evidence behind it may very well be wrong, even if the attitude is still important.

Notes

Prologue: Victorian Social Science in a Twentieth-Century World

1. Charles Murray, *Losing Ground: American Social Policy 1950–1980* (New York: Basic Books, 1994), *xv*. This is the second edition, with an author's introduction from which this quote is taken. The first edition was published in 1984.
2. William Julius Wilson, *The Truly Disadvantaged: The Inner City, the Underclass, and Public Policy* (Chicago: University of Chicago Press, 1987), 16.
3. Michael B. Katz, *In the Shadow of the Poorhouse: A Social History of Welfare in America* (New York: Basic Books, 1996), 364n38.
4. Murray, *Losing Ground*, 176.
5. Katz makes this comment in *In the Shadow of the Poorhouse*, 364n38. He directs the reader to two analyses of Murray's statistics, both of them quite effective in demonstrating why Murray's figures do not prove what he says they do. Another good source on the subject is Wilson, *The Truly Disadvantaged*, 16–18. Murray's claim that there are no errors to fix is made in his introduction to the anniversary edition of *Losing Ground*, *xx*.
6. Wilson, *The Truly Disadvantaged*, 104, 162.
7. Murray, *Losing Ground*, *xvii*.

Chapter 1   Introduction to Victorian Poverty Studies

1. Throughout the nineteenth century Scotland had its own system of poor relief, separately administered by local authorities, which is outside the scope of this study.
2. S.G. and E.O.A. Checkland, eds, *The Poor Law Report of 1834* (Hammondsworth, Middlesex: Penguin Ltd, 1974), 17.
3. For the full extent of this literature, see the bibliography at the end of this volume.
4. R.H. Tawney, "The Theory of Pauperism" *The Sociological Review* 2 (October, 1909): 363, 366.
5. Sidney and Beatrice Webb, *English Local Government*, Vol. 7 *The Old Poor Law* (London: Longmans, Green and Co., Ltd, 1927), 298.
6. *Ibid.*, 311. That this conclusion might be in direct conflict with their earlier assertion that allowances were generally inadequate they do not appear to have considered. "The Speenhamland counties" were the counties, mostly rural, in which child allowance in supplement of wages was granted by the local overseers under the Old Poor Law. The allowance was also granted on a per capita basis for the maintenance of illegitimate children. For more on how the system operated, see J.D. Marshall, *The Old Poor Law, 1795–1834* or Ursula Henriques, "Bastardy and the New Poor Law." Details of publication are contained in this book's bibliography.

7. Sidney and Beatrice Webb, *English Local Government*, Vol. 9 *English Poor Law History Part II: The Last Hundred Years* (London: Longmans, Green and Co., Ltd, 1929), 476, 471.

8. *Ibid.*, 512.

9. *Ibid.*, 546.

10. *Ibid.*, 548, 556.

11. See, for example, Hanser's claim that the Minority Report was "more radical" than the Majority Report and that the former "discarded completely the long-established principle that 'character' had something to do with poverty." Charles J. Hanser, *Guide to Decision: The Royal Commission* (Totowa, NJ: The Bedminster Press, 1965), 186, 188.

12. *Ibid.*, 826–34.

13. Ian Anstruther, *The Scandal of the Andover Workhouse* (London: Geoffrey Bles, 1973).

14. See for example Michael E. Rose, *The English Poor Law, 1780–1930* (New York: Barnes and Noble, 1971); *The Relief of Poverty, 1834–1914* (London: Macmillan, 1972).

15. *Ibid.*, 297, 286.

16. *Ibid.*, 246.

17. A.W. Vincent, "The Poor Law Reports of 1909 and the Social Theory of the Charity Organization Society" *Victorian Studies*, 27 (1984): 363.

18. Gertrude Himmelfarb, *The Idea of Poverty: England in the Early Industrial Age* (New York: Alfred A. Knopf, 1984), 366–7.

19. *Ibid.*, 521.

20. Gertrude Himmelfarb, *Poverty and Compassion: The Moral Imagination of the Late Victorians* (New York: Alfred A. Knopf, 1991), 7.

21. See for example "The Victorians Get a Bad Rap" *New York Times* January 9, 1995.

22. *Ibid.*, 382.

23. *Ibid.*, 384.

24. *Ibid.*, 321–2.

25. *The Solidarities of Strangers*, 321.

Chapter 2   Two Royal Commissions

1. Checkland and Checkland, *The Poor Law Report of 1834*, 497.

2. Raymond G. Cowherd, *Political Economists and the English Poor Laws: A Historical Study of the Influence of Classical Economics on the Formation of Social Welfare Policy* (Athens, OH: Ohio University Press, 1977), 215.

3. *Ibid.*

4. *Ibid.*

5. Anne Digby, "Malthus and Reform of the Poor Law," in *Malthus Past and Present*, ed. by J. Dupaquier (New York: Academic Press, Inc., 1983), 106.

6. Himmelfarb, *The Idea of Poverty*, 156.

7. Lees, *The Solidarities of Strangers*, 119.

8. S.E. Finer, "The transmission of Benthamite ideas 1820–50," 15.

9. Marian Bowley, *Nassau Senior and Classical Economics* (New York: Augustus M. Kelly, 1949), 329.

10. Checkland and Checkland, *The Poor Law Report of 1834*, 30.
11. Cowherd, *Political Economists*, 231–3.
12. *Ibid.*, 239.
13. John Roach, *Social Reform in England 1780–1880* (New York: St Martin's Press, 1978), 97; Himmelfarb, *The Idea of Poverty*, 156.
14. Bowley, *Nassau Senior*, 328.
15. *Ibid.*, 19.
16. *Ibid.*, 329.
17. Finer, *Life and Times of Sir Edwin Chadwick*, 70.
18. Finer, "Transmission of Benthamite Ideas," 26.
19. R.K. Webb, *Harriet Martineau: A Radical Victorian* (New York: Columbia University Press, 1960), 129.
20. R.K. Webb, *The British Working Class Reader 1790–1848: Literacy and Social Tension* (London: George Allen & Unwin Ltd, 1955), 127.
21. R.H. Tawney, "The Theory of Pauperism": 363; Sydney Checkland, *British Public Policy*, 90.
22. Himmelfarb, *The Idea of Poverty*, 155, 153.
23. Ironically, a tactical decision to alter the details of Settlement rather than take the controversial step of abolishing it meant that this impairment to labor mobility remained. In the long run, industrialization proceeded anyway.
24. Digby, "Malthus and Reform of the Poor Law," 104.
25. Checkland, *British Public Policy*, 92.
26. Checkland and Checkland, *The Poor Law Report of 1834*, 42–3.
27. Beatrice Webb, *Our Partnership*, ed. by Barbara Drake and Margaret Cole (London: Longmans, Green and Co., 1948), 320.
28. *Ibid.*, 420.
29. *Ibid.*, 321.
30. McBriar, *An Edwardian Mixed Doubles: The Bosanquets versus the Webbs: A Study in British Social Policy 1890–1929* (Oxford: Clarendon Press, 1987), 179; Lees, *The Solidarities of Strangers*, 319.
31. George Lansbury, *My Life* (London: Constable and Co., 1928), 138.
32. McBriar, *An Edwardian Mixed Doubles*, 187–8. McBriar also sees the influence of Daniel O'Connell at work; this assertion seems more problematic.
33. *Ibid.*, 183–4.
34. *Ibid.*, 189.
35. McBriar, *An Edwardian Mixed Doubles*, 181.
36. *Ibid.*, 192.
37. *Ibid.*, 191.
38. Lansbury, *My Life*, 52, 79.
39. *Ibid.*, 25, 132.
40. C.L. Mowatt, *The Charity Organisation Society 1869–1913: Its Ideas and Work* (London: Methuen & Co. Ltd., 1961), 63.
41. *Ibid.*, 63–5.
42. A.W. Vincent, "The Poor Law Reports of 1909 and the Social Theory of the Charity Organisation Society," 346; David Owen, *English Philanthropy*, 229.
43. E. Moberly Bell, *Octavia Hill, a Biography* (London: Constable and Co., 1942), 113, 205. The National Trust is the National Trust for Places of Historic Interest or Natural Beauty.

44. Jane Lewis, *Women and Social Action in Victorian and Edwardian England* (Stanford, CA: Stanford University Press, 1991), 49.
45. McBriar, *An Edwardian Mixed Doubles*, 191.
46. *Ibid.*, 49.
47. T.S. Simey, *Charles Booth: Social Scientist* (London: Oxford University Press, 1960), 175.
48. *Ibid.*, 175.
49. Lees, *The Solidarities of Strangers*, 320.
50. Lewis, *Women and Social Action*, 146.
51. *Ibid.*
52. McBriar, *An Edwardian Mixed Doubles*, 55.
53. Vincent, "The Poor Law Reports of 1909," 346.
54. McBriar, *An Edwardian Mixed Doubles*, 252.
55. *Ibid.*
56. *Ibid.*, 282–3.
57. Ross, *Love and Toil: Motherhood in Outcast London 1870–1918* (New York: Oxford University Press, 1993), 20.
58. Ross McKibbon, "Class and Poverty in Edwardian England," in *The Ideologies of Class: Social Relations in Britain 1880–1950*, ed. by Ross McKibbon (Oxford: Clarendon Press, 1990), 169.
59. Paul Johnson, *Saving and Spending: The Working-Class Economy in Britain 1870–1939* (Oxford: Clarendon Press, 1985), 228.
60. Margaret Cole, *Beatrice Webb* (London: Longmans, Green & Co., 1945), 59.
61. Mary Ann Romano, *Beatrice Webb (1858–1943): The Socialist with a Sociological Imagination* (Lewiston, NY: The Edwin Mellen Press, 1998), 47.
62. Jeanne MacKenzie, *A Victorian Courtship: The Story of Beatrice Potter and Sidney Webb* (New York: Oxford University Press, 1979), 52.
63. Lewis, *Women and Social Action*, 127–8.
64. Cole, *Beatrice Webb*, 89.
65. Lewis, *Women and Social Action*, 107.
66. Lees, *The Solidarities of Strangers*, 320.
67. *Ibid.*, 321
68. McBriar, *An Edwardian Mixed Doubles*, 294–5.
69. *Ibid.*
70. Sidney and Beatrice Webb, *The Prevention of Destitution* Special Edition Presented By the Authors to Their Fellow Members of the National Committee for the Prevention of Destitution (London: 1911), 47.
71. Lansbury, *My Life*, 152–3.
72. *Ibid.*, 154.

Chapter 3   Protestant Paradigms in Victorian Poverty Studies

1. Max Weber, *The Protestant Ethic and the Spirit of Capitalism* (New York: Charles Scribners Sons, 1930), 178 [first published in 1904–5].
2. *Ibid.*, 177.
3. *Ibid.*, 159, 164.
4. *Ibid.*, 175.

5. Michael Walzer, *The Revolution of the Saints: A Study in the Origins of Radical Politics* (Cambridge, MA: Harvard University Press, 1965), 218.
6. James Obelkevich, "Religion," in *The Cambridge Social History of Britain, 1750–1950*, ed. F.M.L. Thompson, Vol. 3 (Cambridge: Cambridge University Press, 1990), 336.
7. The one Catholic member of the Edwardian Royal Commission, Irish Bishop Denis Kelly, was as we have seen neither active nor influential in its proceedings.
8. Obelkevich, "Religion," 318.
9. John Bunyan, *The Pilgrim's Progress from This World to That Which Is to Come* (Laurel, NY: Lightyear Press, 1984), 33.
10. *Ibid.*, 47.
11. Samuel Smiles, *Self-Help; with Illustrations of Character, Conduct, and Perseverance* (London: John Murray, 1871), 342. The book was first published in 1859.
12. On the extensive use of Bunyan in the Sunday School movement, see W.R. Owens, "The Reception of *The Pilgrim's Progress* in England", in *Bunyan in England and Abroad,* ed. M. van Os and G.J. Schutte (Amsterdam: Vrije Universiteit Press, 1990), 91–104.
13. Smiles, *Self-Help*, 317.
14. Bunyan, *The Pilgrim's Progress*, 65.
15. Smiles, *Self-Help*, 302–3.
16. Gerald Parsons, "From Dissenters to Free Churchmen: The Transitions of Victorian Nonconformity," in *Religion in Victorian Britain*, Vol. 1: *Traditions*, ed. by Gerald Parsons (Manchester, UK: Manchester University Press, 1988), 71.
17. *Ibid.*, 71–2.
18. Richard Helmstadter, "The Nonconformist Conscience," in *The Conscience of the Victorian State*, ed. by Peter Marsh (Syracuse, NY: Syracuse University Press, 1979), 140.
19. *Ibid.*, 145.
20. Parsons, "From Dissenters to Free Churchmen," 73.
21. Boyd Hilton, *The Age of Atonement: The Influence of Evangelicalism on Social and Economic Thought, 1795–1865* (New York: Oxford University Press, 1988), 8.
22. Mary Poovey, *Making a Social Body: British Cultural Formation 1830–1864* (Chicago, IL: University of Chicago Press, 1995), 51.
23. Hilton, *Age of Atonement*, 16.
24. *Ibid.*
25. *Ibid.*
26. Helmstadter, "Nonconformist Conscience", 142.
27. Boyd Hilton, "The role of Providence in evangelical thought," in *History, Society and the Churches: Essays in honour of Owen Chadwick*, ed. by Derek Beales and Geoffrey Best (Cambridge: Cambridge University Press, 1985), 219.
28. Hilton, *Age of Atonement, ix.*
29. Gertrude Himmelfarb, *The Idea of Poverty*, 12.
30. Nassau William Senior, *A Letter to Lord Howick on a Legal Provision for the Irish Poor; Commutation of Tithes, and a Provision for the Irish Roman*

Catholic Clergy, 3rd edition *with a Preface, containing Suggestions as to the Measures to be adopted in the Present Emergency* (London: John Murray, 1832), 57.

31.   Nassau William Senior to the Lord Chancellor, January 1833, Chadwick Papers, University College, London.

32.   R.K. Webb, *The British Working Class Reader 1790–1848: Literacy and Social Tension* (London: George Allen & Unwin Ltd, 1955), 130.

33.   Checkland and Checkland, *The Poor Law Report of 1834*, 173. No claims about the gossip and drinking habits of people who are not paupers were offered or requested.

34.   *Ibid.*, 170.

35.   Sidney and Beatrice Webb, *English Local Government*, Vol. 8, 84.

36.   R.K. Webb, *Harriet Martineau*, 48.

37.   *Ibid.*, 251.

38.   Jeremy Bentham, *Essays on the subject of the Poor Laws CLIII*(a) Folder 1, Bentham Archives, University College, London; 2.

39.   *Ibid.*

40.   Jenifer Hart, "Religion and Social Control in the mid-Nineteenth Century", in *Social Control in Nineteenth Century Britain*, ed. by A.P. Donajgrodzki (London: Croom Helm, 1977), 112.

41.   *Ibid.*, 113.

42.   *Hansard Parliamentary Debates*, 3d ser., Vol. 22 (1834), col. 877.

43.   *Ibid.*, cols. 877–8.

44.   Himmelfarb, *The Idea of Poverty*, 4; 126–7.

45.   *Ibid.*, 4.

46.   Hilton, *The Age of Atonement*, 26.

47.   Mary Poovey, *A History of the Modern Fact: Problems of Knowledge in the Sciences of Wealth and Society* (Chicago: University of Chicago Press, 1998), 289.

48.   Patricia James, *Population Malthus: His Life and Times* (London: Routledge and Kegan Paul, 1979), 24.

49.   T.R. Malthus, *An Essay on the Principle of Population*, 2nd edn, (London: J. Johnson, 1803), 531–2. Italics in original.

50.   James, *Population Malthus*, 100.

51.   Himmelfarb, *The Idea of Poverty*, 156.

52.   Owen Chadwick, *The Secularization of the European Mind in the Nineteenth Century* (Cambridge: Cambridge University Press, 1975), 231.

53.   Gertrude Himmelfarb, *Marriage and Morals Among the Victorians* (New York: Alfred A. Knopf, 1986), 21.

54.   Lees, *The Solidarities of Strangers*, 282.

55.   T.S. Simey, *Charles Booth: Social Scientist*, 41.

56.   Helen Dendy Bosanquet, *Rich and Poor* (London: Macmillan and Co., 1898), 29.

57.   Helen Dendy Bosanquet, *The Strength of the People: A Study in Social Economics* (London: Macmillan and Co., 1903), 36.

58.   Bunyan, *Pilgrim's Progress*, 23.

59.   General [William] Booth, *In Darkest England, And the Way Out* (London: Funk & Wagnalls, 1890), 13.

60.   Helen Dendy Bosanquet, *Rich and Poor*, 137.

61. Galatians 6:7; 2 Thessalonians 3:10.
62. Robert Humphreys, *Sin, Organized Charity and the Poor Law in Victorian England* (New York: St Martin's Press, 1995), 61.
63. *Ibid.*, 90.
64. Clyde Binfield, *So Down to Prayers: Studies in English Nonconformity 1780–1920* (London: J.M. Dent and Sons, 1977), 5.
65. *Ibid.*
66. R.K. Webb, *Harriet Martineau*, 200.
67. *Ibid.*, 68.
68. *Ibid.*, 71.
69. F.K. Prochaska, "Philanthropy," in *The Cambridge Social History of Britain 1750–1950*, ed. by F.M.L. Thompson, Vol. 3 (Cambridge: Cambridge University Press, 1990), 379.
70. R.K. Webb, *Harriet Martineau*, 73.
71. This attitude was particularly evident in the career of Octavia Hill.
72. Simey, *Charles Booth*, 42.
73. C.S. Loch, *How to Help Cases of Distress: A Handy Reference Book for Almoners and Others*, 4th edn (London: Longmans, Green for the C.O.S., 1890), xviii.
74. Bosanquet, *Strength of the People*, 108.
75. Genesis 25:29–34.
76. Sidney and Beatrice Webb, *The Prevention of Destitution*, 238.
77. Himmelfarb, *The Idea of Poverty*, 406.
78. Pamela J. Walker, *Pulling the Devil's Kingdom Down: The Salvation Army in Victorian Britain* (Berkeley and Los Angeles: University of California Press, 2001), 53.
79. *Ibid.*, 176.
80. *Ibid.*, 180.
81. W. Booth, *In Darkest England*, 14.
82. *Ibid.*
83. *Ibid.*, 13.
84. Helen Dendy Bosanquet, *The Standard of Life and Other Studies* (London: Macmillan and Co., 1898), 50–1.
85. George Orwell's experience among tramps led him to reject the notion that they are "atavistic" wanderers; in his view "A tramp tramps, not because he likes it, but for the same reason as a car keeps to the left; because there happens to be a law compelling him to do so." *Down and Out in Paris and London* (London: Secker and Warburg, 1986). The work was first published in 1933.
86. Bosanquet, *The Standard of Life*, 52.
87. Malthus, *Essay on the Principle of Population*, 2nd edn, 488.
88. Bosanquet, *Rich and Poor*, 73.
89. Bosanquet, *Strength of the People*, 205.
90. Robert Roberts, *The Classic Slum: Salford Life in the First Quarter of the Century* (Manchester: Manchester University Press, 1971), 66.
91. *Ibid.*, 45.
92. *Ibid.*, 176–7.
93. Bosanquet, *Rich and Poor*, 106.
94. Bell, *Octavia Hill*, 203.

95.   Himmelfarb, *Poverty and Compassion*, 151.

96.   Webb, *The Prevention of Destitution*, 238.

97.   *Alcohol and Alcoholism: The Report of a Special Committee of the Royal College of Psychiatrists* (New York: The Free Press, 1979), 22–3.

98.   *Ibid.*, 104.

99.   McBriar, *An Edwardian Mixed Doubles*, 56.

100.   Digby, "Malthus and Reform of the Poor Law," 100.

101.   McBriar, *An Edwardian Mixed Doubles*, 369.

102.   *Ibid.*

103.   Lewis, *Women and Social Action*, 147.

104.   Himmelfarb, *Poverty and Compassion*, 248.

105.   *Ibid.*

106.   Smiles, *Self-Help*, 226.

107.   Bosanquet, *The Strength of the People*, 1. Bosanquet quotes Morley's *Life of Cromwell*, 417.

108.   Nathan Irvin Huggins, *Protestants Against Poverty: Boston's Charities 1870–1900* (Westport, CT: Greenwood Publishing, 1971), 166.

109.   Samuel Smiles, *Character* (NY: Harper & Brothers, 1872), 46.

110.   Beatrice Webb, *Our Partnership*, 300. The appeal of Puritan asceticism to a sensual man would undoubtedly be rather limited.

111.   Helen Bosanquet, "Reconstruction – Of What?" *The Hibbert Journal*, Vol. 15 (June 1917): 544.

112.   Owen, *English Philanthropy*, 136.

113.   Jenifer Hart, "Nineteenth-Century Social Reform: A Tory Interpretation of History" *Past and Present*, 31 (July 1965): 52.

114.   Hart, "Religion and Social Control," 119.

115.   Smiles, *Self-Help*, 19. Smiles made a bit of a specialty of this theme.

116.   *Ibid.*, 268. Smiles apparently has not considered the full theological import of his argument, which could easily be taken to imply that the expulsion from the Garden of Eden in penalty for Adam's sin was a very good thing.

117.   Owen, *English Philanthropy*, 149–50.

118.   Bosanquet, *Strength of the People*, 36.

119.   Bell, *Octavia Hill*, 204.

120.   Alon Kadish, *Apostle Arnold: The Life and Death of Arnold Toynbee 1852–1883* (Durham, NC: Duke University Press, 1986), 80.

121.   C.S. Loch, *Cheap Dinners for Poor School Children* (London: about 1885) [edition made from bound galleys, most pages unnumbered] cataloged B.885, Goldsmith's Library, University of London.

122.   Sidney and Beatrice Webb, *Break-Up of the Poor Law*, 203.

Chapter 4   Political Economy and the New Poor Law

1. James Bonar, *Malthus and His Work* (London: Macmillan and Co., 1885), 304–5.

2. Digby, "Malthus and Reform of the Poor Law": 106.

3. Finer, "The transmission of Benthamite ideas": 16.

4. *Ibid.*, 16.

5. James, *Population Malthus*, 355.

6. *Ibid.*

7. Finer, "The transmission of Benthamite ideas": 17.

8. Hilton, *Age of Atonement*, 240.

9. O.R. McGregor, "Social Research and Social Policy in the Nineteenth Century," *British Journal of Sociology*, Vol. 8 (1957): 148.

10. Nassau William Senior, *Two Lectures on Population, Delivered before The University of Oxford in Easter Term, 1828, to which is Added, a Correspondence between the Author and the Revd.T.R. Malthus* (London: Saunders and Otley, 1828), 63.

11. Himmelfarb, *The Idea of Poverty*, 101. The latter assumption reflects the "wage fund theory" commonly accepted by political economists of the era. This theory held that the amount of circulating capital available for wages was fixed; therefore individual wages would be governed entirely by the laws of supply and demand, with more laborers inevitably meaning lower wages for each. For a fuller history and explication, see *The New Palgrave: A Dictionary of Economics*, ed. by John Eatwell, Murray Milgate and Peter Newman, Vol. 4 (New York: Stockton Press, 1987), 835–7.

12. T.R. Malthus, *Letter to Samuel Whitbread, Esq. MP on His Proposed Bill for the Amendment of the Poor Laws*, 1807, reprinted in *Introduction to Malthus*, ed. by D.V. Glass (New York: John Wiley & Sons, 1953), 190.

13. *Ibid.*

14. Himmelfarb, *The Idea of Poverty*, 63.

15. *Ibid.*, 61.

16. Senior, *Two Lectures on Population*, 14.

17. *Ibid.*, 3.

18. Senior, *Letter to Lord Howick*, 43.

19. Senior, *Two Lectures on Population*, 75.

20. *Ibid.*, 79.

21. Finer, *The Life and Times of Sir Edwin Chadwick*, 23.

22. *Ibid.*, 25.

23. *Ibid.*, 26.

24. Bentham, *Essays on the subject of the Poor Laws*, 25. Essay dated 28 April, 1796.

25. *Ibid.*, 25/3.

26. *Ibid.*, 26.

27. *Ibid.*, 25/3–26.

28. Himmelfarb, *The Idea of Poverty*, 85.

29. Item 18, Circular from the Poor Law Commissioners, 20 January 1835, Chadwick Papers, University College, London.

30. Himmelfarb, *The Idea of Poverty*, 112.

31. Malthus, *An Essay on the Principle of Population*, 2nd edn (London: J. Johnson, 1803), 507.

32. Ursula Henriques, "Bastardy and the New Poor Law": 111.

33. *Report from His Majesty's Commissioners for Inquiring into the Administration and Practical Operation of the Poor Laws*, Appendix C, Communications (1834), 126. Henceforth Royal Commission (1834).

34. Henriques, "Bastardy and the New Poor Law": 127–9.

35. James, *Population Malthus*, 123.

36. *Ibid.*
37. Lord Byron, *Don Juan and Other Satirical Poems* (New York: The Odyssey Press, 1935), 664.
38. Nassau William Senior, *Two Lectures on Population*, 32–3.
39. Checkland and Checkland, *The Poor Law Report of 1834*, 94.
40. Royal Commission (1834), Appendix A, XXVIII, 4.
41. Item 18, Chadwick Papers, University College, London.
42. John Stuart Mill, "On the Definition of Political Economy; and on the Method of Investigation proper to it," in *Essays on Some Unsettled Questions of Political Economy*, 2nd edn (London: Longmans, Green, Reader, and Dyer, 1874), 137.
43. J.S. Mill, "On the Definition of Political Economy," 139.
44. *Ibid.*, 156–7.
45. James, *Population Malthus*, 102.
46. *Ibid.*, 201.
47. Royal Commission (1834), Appendix C, 126.
48. *Ibid.*, 127.
49. *Ibid.*, 128.
50. Royal Commission (1834), Appendix A, 8.
51. Lees, *The Solidarities of Strangers*, 141.
52. Edwin Chadwick, "The New Poor Law" *Edinburgh Review*, LXIII (1836): 488.
53. Harriet Martineau, *Poor Laws and Paupers Illustrated* (London: Charles Fox, 1833), *i.*
54. *Ibid.*, 127.
55. Checkland and Checkland, *The Poor Law Report of 1834*, 263.
56. *Ibid.*, 272. This testimony was attached to the Report of the Royal Commission as an appendix.
57. *Hansard Parliamentary Debates*, 3d ser., Vol. 24 (1834) col. 522.
58. *Ibid.*
59. *Ibid.*
60. *Ibid.*, col. 529.
61. *Ibid.*, col. 530.
62. *Ibid.*, col. 533.
63. *Ibid.*, col. 536–7.
64. *Hansard Parliamentary Debates*, 3d ser., Vol. 25 (1834), col. 248.
65. *Ibid.*, col. 586–7.
66. *Ibid.*, col. 597.
67. *Ibid.*, col. 784.
68. *Ibid.*, col. 248.
69. Murray, *Losing Ground*, 156.
70. Checkland and Checkland, *The Poor Law Report of 1834*, 265.
71. George W. Zinke, "Six Letters from Malthus to Pierre Prevost," *Journal of Economic History*, Vol. 2 (1942): 185.
72. Senior, *Two Lectures on Population*, 32.
73. The assertion of complete rationality, of course, is in keeping not only with political economy but also with the viewpoint of the widely accepted Lockean psychology of pleasure and pain. In this as in so many aspects of Victorian thought, many streams led to the same river, each adding force to the others.

74. Consider, for example, Charles Murray, who seems quite comfortable in confining the decision-making process of "Harold and Phyllis" to economic incentives.
75. *Hansard Parliamentary Debates*, 3d ser., Vol. 24 (1834), col. 530.
76. *Ibid.*, col. 531.
77. Chadwick, "The New Poor Law," 488.
78. Checkland and Checkland, *The Poor Law Report of* 1834, 267.
79. James, *Population Malthus*, 56.

Chapter 5   From Political Economy to Social Science

1. For a full and fairly typical account see Derek Fraser, *The Evolution of the British Welfare State* (London: The Macmillan Press, 1973).
2. Fraser, *The Evolution of the British Welfare State*, 54. Cholera, Fraser comments, caused more public concern than the endemic diseases that claimed far more victims but affected primarily the poor.
3. Dr Southwood Smith, as it happens, was the grandfather of Octavia Hill, a member of the Edwardian Royal Commission on the Poor Laws. He therefore represents, in human form, an element of continuity between the two Commissions.
4. Finer, *The Life and Times of Sir Edwin Chadwick*, 209.
5. *Ibid.*, 157.
6. Charles Singer and E. Ashworth Underwood, *A Short History of Medicine*, 2nd edn (New York: Oxford University Press, 1962), 214–15.
7. Rachel Vorspan, "Vagrancy and the New Poor Law in late-Victorian and Edwardian England," *The English Historical Review*, 92 (January 1977): 68.
8. Senior, *A Letter to Lord Howick*, 28.
9. Chadwick, "The New Poor Law," 498.
10. Lynn Hollen Lees, "The Survival of the Unfit: Welfare Policies and Family Maintenance in Nineteenth-Century London", in *The Uses of Charity*, ed. by Peter Mandler (Philadelphia: University of Pennsylvania Press, 1990), 82.
11. *Ibid.*
12. Himmelfarb, *The Idea of Poverty*, 175.
13. Poovey, *Making a Social Body*, 64.
14. Hilton, *The Age of Atonement*, 155.
15. C.S. Loch, *How to Help Cases of Distress*, vi–vii.
16. Bosanquet, *Rich and Poor*, 73.
17. Sidney and Beatrice Webb, *English Local Government*, Vol. 8, 556.
18. Philip Abrams, *The Origins of British Sociology: 1834–1914, An Essay with Selected Papers* (Chicago and London: University of Chicago Press, 1968), vi.
19. M.J. Cullen, *The Statistical Movement in Early Victorian Britain: The Foundations of Empirical Social Research* (New York: The Harvester Press/Barnes & Noble Books, 1975).
20. *Ibid.*, 10–20.
21. Romano, *Beatrice Webb*, 19.
22. Abrams, *The Origins of British Sociology*, 16–18.

23. Mary Poovey, *Making a Social Body: British Cultural Formation 1830–1864* (Chicago: University of Chicago Press, 1995), 10–11.
24. *Ibid.*
25. Mary Poovey, *A History of the Modern Fact: Problems of Knowledge in the Sciences of Wealth and Society* (Chicago: University of Chicago Press, 1998), 290.
26. Checkland and Checkland, *The Poor Law Report of 1834*, 272.
27. Edwin Chadwick to Nassau William Senior, 30 July 1834, Item 1782, Chadwick Papers, University College, London.
28. *Ibid.*
29. Checkland and Checkland, *The Poor Law Report of 1834*, 265.
30. Poovey, *Making a Social Body*, 87.
31. *Ibid.*, 118.
32. Abrams, *The Origins of British Sociology*, 31.
33. Mary Poovey, "Figures of Arithmetic, Figures of Speech: The Discourse of Statistics in the 1830s," *Critical Inquiry*, 19 (Winter 1993): 270.
34. Abrams, *The Origins of British Sociology*, 32.
35. As we shall see, much the same might be said about many twentieth-century poverty studies as well.
36. Friedrich Engels, *The Condition of the Working Class in England* (Oxford: Oxford University Press, 1993), 103–4. The work was first published in 1844.
37. Himmelfarb, *The Idea of Poverty*, 329.
38. Helen Dendy [Bosanquet], "The Children of Working London," in *Aspects of the Social Problem*, ed. by Bernard Bosanquet (London: Macmillan and Co., 1895), 38.
39. Helen Dendy [Bosanquet], "The Meaning and Methods of True Charity," in *Aspects of the Social Problem,* 176 (Italics in the original.)
40. Sidney and Beatrice Webb, *Industrial Democracy* (London: Longmans, Green and Co., 1902), 638.
41. B. Seebohm Rowntree, *Poverty: A Study of Town Life*, 2nd edn (London: Longmans, Green and Co., 1922), 176. The first edition, published in 1901, differed only trivially from the second.
42. Abrams, *The Origins of British Sociology*, 24.
43. Charles Booth, *Life and Labour of the People in London*, First Series: *Poverty*, Volume I: *East, Central and South London* (New York: AMS Press, Inc., 1970), 42–3. This is a reprint of the 1902–1904 edition, New York and London.
44. Charles Booth, *Life and Labour of the People in London, Final Volume: Notes on Social Influences and Conclusion* (New York: AMS Press, Inc., 1970), 122.
45. Himmelfarb, *Poverty and Compassion*, 120.
46. T.S. Simey, *Charles Booth: Social Scientist*, 68.
47. Reproduced in Poovey, "Figures of Arithmetic", 270.
48. Brian Rodgers, "The Social Science Association, 1857–1886," *The Manchester School of Economics and Social Studies* 20 (Sept. 1952): 295.
49. *Ibid.*, 288.
50. Abrams, *The Origins of British Sociology*, 45.
51. *Ibid.*, 44.
52. Rodgers, "The Social Science Association," 290.

53. Abrams, *The Origins of British Sociology*, 48.
54. *Ibid.*, 45.
55. Rodgers, "The Social Science Association," 302.
56. Abrams, *The Origins of British Sociology*, 43.
57. *Ibid.*
58. Himmelfarb, *Poverty and Compassion*, 120.
59. Brian Harrison, *Drink and the Victorians: The Temperance Question in England 1815–1872* (Pittsburgh: University of Pittsburgh Press, 1971), 371.
60. Abrams, *The Origins of British Sociology*, 49–52.
61. Owen, *English Philanthropy*, 231.
62. Humphreys, *Sin, Organized Charity and the Poor Law*, 7.
63. Richard Titmuss, review of C.L. Mowatt's *The Charity Organisation Society* in *New Statesman*, 61 (June 1961): 962.
64. Lees, *The Solidarities of Strangers*, 270.
65. Humphreys, *Sin, Organized Charity and the Poor Law*, 10.
66. Lees, *The Solidarities of Strangers*, 270.
67. Daniel Patrick Moynihan, "The Professors and the Poor," in *On Understanding Poverty: Perspectives from the Social Sciences*, ed. by Daniel Patrick Moynihan (New York: Basic Books, Inc., 1968), 28.
68. Bell, *Octavia Hill*, 203.
69. Octavia Hill, "Common Sense and the Dwellings of the Poor," *The Nineteenth Century*, 14 (December 1883): 932.
70. Bell, *Octavia Hill*, 109.
71. *Ibid.*, 113.
72. Himmelfarb, *Poverty and Compassion*, 161.
73. *Ibid.*, 163.
74. Lansbury, *My Life*, 129.
75. *Ibid.*, 132.
76. *Ibid.*
77. As Humphreys notes, institutional turf wars undoubtedly played a role, as well.
78. Humphreys, *Sin, Organized Charity, and the Poor Law*, 80.
79. *Ibid.*, 185.
80. Himmelfarb, *Poverty and Compassion*, 192.
81. C.S. Loch, "Manufacturing a New Pauperism," *The Nineteenth Century*, 37 (April 1895): 698.
82. *Ibid.*, 708.
83. Loch, *How to Help Cases of Distress*, clxxxi.
84. Charles Loch Mowatt, *The Charity Organisation Society 1869–1913: Its Ideas and Work* (London: Methuen & Co. Ltd, 1961), 35. This is the Society's semi-official history, written by the grandson of C.S. Loch.
85. *Ibid.*, 36.
86. *Ibid.*, 27.
87. Kathleen Woodroofe, *From Charity to Social Work in England and the United States* (London: Routledge and Kegan Paul, 1962), 24.
88. Lees, *The Solidarities of Strangers*, 179.
89. A.W. Vincent, "The Poor Law Reports of 1909 and the Social Theory of the Charity Organization Society" *Victorian Studies*, 27 (1984): 346.

90. Bernard Bosanquet, "The Reports of the Poor Law Commission," *The Sociological Review*, 2 (April 1909): 116.
91. *Ibid.*, 114.
92. *Ibid.*, 114–15.
93. Himmelfarb, *Poverty and Compassion*, 248.
94. *Ibid.*
95. Vytautas Kavolis, *Moralizing Cultures* (Lanham, MD: University Press of America, 1993), 103.
96. *Ibid.*, 109.
97. Jane Lewis, *The Politics of Motherhood: Child and Maternal Welfare in England 1900–1939* (Montreal: McGill-Queen's University Press, 1980), 11.
98. Lewis, *Women and Social Action*, 180–1.
99. Sidney and Beatrice Webb, eds, *The Break-Up of the Poor Law: Being Part One of the Minority Report* (London: Longmans, Green and Co., 1909), 127. Italics are in the original text.
100. Lewis, *Women and Social Action*, 184.
101. Frances Fox Piven and Richard A. Cloward, *Regulating the Poor: The Functions of Public Welfare* (New York: Pantheon Books, 1971), 177.
102. Jones, *Outcast London*, 257.
103. Humphreys, *Sin, Organized Charity, and the Poor Law*, 12.

Chapter 6   Ignoble Savages on Relief: Social Darwinism in Late Victorian Poverty Studies

1. Gertrude Himmelfarb, *Darwin and the Darwinian Revolution* (New York: W.W. Norton, 1968), 431.
2. *Ibid.*
3. Gertrude Himmelfarb, "Social Darwinism, Sociobiology, and the Two Cultures," in *Marriage and Morals Among the Victorians* (New York: Alfred A. Knopf, 1986), 77.
4. Henrika Kuklick sums up both the vastness and the chaos of the phenomenon in saying that it would be extremely difficult to catalogue fully all of the ways in which the ideas of anthropology influenced social policy precisely because "evolutionist notions suffused Victorian culture." *The Savage Within: The Social History of British Anthropology* (Cambridge: Cambridge University Press, 1991), 77–8.
5. George W. Stocking, Jr, *Victorian Anthropology* (New York: The Free Press, 1987), 146.
6. George F. McCleary, *The Malthusian Population Theory* (London: Faber & Faber Ltd, 1953), 171.
7. Smiles, *Self-Help*, 296.
8. Kuklick, *The Savage Within*, 81.
9. Helen Dendy [Bosanquet], "The Children of Working London," 34.
10. Stephen Jay Gould, *The Mismeasure of Man* (New York: W.W. Norton & Co., 1981), 40.
11. *Ibid.*, 114.
12. *Ibid.*

13. Kuklick, *The Savage Within*, 161.
14. Gould, *Mismeasure of Man*, 115. Italics in the original.
15. Stephen Jay Gould, *Ever Since Darwin: Reflections in Natural History* (New York: W.W. Norton & Co., 1977), 215–17.
16. Stocking, *Victorian Anthropology*, 229.
17. *Ibid.*
18. Helen [Dendy] Bosanquet, *The Standard of Life*, 70.
19. *Ibid.*, 80.
20. Helen [Dendy] Bosanquet, *The Strength of the People*, 106.
21. Interestingly enough, anthropologist Oscar Lewis later explicitly argued that these same characteristics are present, not in primitive peoples, but in the poor of a "class-stratified, highly individuated, capitalistic society." See "The Culture of Poverty," in D.P. Moynihan, ed., *On Understanding Poverty*: 187–8.
22. Quoted in Poovey, *A History of the Modern Fact*, 231.
23. Poovey, *Making a Social Body*, 64.
24. Samuel Smiles, *Character* (New York: Harper & Brothers, 1872), 165. The book was first published in Britain in 1871.
25. Cited in Paul Johnson, "Class Law in Victorian England," *Past and Present*, 141 (1993): 164. The original article was published in 1860 in the *Quarterly Review*.
26. Sidney Webb, *The Difficulties of Individualism*, Fabian Tract #69 (London: 1896).
27. Kuklick, *The Savage Within*, 100.
28. Himmelfarb, *The Idea of Poverty*, 366–7.
29. Abrams, *The Origins of British Sociology*, 97.
30. *Ibid.*
31. Stocking, *Victorian Anthropology*, 227–8.
32. *Ibid.*
33. Therefore Christopher Herbert is more inclined to see the central preoccupation of nineteenth-century social thought, "the myth of a state of ungoverned human desire," as derived from "the Wesleyan mythology of sin." *Culture and Anomie: Ethnographic Imagination in the Nineteenth Century* (Chicago: University of Chicago Press, 1991), 29, 32.
34. Cited in Stocking, *Victorian Anthropology*, 153.
35. Kuklick, *The Savage Within*, 303.
36. *Encyclopaedia Britannica*, 9th edn, s.v. "cannibalism."
37. George W. Stocking, Jr, *After Tylor: British Social Anthropology 1888–1951* (Madison, WI: University of Wisconsin Press, 1995), 15.
38. *Ibid.*, 16.
39. Herbert, *Culture and Anomie*, 160–1.
40. *Ibid.*, 157.
41. Stocking, *Victorian Anthropology*, 225.
42. Thorstein Veblen, *The Theory of the Leisure Class* (New York: Dover Publications, 1994), 26.
43. Karl Marx and Friedrich Engels, *The Communist Manifesto* (Baltimore, MD: Penguin Books, 1967), 99.
44. Veblen, *Theory of the Leisure Class*, 47.
45. *Ibid.*, 137.

46. *Ibid.*, 149.
47. Helen Dendy [Bosanquet], "The Industrial Residuum," in *Aspects of the Social Problem*, 83–4.
48. Sidney Webb, *The Decline in the Birth-Rate*, Fabian Tract #131 (London: March 1907), 17.
49. *Ibid.*
50. Beatrice Webb, *Our Partnership*, 83 Diary entry for July, 1894.
51. *Ibid.*, 299–300. Diary entry of January, 1905.
52. Mill quoted in Owen Chadwick, *The Secularization of the European Mind in the Nineteenth Century*, 28.
53. Himmelfarb, *The Idea of Poverty*, 301–2.
54. Bernard Bosanquet, "The Reports of the Poor Law Commission," 117.
55. Beatrice Webb, *Our Partnership*, 417, 474.
56. *Ibid.*, 474.

Chapter 7   Science and Pseudoscience in Victorian and Edwardian Poverty Studies

1. Gertrude Himmelfarb, "The Age of Philanthropy," *The Wilson Quarterly* (Spring 1997): 51.
2. *Ibid.*
3. Beatrice Webb, *Our Partnership*, 88.
4. *Ibid.*, 87–8.
5. McBriar, *An Edwardian Mixed Doubles*, 17.
6. C. Wright Mills, *The Sociological Imagination* (New York: Oxford University Press, 1959), 13.
7. *Ibid.*
8. Stefan Collini, *Liberalism and Sociology: L.T. Hobhouse and Political Argument in England 1880–1914* (Cambridge: Cambridge University Press, 1979), 26–7.
9. Lees, *The Solidarities of Strangers*, 122.
10. R.K. Webb, *Harriet Martineau*, 37.
11. *Ibid.*, 119.
12. Smiles, *Character*, 168.
13. John Maynard Keynes, "Robert Malthus: The First of the Cambridge Economists," in *Essays in Biography*, 2nd edn (London: Mercury Books, 1961), 99.
14. Ronald L. Meek, ed., *Marx and Engels on Malthus* (New York: International Publishers, 1954), 176.
15. Rodgers, "The Social Science Association," 302.
16. Huggins, *Protestants Against Poverty*, 78–9.
17. Diana Strassman, "Not a Free Market: The Rhetoric of Disciplinary Authority in Economics," in *Beyond Economic Man: Feminist Theory and Economics*, ed. by Marianne A. Ferber and Julie A. Nelson (Chicago: University of Chicago Press, 1993), 63.
18. *Ibid.*, 61.
19. Michael B. Katz, *The Undeserving Poor: From the War on Poverty to the War on Welfare* (New York: Pantheon Books, 1989), 41–2.

20. Moynihan, "The Professors and the Poor," 9.
21. Sidney & Beatrice Webb, *English Local Government*, Vol. 8, 84.
22. Kingsley Davis, "Malthus and the Theory of Population," in *The Language of Social Research: A Reader in the Methodology of Social Research*, ed. by Paul F. Lazarsfeld and Morris Rosenberg (Glencoe, IL: The Free Press, 1955), 549.
23. McKibbon, "Class and Poverty in Edwardian England," 169, 171.
24. Helen [Dendy] Bosanquet, *Rich and Poor*, 26.
25. *Ibid.*
26. Himmelfarb, *Poverty and Compassion*, 233.
27. H. Bosanquet, *Rich and Poor*, 27.
28. Charles Dickens, *Oliver Twist* (London: Penguin Books, 1985), 55. The novel was first published, serially, in 1837–1839.
29. H. Bosanquet, *Rich and Poor*, 92. The coroner had enumerated several recent cases that were, in his opinion, the result of inappropriate feeding.
30. *Ibid.*, 93–4.
31. Maud Pember Reeves, *Round About a Pound A Week* (New York: Garland Publishing Inc., 1980), 87. This is a reprint of the 1913 edition.
32. Reeves does, by the way, draw an environmentalist conclusion from her anecdote; immediately after the last sentence of the passage quoted above, she adds: "The rent is far too low for healthy rooms."
33. S. & B. Webb, *The Prevention of Destitution*, 237.
34. Stephen Jay Gould, "Jim Bowie's Letter and Bill Buckner's Legs," *Natural History*, 109 (May, 2000): 39. It influences, he argues, not just baseball fans remembering the events of a World Series game but earnest scientists attempting to be rigorous and objective in their pursuit of truth.
35. Seth Koven, "Dr. Barnardo's 'Artistic Fictions': Photography, Sexuality, and the Ragged Child in Victorian London," *Radical History Review*, 69 (Fall 1997), 29.
36. R.K. Webb, *Harriet Martineau*, 192.
37. Poovey, *Making a Social Body*, 133.
38. Helen Dendy [Bosanquet], "The Children of Working London," 30.
39. H. Bosanquet, *Rich and Poor*, 106.
40. Bernard Bosanquet, "Character in Its Bearing on Social Causation," in *Aspects of the Social Problem*, 117.
41. Charles Murray, *Losing Ground: American Social Policy, 1950–1980* (New York: Basic Books, Inc., 1984), 156–62.
42. Katz, *The Undeserving Poor*, 170.
43. Lewis Coser, *Masters of Sociological Thought: Ideas in Historical and Social Context*, 2nd edn (New York: Harcourt Brace Jovanovich, 1977), 221.
44. *Ibid.*, 223–4.
45. Max Weber, "'Objectivity' in Social Science and Social Policy," in *Max Weber on the Methodology of the Social Sciences* translated and edited by Edward A. Shils and Henry A. Finch (Glencoe, IL: The Free Press, 1949), 97. Italics in original.
46. Angus McLaren, "Sex and Socialism: The Opposition of the French Left to Birth Control in the Nineteenth Century," *Journal of the History of Ideas*, 38 (1976): 491.

47. For a thorough analysis of precisely what's wrong with Murray's statistics see Christopher Jencks, "How Poor Are the Poor?" *New York Review of Books xxxii*, no. 8 (May 9, 1985), 41–9; and Robert Greenstein, "Losing Faith in 'Losing Ground'" *New Republic*, March 25, 1985. Also illuminating are the critiques in Michael B. Katz, *The Undeserving Poor*, 151–6, and William Julius Wilson, *The Truly Disadvantaged*, 16–18.

48. Himmelfarb, *Poverty and Compassion*, 133.

49. Poovey, *History of the Modern Fact, xii*.

50. John A. Hobson, "The Social Philosophy of Charity Organisation," *The Contemporary Review*, 70 (November 1896): 719.

51. Mills, *The Sociological Imagination*, 67.

52. Humphreys, *Sin, Organized Charity, and the Poor Law*, 10.

53. Himmelfarb, *Poverty and Compassion*, 120.

54. Lewis, *The Politics of Motherhood*, 89.

55. Gould, *The Mismeasure of Man*, 22.

56. Sidney and Beatrice Webb, *Methods of Social Study* (London: Longmans, Green & Co., 1932), 36.

57. *Ibid.*, 47.

58. S. & B. Webb, *Industrial Democracy*, 638.

59. H.L. Malchow, "A Victorian Mind: Gertrude Himmelfarb, Poverty, and the Moral Imagination," *Victorian Studies*, 35 (Spring 1992): 314.

60. Himmelfarb, *Poverty and Compassion*, 98. Beatrice Webb, then Beatrice Potter, had taken a serious interest in the methodology of the survey and participated in some of the earliest phases of it.

61. United Kingdom. Parliament. *Report of the Royal Commission on the Poor Laws and Relief of Distress*. Appendix 18. Cmd. 5037. 1910, 61.

62. *Ibid.*

63. Smiles, *Self-Help*, 242.

64. Finer, *The Life and Times of Sir Edwin Chadwick*, 59.

65. *Ibid.*, 3.

66. H. Bosanquet, *Rich and Poor*, 105.

67. Paul Johnson, "Class Law in Victorian England," *Past and Present*, 141 (1993): 157–8.

68. H. Bosanquet, *The Standard of Life*, 12.

69. Bell, *Octavia Hill*, 85.

70. Lewis, *Women and Social Action*, 61.

71. Lansbury, *My Life*, 131.

72. *Ibid.*, 130.

73. *Ibid.*, 133.

74. *Ibid.*, 52.

75. *Ibid.*, 138.

76. *Ibid.*, 133.

77. Hobson, "The Social Philosophy of Charity Organisation," 712–13.

78. [George] Bernard Shaw, "Socialism and Human Nature," in *The Road to Equality: Ten Unpublished Lectures and Essays, 1884–1918*, ed. Louis Crompton (Boston: Beacon Press, 1971), 99. This essay was read to the Fabian Society in 1890.

79. G.B. Shaw, *Pygmalion*, Act 2, in *Selected Plays of Bernard Shaw* (New York: Dodd, Mead & Co, 1948). The play is dated 1913.

80. F.K. Prochaska, "Philanthropy," 362.
81. George Orwell, *The Road to Wigan Pier*, Left Book Club Edition (London: Victor Gollancz Ltd, 1937), 87–8.
82. Margaret Hewitt, *Wives and Mothers in Victorian Industry* (Westport, CT: Greenwood Press, 1958), 46.
83. Linda Gordon has described a similar process in the workings of the Massachusetts Society for the Prevention of Cruelty to Children from its founding in 1878; in their studies "single mothers are consistently over-represented as neglectful parents," as are the very poor and especially the immigrant poor, whose cultural traditions the largely Anglo-Saxon Protestants of the MSPCC made no attempt to understand. "Single Mothers and Child Neglect, 1880–1920," *American Quarterly*, 37 (Summer 1985), 174, 177–8.
84. Ellen Ross, *Love and Toil: Motherhood in Outcast London 1870–1918* (New York: Oxford University Press, 1993), 217.
85. S. & B. Webb, *The Break-Up of the Poor Law*, 122.
86. *Ibid.*
87. *Ibid.*, 124.
88. Paul Johnson, "Conspicuous Consumption and Working-Class Culture in Late Victorian and Edwardian Britain," *Transactions of the Royal Historical Society*, 38 (1988): 40–1.
89. *Ibid.*
90. Hewitt, *Wives and Mothers in Victorian Industry*, 80.
91. Paul Johnson, *Saving and Spending: The Working-Class Economy in Britain, 1870–1939* (Oxford: Clarendon Press, 1985), 25.
92. Reeves, *Round About a Pound a Week*, 75.
93. Himmelfarb, *The Idea of Poverty*, 404.
94. *Ibid.*
95. Helen Dendy [Bosanquet], "The Children of Working London," 30.
96. H. Bosanquet, *The Strength of the People*, 1; the Cromwell quotation is taken from Morley's *Life*.
97. *Ibid.*, 6.
98. *Ibid.*, 18.
99. *Ibid.*, 18–19.
100. *Ibid.*, 155.
101. It also reminds us that male social thinkers don't have a monopoly on misogyny.
102. H. Bosanquet, *The Strength of the People*, 150.
103. *Ibid.*, 154.
104. Albert Fried and Richard M. Elman, eds, *Charles Booth's London: A Portrait of the Poor at the Turn of the Century, Drawn from His "Life and Labour of the People in London"* (New York: Pantheon Books, 1968), *xxix*.
105. Jeanne MacKenzie, *A Victorian Courtship: The Story of Beatrice Potter and Sidney Webb* (New York: Oxford University Press, 1979), 52.
106. *Ibid.*
107. Charles Booth, *Life and Labour of the People in London*, First Series: *Poverty*, Volume 2: *Streets and Population Classified* (New York: AMS Press, Inc., 1970), 54. This is a reprint from the edition of 1902–1904, New York and London.

108.   It should be noted that this multiplication of Christmas dinners rep-
       resents precisely the type of unscientific, unsystematic distribution of
       charity so deplored by the COS, although it is harder for this reader than
       for COS members to interpret it as a product of chicanery rather than of
       desperation.
109.   C. Booth, *Life and Labour*, First Series, Vol. 2, 81.
110.   Simey, *Charles Booth: Social Scientist*, 113.
111.   Charles Booth, *Life and Labour of the People in London*, Final Volume:
       Notes on Social Influences and Conclusion (1902–1904; reprint, New York:
       AMS Press, 1970), 62, 59.
112.   *Ibid.*, 62.
113.   *Ibid.*, 72.
114.   At the time, ill health was often seen as well within the control of the
       poor, as we have seen in our survey of the Public Health Movement.
115.   In other contexts Booth was more open to environmentalist considera-
       tions, commenting, for example, that the condition of the disreputable
       denizens of Class A, who "degrade whatever they touch," is affected by
       the economic condition of the classes above them. They are depraved, in
       other words, but are unavoidably harmed by economic currents beyond
       their control. *Life and Labour*, First Series, Vol. 1, 38.
116.   Himmelfarb, *Poverty and Compassion*, 102.
117.   *Ibid.*, 163.
118.   H. Bosanquet, *The Strength of the People*, 101–2.
119.   *Ibid.*, 102.
120.   C. Booth, *Life and Labour of the People in London*, Vol. 1, 41.
121.   *Ibid.*, 47.
122.   B. Seebohm Rowntree, *Poverty: A Study of Town Life*, 2nd edn (London:
       Longmans, Green & Co., 1922), 154, first edition 1901.
123.   *Ibid.*, 73.
124.   *The Poor Law Report of 1909*, 77.
125.   H. Bosanquet, *The Strength of the People*, 102.
126.   *Ibid.*
127.   Reeves, *Round About A Pound A Week*, 8.
128.   *Ibid.*, 176.
129.   *Ibid.*, 9–10.
130.   *Ibid.*, 9.
131.   *Ibid.*
132.   *Ibid.*, 93.
133.   *Ibid.*, 80.
134.   Judith Fido, "The Charity Organisation Society and Social Casework
       in London, 1869–1900," in *Social Control in Nineteenth Century Britain*,
       ed. A.P. Donajgrodzki (London: Croom Helm, 1977), 218.
135.   The decision to raise the upper limit of income after two years' study is a
       case in point.
136.   Reeves, *Round About A Pound A Week*, 193.
137.   *Ibid.*
138.   *Ibid.*, 76.
139.   Helen Bosanquet, review of Mrs Pember Reeves, *Round About A Pound
       A Week* in *Economic Journal*, 24 (March 1914): 110.

140. Reeves, *Round About A Pound A Week*, 151.
141. H. Bosanquet, review of *Round About A Pound A Week*, 110.
142. *Ibid.*, 111.
143. *Ibid.*, 112.
144. Michael Young and Peter Willmott, *Family and Kinship in East London* (Glencoe, IL: The Free Press, 1957), 157–8.
145. Edward T. Devine, *Misery and Its Causes* (New York: Macmillan, 1913). The book was first published in 1909; this edition was a second printing, apparently unrevised. Devine was Schiff Professor of Social Economy at Columbia University and editor of the chapter's journal, *The Survey*.
146. *Ibid.*, 178.
147. *Ibid.*
148. *Ibid.*, 192.
149. *Ibid.*, 225.
150. *Ibid.*, 225–6.
151. *Ibid.*, 11.
152. *Ibid.*, 13.
153. *Ibid.*, 35.
154. *Ibid.*, 74.
155. *Ibid.*, 76.
156. Harrison, *Drink and the Victorians*, 299.
157. Finer, *The Life and Times of Sir Edwin Chadwick*, 209.
158. Chadwick, "The New Poor Law," 498.
159. Loch, *How to Help Cases of Distress*, liv.
160. Katz, *The Undeserving Poor*, 41–2.
161. Simey, *Charles Booth: Social Scientist*, 180.
162. *Ibid.*, 163, citing Booth's *Pauperism, a Picture, and Endowment of Old Age*, 1892.
163. *Ibid.*, 158–9.
164. *Ibid.*, 163.
165. Helen Dendy [Bosanquet], "The Children of Working London," 38.
166. *Ibid.*, 39.
167. *Ibid.*
168. *Ibid.*, 84.
169. *Ibid.*, 87.
170. *Ibid.*, 88.
171. H. Bosanquet, *The Standard of Life*, 22.
172. Easily the most detailed study is Brian Harrison's *Drink and the Victorians*.
173. Rowntree, *Poverty*, 175.
174. *Ibid.*, 144, 152–3.
175. *Ibid.*, 152–3.
176. Helen Dendy [Bosanquet], "The Meaning and Methods of True Charity," in *Aspects of the Social Problem*, 176.
177. Rowntree, *Poverty*, 166.
178. *Ibid.*, 176.
179. *Ibid.*, 176, 179.
180. *Ibid.*, 179.
181. This inquiry was undertaken in response to the large number of recruits who failed Army induction physicals during the Boer War.

182.   S. & B. Webb, *English Local Government*, Vol. 8, 603.
183.   *Ibid.*, 606.
184.   *Ibid.*, 613.
185.   *Ibid.*
186.   *Ibid.*
187.   S. & B. Webb, *The Prevention of Destitution*, 6–7.
188.   *Ibid.*, 14.
189.   *Ibid.*, 49.
190.   Note the revealing phrase "class atmosphere."

Chapter 8   Three Case Studies in *a priori* Social Science

1.   Ross, *Love and Toil*, 201. The contemporary French debate on infant and child welfare paid little attention to this issue, concerning itself instead with nursing and maternal employment.
2.   Rowntree, *Poverty*, 55.
3.   *Ibid.*, 176.
4.   H. Bosanquet, *Rich and Poor*, 90–1.
5.   *Ibid.*, 85. This seems an unlikely error for a shopper who can "choose and buy as skillfully as any one," of course, but it is in keeping with the assumption of primitive ignorance.
6.   H. Bosanquet, *The Standard of Life*, 70.
7.   H. Bosanquet, *The Standard of Life*, 70.
8.   *Ibid.*
9.   *Ibid.*, 83. Italics in original text. The use of the male pronoun here is anomalous, not only because Bosanquet generally criticizes the household management of women, but because pawning and shopping on credit, as Bosanquet clearly knew, were generally the province of the housewife. Elsewhere Bosanquet consistently discusses shopping as the province of women. It seems probable that she uses the male pronoun here purely because of grammatical convention, since she is contrasting the slum resident to Economic *Man*.
10.   H. Bosanquet, "Marriage in East London," in *Aspects of the Social Problem*, 78.
11.   Smiles, *Self-Help*, 292.
12.   H. Bosanquet, *Strength of the People*, 95.
13.   Reeves, *Round About a Pound a Week*, 78.
14.   *Ibid.*, 110.
15.   Robert Roberts has left us a rich account of the grocery shop that his parents owned in Edwardian Salford, Manchester's worst slum. He recalls that his father disdained to sell extremely small quantities of food but that his mother and sister were more accommodating to their poorest customers, knowing that these tiny amounts were all they could afford. *The Classic Slum*, 105–6.
16.   Ross, *Love and Toil*, 52.
17.   Paul Johnson, Saving and Spending: The Working-Class Economy in Britain 1870–1939 (Oxford: Clarendon Press, 1985), 145.
18.   *Ibid.*, 147.

19. Roberts, *The Classic Slum*, 81–3.
20. Johnson, *Saving and Spending*, 150.
21. Roberts, *The Classic Slum*, 105–6.
22. *Ibid.*, 81.
23. *Ibid.*, 81–2.
24. *Ibid.*, 13.
25. See for example Ross, *Love and Toil*, 39.
26. *Ibid.*
27. Roberts, *The Classic Slum*, 174.
28. Johnson, *Conspicuous Consumption*, 36.
29. Veblen, *Theory of the Leisure Class*, 105.
30. *Ibid.*, 60.
31. Roberts, *The Classic Slum*, 25.
32. H. Bosanquet, "Marriage in East London," 78.
33. Johnson, *Saving and Spending*, 175–6.
34. *Ibid.*, 176–7.
35. *Ibid.*, 177.
36. *Ibid.*, 179.
37. Reeves, *Round About a Pound a Week*, 76.
38. Rowntree, *Poverty*, 142.
39. Orwell, *The Road to Wigan Pier*, 95.
40. Peter Townsend, "The Meaning of Poverty," *British Journal of Sociology*, 13 (1962): 217–19.
41. Rowntree, *Poverty*, 307.
42. Smiles, *Character*, 52.
43. *Ibid.*, 65–6.
44. R.K. Webb, *Harriet Martineau*, 270.
45. Jeremy Bentham, *Essays on the subject of the Poor Laws* CLIV (b) Folder 13, Bentham Archives, University College, London; 533 (Probable date 1797) Segregation by sex in the workhouse would also, of course, limit reproduction by the destitute.
46. H. Bosanquet, "The Children of Working London," 36.
47. S. & B. Webb, *The Break-Up of the Poor Law*, 86–7.
48. *Ibid.*, 7.
49. W. Booth, *In Darkest England*, 65.
50. H. Bosanquet, *Strength of the People*, 64.
51. H. Bosanquet, *Rich and Poor*, 92.
52. S. & B. Webb, *The Break-Up of the Poor Law*, 98.
53. S. & B. Webb, *English Poor Law History*, 606.
54. H. Bosanquet, *Rich and Poor*, 148.
55. H. Bosanquet, "The Children of Working London," 37.
56. H. Bosanquet, *Rich and Poor*, 81.
57. Ross, *Love and Toil*, 36.
58. *Ibid.*
59. Jack Goody, *Cooking, Cuisine and Class: A Study in Comparative Sociology* (Cambridge: Cambridge University Press, 1982), 150.
60. *Ibid.*, 151.
61. Ross, *Love and Toil*, 36.
62. Reeves, *Round About a Pound a Week*, 57.

63. *Ibid.* On the basis of numerous memoirs of working-class London, Ellen Ross gives a similar list of objections to the practicality of oatmeal, concluding that it "was a food that middle-class officials of various kinds attempted literally to stuff down the throats of the workers, a nauseating reminder of their social status." Ross, *Love and Toil*, 37.
64. Harrison, *Drink and the Victorians*, 38.
65. Goody, *Cooking, Cuisine and Class*, 160.
66. Reeves, *Round About a Pound a Week*, 99.
67. *Ibid.*
68. Lewis, *Politics of Motherhood*, 89.
69. S. & B. Webb, *The Prevention of Destitution*, 124–5.
70. *Ibid.*, 125.
71. United Kingdom. Parliament. *Report of the Royal Commission on the Poor Laws and Relief of Distress.* Cmd. 4499. 1909, 248–50.
72. Bosanquet, *Rich and Poor*, 27. This anecdote was discussed in detail in the previous chapter.
73. Octavia Hill, *The Charity Organisation Society*, Occasional Paper #15 (COS, 1896), 17; cited in Lewis, *Women and Social Action*, 50.
74. Lewis, *Women and Social Action*, 177.
75. S. & B. Webb, *The Prevention of Destitution*, 210.
76. *Ibid.*, 134–5.
77. S. & B. Webb, *English Local Government*, Vol. 8, 606.
78. S. & B. Webb, *The Prevention of Destitution*, 98.
79. *Ibid.*
80. Anna Davin, "Loaves and Fishes: Food in Poor Households in Late Nineteenth-Century London," *History Workshop Journal*, 41 (Spring 1996), 184.
81. Young and Willmott, *Family and Kinship in East London*, 32.
82. Midge Gillies, *Marie Lloyd: The One and Only* (London: Victor Gollancz, 1999), 80–1.
83. Roberts, *The Classic Slum*, 92.
84. Gordon, "Single Mothers and Child Neglect," 180.
85. *Ibid.*, 180–1.
86. Edward Berdoe, "Slum Mothers and Death-Clubs: A Vindication," *The Nineteenth Century* (April 1891): 562.
87. Lewis, *Politics of Motherhood*, 61, 77.
88. S. & B. Webb, *The Prevention of Destitution*, 123.
89. On the childlessness of district nurses and health visitors, see Ellen Ross, "Good and Bad Mothers: Lady Philanthropists and London Housewives before the First World War," in *Lady Bountiful Revisited: Women, Philanthropy, and Power*, ed. by Kathleen D. McCarthy (New Brunswick, NJ: Rutgers University Press, 1990), 181.
90. Young and Willmott, *Family and Kinship in East London*, 36.
91. S. & B. Webb, *Break-Up of the Poor Law*, 507.
92. Ross, *Love and Toil*, 180.
93. Bunyan, *The Pilgrim's Progress*, 47.
94. Malthus, *Essay on the Principle of Population*, 2nd edn, 491.
95. Veblen, *Theory of the Leisure Class*, 26.

96. Helen Bosanquet, *The Poor Law Report of 1909: A Summary Explaining the Defects of the Present System and the Principal Recommendations of the Commission, so far as relates to England and Wales* (London: Macmillan and Co., 1909), 4.
97. Beatrice Webb, *Our Partnership*, 474.
98. Charles Booth, *Life and Labour of the People in London; Final Volume*, 125.
99. Susan Kingsley Kent, *Sex and Suffrage in Britain, 1860–1914* (Princeton, NJ: Princeton University Press, 1987); Judith R. Walkowitz, *Prostitution and Victorian Society: Women, Class and the State* (Cambridge: Cambridge University Press, 1980).
100. Octavia Hill, "Cottage Property in London," in *Homes of the London Poor* (London: Macmillan and Co., 1883), 10. This essay was first published in the *Fortnightly Review* in November, 1866.
101. *Ibid.*
102. *Ibid.*
103. Checkland & Checkland, *The Poor Law Report of 1834*, 173.
104. Bosanquet, *Strength of the People*, 103–4. For sheer naked misogyny this passage would be difficult to match in the writings of male social theorists, although it does acknowledge that the behavior attributed to poor women is not unique to their class.
105. Ellen Ross, "Survival Networks: Women's Neighborhood Sharing in London before World War One," *History Workshop Journal*, 15 (1983): 10; Roberts, *The Classic Slum*, 26.
106. W. Booth, *In Darkest England*, 165 (The odd punctuation is in the original.)
107. Octavia Hill, "Four Years' Management of a London court," in *Homes of the London Poor*, 27. This essay was first published in *Macmillan's Magazine* in July, 1869.
108. Octavia Hill, "Landlords and Tenants in London," in *Homes of the London Poor*, 41.
109. Octavia Hill, "Common Sense and the Dwellings of the Poor," 932.
110. Ross, *Love and Toil*, 137.
111. Lewis, *Politics of Motherhood*, 62–5.
112. *Ibid.*
113. Paul Thompson, *The Edwardians* (Chicago: Academy Chicago Publishers, 1975), 283.
114. Lewis, *Politics of Motherhood*, 62–5.
115. Ross, *Love and Toil*, 54.
116. Singer and Ashworth, *A Short History of Medicine*, 613–14.
117. Ross, *Love and Toil*, 181.
118. H. Bosanquet, *Rich and Poor*, 93–4.
119. *Ibid.*, 94.
120. B. Bosanquet, "The Reports of the Poor Law Commission," 120–1.
121. Berdoe, "Slum Mothers and Death-Clubs," 562.
122. H. Bosanquet, *Rich and Poor*, 108.
123. *Ibid.*
124. Ross, *Love and Toil*, 146–8.

125.   Yvonne M. Lassalle and Maureen O'Dougherty, "In Search of Weeping Worlds, Economies of Agency and Politics of Representation in the Ethnography of Inequality," *Radical History Review*, 69 (Fall 1997): 247.
126.   Johnson, "Class Law in Victorian England," 155.
127.   *Ibid.*, 156.
128.   Johnson, *Saving and Spending*, 13.
129.   *Lancet*, 14 September, 1861: 256–7.
130.   *Ibid.*
131.   *Lancet*, 28 September, 1861: 299.
132.   *Ibid.*
133.   J.I. Ikin, "On the undue Mortality of Infants and Children in connection with the Questions of Early Marriages, Drugging Children, Bad Nursing, Death Clubs, and Certificates of Death, &c," *Transactions* of the National Association for the Promotion of Social Science, York Meeting, 1864 (London: Longman, Green, Longman, Roberts, and Green, 1865), 510–11.
134.   W. Booth, *In Darkest England*, 65.
135.   S. & B. Webb, *The Break-up of the Poor Law*, 87.
136.   Berdoe, "Slum Mothers and Death Clubs," 560.
137.   *Ibid.*, 562.
138.   *Ibid.*, 562, 563.
139.   *Ibid.*
140.   Smiles, *Self-Help*, 247.
141.   Himmelfarb, *Poverty and Compassion*, 233.
142.   Lees, "The Survival of the Unfit," 86.
143.   Rowntree, *Poverty*, 142.
144.   Reeves, *Round About a Pound a Week*, 66.
145.   *Ibid.*, 67–8.
146.   Johnson, *Saving and Spending*, 43.
147.   *Ibid.*, 45. Most of the very poor were unlikely to have the vote in this period, so disenfranchisement, while stigmatizing, would not carry a practical penalty.
148.   Berdoe, "Slum Mothers and Death Clubs," 561.
149.   Johnson, *Saving and Spending*, 45.
150.   Himmelfarb, *The Idea of Poverty*, 186.
151.   Johnson, *Saving and Spending*, 25.
152.   Berdoe, "Slum Mothers and Death Clubs," 561.
153.   Jeremy Bentham, *Essays on the subject of the Poor Laws* CLIII(a) Folder 6, Bentham Archives, University College, London; 219.
154.   Erving Goffman, *Stigma: Notes on the Management of Spoiled Identity* (Englewood Cliffs, NJ: Prentice-Hall, Inc., 1963), 5.
155.   Veblen, *Theory of the Leisure Class*, 20.
156.   Ross, *Love and Toil*, 192.
157.   *Ibid.*
158.   Veblen, *Theory of the Leisure Class*, 45.
159.   Reeves, *Round About a Pound a Week*, 69.
160.   *Ibid.*, 73.
161.   Ross, *Love and Toil*, 191.

Chapter 9   Unanswered Questions, Unasked Questions, and an Experimental Counter-Hypothesis

1. Abrams, *The Origins of British Sociology*, 43. Italics in original.
2. Himmelfarb, *Poverty and Compassion*, 120.
3. Roberts, *The Classic Slum*, 95.
4. *Ibid.*, 96, 66.
5. Lansbury, *My Life*, 142.
6. McBriar, *An Edwardian Mixed Doubles*, 219.
7. *Ibid.*, 269. William Beveridge (1879–1963), later to become the architect of the British welfare state, did not play a major role in the work of the Royal Commission. He was at this time affiliated with Toynbee Hall, where he met the Webbs. A minor official at the Board of Trade engaged in the planning of labor exchanges, he was pressed into service by Beatrice Webb for expert testimony on the subject of unemployment.
8. Katz, *The Undeserving Poor*, 122.
9. Walter Korpi, "Approaches to the Study of Poverty in the United States: Critical Notes from a European Perspective," in *Poverty and Public Policy: an Evaluation of Social Science Research*, ed. by Vincent T. Covello (Cambridge, MA: Schenkman Publishing Co., 1980), 299.
10. *Ibid.*, 306.
11. Thomas Pettigrew, "Social Psychology's Potential Contributions to an Understanding of Poverty," in *Poverty and Public Policy*, 196.
12. *Ibid.*, 216.
13. Roberts, *The Classic Slum*, 176–7.
14. Berdoe, "Slum Mothers and Death Clubs," 562.
15. Reeves, *Round About a Pound a Week*, 92.
16. Roberts, *The Classic Slum*, 11.
17. S. & B. Webb, *English Local Government*, Vol. 8, 613.
18. This is what Linda Gordon found to be true in the slums of Boston in the late nineteenth and early twentieth century. "Single Mothers and Child Neglect": 80–1.
19. Devine, *Misery and Its Causes*, 9.
20. *Ibid.*, 13–14.
21. John E. Schrecker, *The Chinese Revolution in Historical Perspective* (New York: Praeger, 1991), 14.
22. Mung Tzu (Mencius), *The Mencius*, excerpted in *Sources of Chinese Tradition*, Vol. 1, compiled by Wm.deBary, Wing-tsit Chan, and Burton Watson (New York: Columbia University Press, 1960), 93.
23. Katz, *The Undeserving Poor*, 174–5.
24. J.D. Marshall, *The Old Poor Law, 1795–1834* (London: Macmillan, 1968), 42. The postwar experience of France and Japan would certainly tend to support this view.
25. Bernice Madison, "Canadian Family Allowances and Their Major Social Implications," *Journal of Marriage and the Family*, 26 (May 1964).
26. Ronald Freedman, "The Sociology of Human Fertility," *Current Sociology*, 10–11 (1961–69): 48.
27. G.B. Shaw, *Pygmalion*, Act V.
28. S. & B. Webb, *Methods of Social Study*, 33.

29. Pettigrew, "Social Psychology's Potential," 196.
30. Sanford F. Schram, *Words of Welfare: the Poverty of Social Science and the Social Science of Poverty* (Minneapolis: University of Minnesota Press, 1995), 64.
31. Walvin, *Victorian Values*, 2.
32. Tawney, "The Theory of Pauperism," 361.
33. Harrison, *Drink and the Victorians*, 372. Harrison is speaking of temperance societies, but he might just as well be speaking of the COS.
34. Cecil Driver, *Tory Radical: The Life of Richard Oastler* (New York: Oxford University Press, 1946), 282 Oastler (1789–1861) was a Tory radical who strongly supported the Established Church and opposed the *laissez-faire* policies of political economy on paternalistic grounds.
35. Kavolis, *Moralizing Cultures*, 51.
36. C.L. Mowatt, *The Charity Organisation Society*, 20.
37. Hazlitt asserted that the policy amounted to "starving the children of the poor to feed the horses of the rich." James, *Population Malthus*, 349.
38. Senior, "An Introductory Lecture on Political Economy, delivered before the University of Oxford, on the 6th of December, 1826," reprinted in *Selected Writings on Economics by Nassau W. Senior* (New York: Augustus M. Kelley, 1966), 34.
39. Sydney Checkland, *British Public Policy*, 93.
40. W.L. Guttsman, *The British Political Elite* (London: MacGibbon & Kee Ltd., 1963), 39–40.
41. Lees, *The Solidarities of Strangers*, 84.
42. Michael E. Rose, "The Allowance System under the New Poor Law," *Economic History Review* 2nd series, 19 (1966): 620.
43. *Hansard Parliamentary Debates*, 3d ser., Vol. 24 (1834), col. 318 comments of Poulett Scrope, MP.
44. Robert, *The Classic Slum*, 92.
45. Piven and Cloward, *Regulating the Poor*, 346.
46. Roberts, *The Classic Slum*, 8.
47. Himmelfarb, *The Idea of Poverty*, 181.
48. *Ibid.*
49. Nor, of course, was it uniformly enforced, especially in the northern manufacturing districts least suited to its provisions, because of cyclical unemployment. Resistance to centralized bureaucratic control had ensured that the local guardians enjoyed some margin of discretion in meeting local conditions.
50. Margaret Gordon explains how the availability of alternative income for the unemployed aids unionization; obviously its absence would deter unionization. *The Economics of Welfare Policies* (New York: Columbia University Press, 1963), 90–1.
51. Roberts, *The Classic Slum*, 66.
52. *Ibid.*, 51.
53. Katz, *The Undeserving Poor*, 209.
54. Piven and Cloward, *Regulating the Poor*, 177.
55. *Ibid.*, 345.
56. Hobson, "The Social Philosophy of Charity Organisation," 714.
57. G.B. Shaw, *Pygmalion* Act II.
58. J.B. Brown, "The Pig or the Stye: Drink and Poverty in Late Victorian Britain," *International Review of Social History*, 18 (1973): 388.

59. Roberts, *The Classic Slum*, 9.
60. Devine, *Misery and Its Causes*, 3.
61. Melvin J. Lerner, "The Desire for Justice and Reaction to Victims," in *Altruism and Helping Behavior: Social Psychological Studies of Some Antecedents and Consequences*, ed. by J. Macaulay and L. Berkowitz (New York: Academic Press, 1970), 207. Lerner studied the reactions of observers to suffering (in the form of electric shocks) imposed on apparently undeserving victims.
62. *Ibid.*, 208. Lerner's experimental subjects did, in fact, construct explanations for the suffering of the electric-shock victim based on some presumed malfeasance on his part.
63. Goffman, *Stigma*, 5.
64. *Ibid.*
65. Malthus, *Essay on the Principle of Population*, 2nd edn, 506–7.
66. Elaine Freedgood, "Banishing Panic: Harriet Martineau and the Popularization of Political Economy," *Victorian Studies*, 39 (Autumn 1995): 36.
67. Webb, *Harriet Martineau*, 82.
68. Simey, *Charles Booth*, 41, 131.
69. *Ibid.*, 176.
70. Lansbury, *My Life*, 186.
71. *Ibid.*, 153.
72. Smiles, *Self-Help*, 267.
73. Thomas Gilovich, *How We Know What Isn't So: The Fallibility of Human Reason in Everyday Life* (New York: The Free Press, 1991), 133.
74. Chadwick, "The New Poor Law," *Edinburgh Review*, 63 (July 1836): 494.

Chapter 10   Why Critique the Victorian Social Science of Poverty?

1. For a look at what a "modern" social science approach to poverty looks like, try the work of William Julius Wilson, Herbert Gans, and Joel F. Handler and Yeheskel Hasenfeld.
2. Quoted in Gertrude Himmelfarb, *Poverty and Compassion*, 235.
3. For an enlightening look at just how significant these structural changes were, see William Julius Wilson, *The Truly Disadvantaged*.
4. Murray, *Losing Ground*, 197.
5. *Ibid.*
6. Edward Banfield, *The Unheavenly City Revisited* (Boston: Little Brown, 1974), 53.
7. *Ibid.*, 54.
8. See his self-contradictory comments on the recklessness of casual laborers in Chapter 6.
9. Banfield, *The Unheavenly City Revisited*, 62. The lower-class individual's probable lack of health insurance is, of course, not discussed as a possible factor in this behavior.
10. *Ibid.*, 61.
11. *Ibid.*, 62.
12. *Ibid.*, 54.

Bibliography

Primary sources

Manuscripts

Bentham Papers. University College, London.
Chadwick Papers. University College, London.

Official and semi-official government papers

Hansard Parliamentary Debates, 3rd series., Vol. 22–25 (1834).
Hansard Parliamentary Debates, 4th series, Vol. 141 (1905).
Hansard Parliamentary Debates, 5th series, Vol. 16 (1910).
United Kingdom. Parliament. *Report of the Royal Commission for Inquiring into the Administration and Practical Operation of the Poor Laws*. 1834
United Kingdom. Parliament. *Report of the Royal Commission on the Poor Laws and Relief of Distress*. Cmd. 4499. 1909
United Kingdom. Parliament. *Report of the Royal Commission on the Poor Laws and Relief of Distress*. Vol. 18, Appendices [Children]. Cmd. 5037. 1910

Other primary sources

Berdoe, Edward, "Slum-Mothers and Death Clubs: A Vindication," *The Nineteenth Century* (April 1891), 560–3
Booth, Charles, *Pauperism, A Picture and the Endowment of Old Age, An Argument* (London: Macmillan and Co., 1892)
——, *Life and Labour of the People in London* First series: *Poverty* (1902–1904; reprint, New York: AMS Press, 1970)
——, *Life and Labour of the People in London* Final volume: *Notes on Social Influences and Conclusion* (1902–1904; reprint, New York: AMS Press, 1970)
Booth, General [William], *In Darkest England, And the Way Out* (London: Funk and Wagnals, 1890)
Bosanquet, Bernard, "The Reports of the Poor Law Commission" *The Sociological Review* 2 (April 1909): 109–26
Bosanquet, Bernard, ed., *Aspects of the Social Problem* by Various Authors (London: Macmillan and Co., 1895; reprint, New York: Kraus Reprint Co., 1968)
Bosanquet, Helen [Dendy], "The Children of Working London," in *Aspects of the Social Problem* ed. by Bernard Bosanquet
——, "The Industrial Residuum," in *Aspects of the Social Problem*
—— "The Meaning and Methods of True Charity," in *Aspects of the Social Problem* ed. by Bernard Bosanquet
——, "Marriage in East London," in *Aspects of the Social Problem*
——, *Rich and Poor* (London: Macmillan and Co., 1898)
——, *The Standard of Life and Other Studies* (London: Macmillan and Co., Ltd, 1898)

——, *The Strength of the People: A Study in Social Economics* (London: Macmillan and Co., Ltd, 1903)

——, *The Family* (London: Macmillan and Co., 1906)

——, *The Poor Law Report of 1909: A Summary Explaining the Defects of the Present System and the Principal Recommendations of the Commission, so far as Relates to England and Wales* (London: Macmillan and Co., 1909)

——, review of *Round About a Pound a Week*, by Mrs. Pember Reeves, *Economic Journal* 24 (March 1914): 109–12

——, *Social Work in London, 1869–1912: A History of the Charity Organisation Society* (London: John Murray, 1914)

——, "Reconstruction – Of What?" *The Hibbert Journal* 15 (June 1917): 542–6

Bunyan, John, *The Pilgrim's Progress from This World to That Which Is to Come* (1678; reprint, Laurel, NY: Lightyear Press, 1984)

Chadwick, Edwin, "The New Poor Law" *Edinburgh Review* 63 (July 1836): 487–573

——, "On the Chief Methods of Preparation for Legislation, Especially as Applicable to the Reform of Parliament" *Frasier's Magazine* 75 (May 1867): 673–90

Checkland, S.G. and E.O.A. Checkland, eds, *The Poor Law Report of 1834* (Harmondsworth, England: Penguin Books, 1974)

Cumming, Rev. J. Elder, "On the Neglect of Infants in Large Towns, with some Remarks on the Creche System" *Transactions* of the National Association for the Promotion of Social Science, Glasgow Meeting, 1874 (London: Longmans, Green, and Co., 1875): 723–9

Devine, Edward T., *Misery and Its Causes* (New York: Macmillan and Co., 1913) first published in 1909

Engels, Friedrich, *The Condition of the Working Class in England* (Oxford: Oxford University Press, 1993) first published in 1844

Hill, Octavia, "Common Sense and the Dwellings of the Poor" *The Nineteenth Century* 14 (December 1883): 925–33

——, *Homes of the London Poor* (London: Macmillan and Co., 1883)

——, "Our Dealings with the Poor" *The Nineteenth Century* 30 (August 1891): 161–70

Ikin, J.I., "On the undue Mortality of Infants and Children in connection with the Questions of Early Marriages, Drugging Children, Bad Nursing, Death Clubs, and Certificates of Death" *Transactions* of the National Association for the Promotion of Social Science, York Meeting, 1864 (London: Longman, Green, Longman, Roberts, and Green, 1865): 509–11

Lansbury, George, *My Life* (London: Constable and Co., Ltd, 1928)

Loch, C.S., *How to Help Cases of Distress: A Handy Reference Book for Almoners and Others* 4th edn (London: Longmans, Green and Co. for the C.O.S., 1890)

——, *Charity Organisation* (London: Swan Sonnenschein and Co., 1892)

——, "Cheap Dinners for Poor School Children" (London: 1885?) Edition made from bound galleys, Goldsmith's Library, University of London

——, "Manufacturing a New Pauperism" *The Nineteenth Century* 37 (April 1895): 697–708

Malthus, T.R., *An Essay on the Principle of Population; or, A view of its past and present effects on Human Happiness, with an Inquiry into our prospects respecting the future of the evils which it occasions* 2nd edn (London: J. Johnson, 1803)

——, *Definitions in Political Economy, Preceded by an Inquiry into the Rules Which Ought to Guide Political Economists in the Definition and Use of Their Terms; with Remarks on the Deviation from These Rules in their Writings* (London: John Murray, 1827)

——, "Six Letters from Malthus to Pierre Prevost" ed. by George W. Zinke, *Journal of Economic History* 2 (November 1942): 174–90

——, *Letter to Samuel Whitbread, Esq. on His Proposed Bill for the Amendment of the Poor Laws* (1807) reproduced in D.V. Glass, *Introduction to Malthus* (New York: John Wiley and Sons, 1953)

Martineau, Harriet, *Poor Laws and Paupers Illustrated* "published under the superintendence of the Society for the Diffusion of Useful Knowledge" (London: Charles Fox, 1833)

Mill, John Stuart, "Thornton on Labour and Its Claims" *Fortnightly Review* 5 (May 1869)

——, "On the Definition of Political Economy; and on the Method of Investigation proper to it," in *Essays on Some Unsettled Questions of Political Economy* 2nd edn (London: Longmans, Green, Reader, and Dye, 1874), 120–64

Reeves, M.S., *Round About a Pound a Week* (New York: Garland Publishing Inc., 1980) reprint of the 1913 edition

Roberts, Robert, *The Classic Slum: Salford Life in the First Quarter of the Century* (Manchester: Manchester University Press, 1971)

Rowntree, B. Seebohm, *Poverty: A Study of Town Life* 2nd edn (London: Longmans, Green and Co., 1922) (first edition 1901)

Senior, Nassau William, *Two Lectures on Population, Delivered before the University of Oxford in Easter Term, 1828, to Which is Added, a Correspondence between the Author and the Rev. T.R. Malthus* (London: Saunders and Otley, 1828)

——, *A Letter to Lord Howick on a Legal Provision for the Irish Poor; Commutation of Tithes, and a Provision for the Irish Roman Catholic Clergy* 3rd edn. *With a Preface, containing Suggestions as to the Measures to be adopted in the Present Emergency* (London: John Murray, 1832)

——, "An Introductory Lecture on Political Economy, delivered before the University of Oxford, on the 6th of December, 1826," in *Selected Writings on Economics by Nassau W. Senior* (New York: Augustus M. Kelly, 1966)

Shaw, G.B., "Preface to *Major Barbara*," in *Selected Plays of Bernard Shaw* (New York: Dodd, Mead and Co., 1948) preface dated June 1906

——, *Pygmalion* in *Selected Plays of Bernard Shaw* (New York: Dodd, Mead and Co., 1948) play dated 1913

——, "Socialism and Human Nature," in *The Road to Equality: Ten Unpublished Lectures and Essays, 1884–1918* ed. Louis Crompton (Boston: Beacon Press, 1971), 89–102

Smiles, Samuel, *Self-help; with Illustrations of Character, Conduct, and Perseverance* (1859; reprint, London: John Murray, 1871)

——, *Character* (New York: Harper and Bros., 1872?)

Tylor, E.B., *Encyclopaedia Britannica* 9th edn, s.v. "cannibalism"

[Webb], Beatrice Potter, *My Apprenticeship* 2nd edn (London: Longmans, Green and Co., 1948)

——, *Our Partnership* ed. by Barbara Drake and Margaret Cole (London: Longmans, Green and Co., 1948)

Webb, Sidney, *The Difficulties of Individualism* Fabian Tract #69 (1896; reprint, London: 1908)
——, "The End of the Poor Law" *Sociological Review* 2 (April 1909): 127–39
——, *The Decline in the Birth-Rate* Fabian Tract #131 (1907; reprint, London: 1910)
Webb, Sydney and Beatrice, *Industrial Democracy* (London: Longmans, Green and Co., 1902)
——, *The Prevention of Destitution* (London: 1911) Special Edition for the National Committee for the Prevention of Destitution
——, *English Local Government* Vol. 7, *The Old Poor Law* (London: Longmans, Green and Co., Ltd, 1927)
——, *English Local Government* Vols. 8 and 9, *English Poor Law History: The Last Hundred Years* (London: Longmans, Green and Co., 1929)
——, *Methods of Social Study* (London: Longmans, Green and Co., 1932)
Webb, Sydney and Beatrice, eds, *The Break-Up of the Poor Law: Being Part One of the Minority Report* (London: Longmans, Green and Co., 1909)
Zinke, George W., "Six Letters from Malthus to Pierre Prevost," *Journal of Economic History* Vol. 2 (1942): 185

Victorian and Edwardian commentators

Bonar, James, *Malthus and His Work* (London: Macmillan and Co., 1885)
Brabrook, Sir Edward, "The Report of the Poor Law Commission" *Eugenics Review* 1 (April 1909–January 1910): 47–50
Dickens, Charles, *Oliver Twist* (London: Penguin Books, 1985) first published 1837–1839
Hobson, John A., "The Social Philosophy of Charity Organisation" *The Contemporary Review* 70 (November 1896): 710–27
Mackay, Thomas, *The English Poor: A Sketch of their Social and Economic History* (London: John Murray, 1889)
Tawney, R.H., "The Theory of Pauperism," *The Sociological Review* 2 (October 1909): 361–74
Veblen, Thorstein, *The Theory of the Leisure Class* (1899; reprint, New York: Dover Publications, 1994)
Weber, Max, *The Protestant Ethic and the Spirit of Capitalism* (1904–1905; reprint, translated by Talcott Parsons (New York: Charles Scribners's Sons, 1930)

Secondary sources

Abrams, Philip, *The Origins of British Sociology, 1834–1914: An Essay with Selected Papers* (Chicago and London: University of Chicago Press, 1968)
Anstruther, Ian, *The Scandal of the Andover Workhouse* (London: Geoffrey Bles, 1973)
Banfield, Edward C., *The Unheavenly City Revisited* (Boston: Little, Brown and Co., 1974)
Beales, H.L., "The New Poor Law" *History* 15 (January 1931): 308–19
Bell, E. Moberly, *Octavia Hill, a Biography* (London: Constable and Co., Ltd, 1942)

Binfield, Clyde, *So Down to Prayers: Studies in English Nonconformity, 1780–1920* (London: J.M. Dent and Sons Ltd, 1977)

Blake, Judith, "Are Babies Consumer Durables? A Critique of the Economic Theory of Reproductive Motivation" *Population Studies* 22 (March 1968): 5–25

Blaug, Mark, "The Poor Law Report Reexamined" *Journal of Economic History* 24 (1964): 229–45

Bowley, Marian, *Nassau Senior and Classical Economics* (New York: Augustus M. Kelly, 1949)

Briggs, Asa, "The Welfare State in Historical Perspective" in *Social Welfare Institutions: A Sociological Reader*, ed. by John N. Zald (New York: John Wiley and Sons, 1965), 37–70

Brown, J.B., "The Pig or the Stye: Drink and Poverty in Late Victorian Britain" *International Review of Social History* 18 (1973): 380–95

Bulmer, Martin, Kevin Bales, and Kathryn Kish Sklar, eds, *The Social Survey in Historical Perspective, 1880–1940* (Cambridge: Cambridge University Press, 1991)

Byron [Lord], *Don Juan and Other Satirical Poems* (New York: The Odyssey Press, 1935), 664

Cartwright, T.J., *Royal Commissions and Departmental Committees in Britain: A Case Study in Institutional Adaptiveness and Public Participation in Government* (London: Hodder and Stoughton, 1975)

Chadwick, Owen, *The Secularization of the European Mind in the Nineteenth Century* (Cambridge: Cambridge University Press, 1975)

Checkland, Sydney, *British Public Policy, 1776–1939: An Economic, Social, and Political Perspective* (Cambridge: Cambridge University Press, 1983)

Cochrane, Susan H., "Children as By-products, Investment Goods and Consumer Goods: A Review of Some Micro-Economic Models of Fertility" *Population Studies* 29 (November 1975): 373–90

Cole, Margaret, *Beatrice Webb* (London: Longmans, Green and Co., 1945)

Collini, Stefan, "Hobhouse, Bosanquet and the State: Philosophical Idealism and Political Argument in England, 1880–1918" *Past and Present* 72 (August 1976): 86–111

——, *Liberalism and Sociology: L.T. Hobhouse and Political Argument in England, 1880–1914* (Cambridge: Cambridge University Press, 1979)

Coser, Lewis A., *Masters of Sociological Thought: Ideas in Historical and Social Context* 2nd edn (New York: Harcourt, Brace, Jovanovich, 1977)

Cowherd, Raymond G., *Political Economists and the English Poor Laws: A Historical Study of the Influence of Classical Economics on the Formation of Social Welfare Policy* (Athens, OH: Ohio State University Press, 1977)

Cullen, M.J., *The Statistical Movement in Early Victorian Britain: The Foundations of Empirical Social Research* (New York: The Harvester Press, 1975)

Davidoff, Leonore, "Class and Gender in Victorian England," in *Sex and Class in Women's History* (London: Routledge and Kegan Paul, 1983) ed. by Judith L. Newton *et al.*

Davin, Anna, "Loaves and Fishes: Food in Poor Households in Late Nineteenth-Century London" *History Workshop Journal* 41 (Spring 1996): 167–92

Davis, Kingsley, "Malthus and the Theory of Population," in *The Language of Social Research: A Reader in the Methodology of Social Research* ed. by Paul F. Lazarsfeld and Morris Rosenberg (Glencoe, IL: The Free Press, 1955), 540–53

Digby, Anne, "Malthus and Reform of the Poor Law," in *Malthus Past and Present*, ed. by J. Dupaquier (New York: Academic Press, Inc., 1983), 97–109

Driver, Cecil, *Tory Radical: The Life of Richard Oastler* (New York: Oxford University Press, 1946)

Englander, David and Rosemary O'Day, eds, *Retrieved Riches: Social Investigation in Britain, 1840–1914* (Aldershot, Hants.: Scholar Press, 1995)

Ferber, Marianne A. and Julie A. Nelson, eds, *Beyond Economic Man: Feminist Theory and Economics* (Chicago: University of Chicago Press, 1993)

Fido, Judith, "The Charity Organisation Society and Social Casework in London, 1869–1900," in *Social Control in Nineteenth Century Britain* ed. by A.P. Donaj-grodzki (London: Croom Helm, 1977), 207–30

Finer, Samuel E., *The Life And Times of Sir Edwin Chadwick* (London: Methuen and Co., Ltd, 1952)

——, "The Transmission of Benthamite Ideas, 1820–50," in *Studies in the Growth of Nineteenth-century Government* ed. by Gillian Sutherland (Totowa, NJ: Rowman and Littlefield, 1972)

Fraser, Derek, *The Evolution of the British Welfare State* (New York: Barnes and Noble, 1973)

Freedgood, Elaine, "Banishing Panic: Harriet Martineau and the Popularization of Political Economy" *Victorian Studies* 39 (Autumn 1995): 33–53

Freedman, Ronald, "The Sociology of Human Fertility" *Current Sociology* 10–11 (1961–1962): 35–9

Fried, Albert and Richard M. Elman, eds, *Charles Booth's London: A Portrait of the Poor at the Turn of the Century, Drawn from his "Life and Labour of the People in London"* (New York: Pantheon Books, 1968)

Gans, Herbert J., "Culture and Class in the Study of Poverty: An Approach to Anti-Poverty Research," in *On Understanding Poverty: Perspectives from the Social Sciences* ed. by Daniel P. Moynihan, 201–28

Gillies, Midge, *Marie Lloyd: The One and Only* (London: Victor Gollancz, 1999)

Gilovich, Thomas, *How We Know What Isn't So: The Fallibility of Human Reason in Everyday Life* (New York: The Free Press, 1991)

Glass, D.V., ed., *Introduction to Malthus* (New York: John Wiley and Sons, 1953)

Goffman, Erving, *Stigma: Notes on the Management of Spoiled Identity* (Englewood Cliffs, NJ: Prentice-Hall, Inc., 1963)

Goody, Jack, *Cooking, Cuisine and Class: A Study in Comparative Sociology* (Cambridge: Cambridge University Press, 1982)

Gordon, Linda, "Single Mothers and Child Neglect, 1880–1920" *American Quarterly* 37 (Summer 1985): 173–92

Gordon, Margaret S., *The Economics of Welfare Policies* (New York: Columbia University Press, 1963)

Gould, Stephen Jay, *Ever Since Darwin: Reflections in Natural History* (New York: W.W. Norton and Co., 1977)

——, *The Mismeasure of Man* (New York: W.W. Norton and Co., 1981)

——, "Jim Bowie's Letter and Bill Buckner's Legs" *Natural History* 109 (May 2000): 26–40

Greenstein, Robert, "Losing Faith in Losing Ground," *New Republic* March 25, 1985

Guttsman, W.L., *The British Political Elite* (London: MacGibbon and Kee Ltd, 1963)

Hanser, Charles J., *Guide to Decision: The Royal Commission* (Totowa, NJ: The Bedminster Press, 1965)

Harrison, Brian, *Drink and the Victorians: The Temperance Question in England, 1815–1872* (Pittsburgh: University of Pittsburgh Press, 1971)

Hart, Jennifer, "Nineteenth-Century Social Reform: A Tory Interpretation of History" *Past and Present* 31 (July 1965): 39–61

——, "Religion and Social Control in the mid-Nineteenth Century," in *Social Control in Nineteenth Century Britain* ed. by A.P. Donajgrodzki (London: Croom-Helm, 1977), 108–37

Helmstadter, Richard, "The Nonconformist Conscience," in *The Conscience of the Victorian State* ed. by Peter Marsh (Syracuse, NY: Syracuse University Press, 1979), 135–72

Henriques, Ursula, "Bastardy and the New Poor Law" *Past and Present* 37 (July 1967): 103–29

——, "How Cruel Was the Victorian Poor Law?" *Historical Journal* 11 (1968): 365–71

Herbert, Christopher, *Culture and Anomie: Ethnographic Imagination in the Nineteenth Century* (Chicago: University of Chicago Press, 1991)

Hewitt, Margaret, *Wives and Mothers in Victorian Industry* (Westport, CT: Greenwood Press, 1958)

Hilton, Boyd, "The Role of Providence in Evangelical Thought," in *History, Society and the Churches: Essays in Honour of Owen Chadwick* ed. by Derek Beales and Geoffrey Best (Cambridge: Cambridge University Press, 1985), 215–34

——, *The Age of Atonement: The Influence of Evangelicalism on Social and Economic Thought, 1795–1865* (New York: Oxford University Press, 1988)

Himmelfarb, Gertrude, *Darwin and the Darwinian Revolution* (New York: W.W. Norton, 1968)

——, "Bentham Scholarship and the Bentham 'Problem'" *Journal of Modern History* 41 (June 1969): 189–206

——, *The Idea of Poverty: England in the Early Industrial Age* (New York: Alfred A. Knopf, 1984)

——, *Marriage and Morals Among the Victorians* (New York: Alfred A. Knopf, 1986)

——, *Poverty and Compassion: The Moral Imagination of the Late Victorians* (New York: Alfred A. Knopf, 1991)

——, "The Age of Philanthropy" *The Wilson Quarterly* (Spring 1997): 48–55

Huggins, Nathan Irvin, *Protestants Against Poverty: Boston's Charities, 1870–1900* (Westport, CT: Greenwood Publishing Corp., 1971)

Humphreys, Robert *Sin, Organized Charity and the Poor Law in Victorian England* (New York: St Martin's Press, 1995)

James, Patricia, *Population Malthus: His Life and Times* (London: Routledge and Kegan Paul, 1979)

Jencks, Christopher, "How Poor are the Poor?" *New York Review of Books* xxxii, no. 8 (May 9, 1985): 41–9

Johnson, Paul, "Class Law in Victorian England" *Past and Present* 141 (1993): 147–69

——, "Conspicuous Consumption and Working-Class Culture in Late-Victorian and Edwardian Britain" *Transactions* of the Royal Historical Society (1988): 27–42

——, *Saving and Spending: The Working-Class Economy in Britain, 1870–1939* (Oxford: Clarendon Press, 1985)

Jones, Gareth Stedman, *Outcast London: A Study in the Relationship between Classes in Victorian Society* (London: Penguin Books, 1976)

Kadish, Alon, *Apostle Arnold: The Life and Death of Arnold Toynbee, 1852–1883* (Durham, NC: Duke University Press, 1986)

Katz, Michael B., *The Undeserving Poor: From the War on Poverty to the War on Welfare* (New York: Pantheon Books, 1989)

——, *In the Shadow of the Poorhouse: A Social History of Welfare in America* (New York: Basic Books, 1996)

Kavolis, Vytautas, *Moralizing Cultures* (Landham, MD: University Press of America, 1993)

Kent, Susan Kingsley, *Sex and Suffrage in Britain, 1860–1914* (Princeton, NJ: Princeton University Press, 1987)

Keynes, John Maynard, "Robert Malthus, The First of the Cambridge Economists," in *Essays in Biography* 2nd edn (London: Mercury Books, 1961), 81–124

Korpi, Walter, "Approaches to the Study of Poverty in the United States: Critical Notes from a European Perspective," in *Poverty and Public Policy: An Evaluation of Social Science Research* ed. Vincent T. Covello (Cambridge, MA: Schenkman Publishing Co., 1980), 287–314

Koven, Seth, "Dr. Barnardo's 'Artistic Fictions': Photography, Sexuality, and the Ragged Child in Victorian London" *Radical History Review* 69 (Fall 1997): 6–45

Kuklik, Henrika, *The Savage Within: The Social History of British Anthropology, 1885–1945* (Cambridge: Cambridge University Press, 1991)

Lassalle, Yvonne M. and Maureen O'Dougherty, "In Search of Weeping Worlds: Economies of Agency and Politics of Representation in the Ethnography of Inequality" *Radical History Review* 69 (Fall 1997): 243–60

Lees, Lynn Hollen, "The Survival of the Unfit: Welfare Policies and Family Maintenance in Nineteenth-Century London," in *The Uses of Charity* ed. by Peter Mandler (Philadelphia: University of Pennsylvania Press, 1990), 68–88

——, *The Solidarities of Strangers: The English Poor Laws and the People, 1700–1948* (New York: Cambridge University Press, 1998)

Lerner, Melvin J., "The Desire for Justice and Reaction to Victims," in *Altruism and Helping Behavior: Social Psychological Studies of Some Antecedents and Consequences* ed. by J. Macauley and L. Berkowitz (New York: Academic Press, 1970), 205–30

Lewis, Jane, *The Politics of Motherhood: Child and Maternal Welfare in England 1900–1939* (Montreal: McGill-Queen's University Press, 1980)

——, *Women and Social Action in Victorian and Edwardian England* (Stanford, CA: Stanford University Press, 1991)

——, "Lone Mothers: the British Case," in *Lone Mothers in European Welfare Regimes* ed. by Jane Lewis (London: Jessica Kingsley Publishers, 1997), 50–75

Lewis, Oscar, "The Culture of Poverty," in *On Understanding Poverty: Perspectives from the Social Sciences* ed. by Daniel P. Moynihan (New York: Basic Books, 1968), 187–200

MacKenzie, Jeanne, *A Victorian Courtship: The Story of Beatrice Potter and Sidney Webb* (New York: Oxford University Press, 1979)

Madison, Bernice, "Canadian Family Allowances and Their Major Social Implications" *Journal of Marriage and the Family* 26 (May 1964): 134–41

Malchow, H.L., "A Victorian Mind: Gertrude Himmelfarb, Poverty, and the Moral Imagination" *Victorian Studies* 35 (Spring 1992): 309–15

Marshall, J.D., *The Old Poor Law, 1795–1834* (London: Macmillan and Co., 1968)

McBriar, A.M., *An Edwardian Mixed Doubles: The Bosanquets versus the Webbs: A Study in British Social Policy, 1890–1929* (Oxford: Clarendon Press, 1987)

McCleary, George F., *The Malthusian Population Theory* (London: Faber and Faber, Ltd, 1953)

McGregor, O.R., "Social Research and Social Policy in the Nineteenth Century" *British Journal of Sociology* 8 (1957): 146–57

McKibbon, Ross, "Class and Poverty in Edwardian England," in *The Ideologies of Class: Social Relations in Britain 1880–1950* ed. by R. McKibbon (Oxford: Clarendon Press, 1990), 167–96

McLaren, Angus, "Contraception and the Working Classes: The Social Ideology of the English Birth Control Movement in its Early Years" *Comparative Studies in Society and History* 18 (April 1976): 236–51

——, "Sex and Socialism: The Opposition of the French Left to Birth Control in the Nineteenth Century" *Journal of the History of Ideas* 37 (July–September 1976): 475–92

Meek, Ronald L., ed., *Marx and Engels on Malthus* (New York: International Publishers, 1954)

Merton, Robert K., "The Perspectives of Insiders and Outsiders," in *The Sociology of Science* (Chicago: University of Chicago Press, 1973), 99–136

Mills, C. Wright, *The Sociological Imagination* (New York: Oxford University Press, 1959)

Mowatt, Charles Loch, *The Charity Organisation Society, 1869–1913: Its Ideas and Work* (London: Methuen and Co., Ltd, 1961)

Moynihan, Daniel Patrick, "The Professors and the Poor," in *On Understanding Poverty: Perspectives from the Social Sciences* ed. by D.P. Moynihan (New York: Basic Books, Inc., 1968), 3–35

Murray, Charles, *Losing Ground: American Social Policy, 1950–1980* (New York: Basic Books, Inc., 1984)

Nelson, Julie A., "The Study of Choice or the Study of Provisioning? Gender and the Definition of Economics," in *Beyond Economic Man: Feminist Theory and Economics*, Marianne A. Ferber and Julie A. Nelson, eds (Chicago: University of Chicago Press, 1993), 23–36

Obelkevich, James, "Religion," in *The Cambridge Social History of Britain, 1750–1990*, Vol. 3, ed. by F.M.L. Thompson (Cambridge: Cambridge University Press, 1990), 311–56

Orwell, George, *The Road to Wigan Pier* Left Book Club Edition (London: Victor Gollancz, Ltd, 1937)

——, *Down and Out in Paris and London* (London: Secker and Warburg, 1986) Originally published in 1933.

Owen, David, *English Philanthropy, 1660–1960* (Cambridge, MA: Harvard University Press, 1964)

Owens, W.R., "The Reception of *The Pilgrim's Progress* in England," in *Bunyan in England and Abroad* ed. by M. van Os and G.J. Schutte (Amsterdam: Vrije Universiteit University Press, 1990), 91–104

Parsons, Gerald, "From Dissenters to Free Churchmen: The Transitions of Victorian Nonconformity," in *Religion in Victorian Britain* Vol. 1: *Traditions* ed. by G. Parsons (Manchester, UK: Manchester University Press, 1988), 67–116

Pettigrew, Thomas F., "Social Psychology's Potential Contributions to an Understanding of Poverty," in *Poverty and Public Policy: An Evaluation of Social Science Research* ed. by Vincent T. Covello (Cambridge, MA: Schenkman Publishing Col, 1980), 189–233

Piven, Frances Fox and Richard A. Cloward, *Regulating the Poor: The Functions of Public Welfare* (New York: Pantheon Books, 1971)

Poovey, Mary, "Figures of Arithmetic, Figures of Speech: The Discourse of Statistics in the 1830s" *Critical Inquiry* 19 (Winter 1993): 256–76

——, *Making a Social Body: British Cultural Formation, 1830–1864* (Chicago: University of Chicago Press, 1995)

——, *A History of the Modern Fact: Problems of Knowledge in the Sciences of Wealth and Society* (Chicago: University of Chicago Press, 1998)

Prochaska, F.K., "Philanthropy," in *The Cambridge Social History of Britain, 1750–1950* Vol. 3, ed. by F.M.L. Thompson (Cambridge: Cambridge University Press, 1990), 357–94

Rapp, Rayna, Ellen Ross and Renate Bridenthal, "Examining Family History," in *Sex and Class in Women's History* ed. by Judith L. Newton *et al.* (London: Routledge and Kegan Paul, 1983), 232–58

Roach, John, *Social Reform in England, 1780–1880* (New York: St Martin's Press, 1978)

Roberts, David, *Victorian Origins of the British Welfare State* (New Haven: Yale University Press, 1960)

——, "How Cruel Was the Victorian Poor Law?" *Historical Journal* 6 (1963): 97–107

——, *The Social Conscience of the Early Victorians* (Stanford, CA: Stanford University Press, 2002)

Rodgers, Brian, "The Social Science Association, 1857–1886" *The Manchester School of Economics and Social Studies* 20 (September 1952): 283–310

Romano, Mary Ann, *Beatrice Webb, 1858–1943: The Socialist with a Sociological Imagination* (Lewiston, NY: The Edwin Mellen Press, 1998)

Rose, Michael E., "The Allowance System under the New Poor Law" *Economic History Review* 2nd series 2 (1966): 607–20

——,*The English Poor Law, 1780–1930* (New York: Barnes and Noble, 1971)

——, *The Relief of Poverty, 1834–1914* (London: Macmillan and Co., 1972)

Ross, Ellen, "Survival Networks: Women's Neighborhood Sharing in London Before World War One" *History Workshop* 15 (1983): 4–27

——, "Good Mothers and Bad Mothers: Lady Philanthropists and London Housewives before the First World War," in *Lady Bountiful Revisited: Women, Philanthropy, and Power* ed. by Kathleen D. McCarthy (New Brunswick, NJ: Rutgers University Press, 1990), 174–98

——, "Hungry Children: Housewives and London Charity, 1870–1918," in *The Uses of Charity* ed. by Peter Mandler (Philadelphia: University of Pennsylvania Press, 1990), 161–96

——, *Love and Toil: Motherhood in Outcast London, 1870–1918* (New York: Oxford University Press, 1993)

Royal College of Psychiatrists, *Alcohol and Alcoholism* The Report of a Special Committee of the Royal College of Psychiatrists (New York: The Free Press, 1979)

Schram, Sanford, *Words of Welfare: The Poverty of Social Science and the Social Science of Poverty* (Minneapolis: University of Minnesota Press, 1995)

Schrecker, John E., *The Chinese Revolution in Historical Perspective* (New York: Praeger, 1991)

Semmel, Bernard, *Imperialism and Social Reform: English Social-Imperial Thought 1895–1914* (London: George Allen & Unwin, Ltd, 1960)

Simey, T.S., *Charles Booth: Social Scientist* (London: Oxford University Press, 1960)

——, "The Contribution of the Webbs to Sociology" *British Journal of Sociology* 12 (June 1961): 106–23

Singer, Charles and E. Ashworth, *A Short History of Medicine* 2nd edn (New York: Oxford University Press, 1962)

Stocking, George W., Jr., *Victorian Anthropology* (New York: The Free Press, 1987)

——, *After Tylor: British Social Anthropology, 1888–1951* (Madison, WI: University of Wisconsin Press, 1995)

Strassman, Diana, "Not a Free Market: The Rhetoric of Disciplinary Authority in Economics," in *Beyond Economic Man* ed. by Marianne Ferber *et al.* (Chicago: University of Chicago Press, 1993), 54–68

Sullivan, Michael, *The Development of the British Welfare State* (London: Prentice Hall, 1996)

Thane, Pat, "Women and the Poor Law in Victorian and Edwardian England" *History Workshop* 6 (Autumn 1978): 29–51

Thompson, Paul, *The Edwardians* (Chicago: Academy Chicago Publishers, 1975)

Titmuss, Richard, review of C.L. Mowat, *The Charity Organisation Society* in *New Statesman* 61 (June 1961): 962

Townsend, Peter, "The Meaning of Poverty" *British Journal of Sociology* 13 (1962): 210–27

Vincent, A.W., "The Poor Law Reports of 1909 and the Social Theory of the Charity Organization Society" *Victorian Studies* 27 (1984): 343–63

Vorspan, Rachel, "Vagrancy and the New Poor Law in late-Victorian and Edwardian England" *The English Historical Review* 92 (January 1977): 59–81

Walker, Pamela J., *Pulling the Devil's Kingdom Down: The Salvation Army in Victorian Britain* (Berkeley and Los Angeles: University of California Press, 2001)

Walkowitz, Judith R., *Prostitution and Victorian Society: Women, Class and the State* (Cambridge: Cambridge University Press, 1980)

Walvin, James, *Victorian Values* (Athens, GA: The University of Georgia Press, 1987)

Walzer, Michael, *The Revolution of the Saints: A Study in the Origins of Radical Politics* (Cambridge: Harvard University Press, 1965)

Webb, R.K., *The British Working Class Reader, 1790–1848: Literacy and Social Tension* (London: George Allen and Unwin, Ltd, 1955)

——, *Harriet Martineau: A Radical Victorian* (New York: Columbia University Press, 1960)

Weber, Max, "'Objectivity' in Social Science and Social Policy," in *Max Weber on the Methodology of the Social Sciences* translated and edited by Edward A. Shils and Henry A. Finch (Glencoe, IL: Free Press, 1949), 50–112

Wilson, William Julius, *The Truly Disadvantaged: The Inner City, the Underclass, and Public Policy* (Chicago: University of Chicago Press, 1987)

Wohl, Anthony S., "The Bitter Cry of Outcast London" *International Review of Social History* 13 (1968) 189–245.
——, *The Eternal Slum: Housing and Social Policy in Victorian London* (Montreal: McGill-Queen's University Press, 1977)
Woodroofe, Kathleen, *From Charity to Social Work in England and the United States* (London: Routledge and Kegan Paul, 1962)
Young, Michael and Peter Willmott, *Family and Kinship in East London* (Glencoe, IL: The Free Press, 1957)

Index